The Columbia River Treaty

D0021403

DISCARDED

RECEIVED

THE COLUMBIA RIVER TREATY
The Economics of an International River Basin Development

BY JOHN V. KRUTILLA

PUBLISHED FOR RESOURCES FOR THE FUTURE, INC.
BY THE JOHNS HOPKINS PRESS, BALTIMORE, MARYLAND

COLORADO MOUNTAIN COLLEGE
LRC---WEST CAMPUS
Glenwood Springs, Colo. 81601

RESOURCES FOR THE FUTURE, INC.

1755 Massachusetts Avenue N.W., Washington, D.C. 20036

Board of Directors:
William S. Paley, *Chairman*, Robert O. Anderson, Harrison Brown, Erwin D. Canham, Edward J. Cleary, Joseph L. Fisher, Luther H. Foster, Charles J. Hitch, Hugh L. Keenleyside, Edward S. Mason, Frank Pace, Jr., Laurance S. Rockefeller, Stanley H. Ruttenberg, Lauren K. Soth, John W. Vanderwilt, P. F. Watzek.
Honorary Directors: Horace M. Albright, Reuben G. Gustavson, Otto H. Liebers, Leslie A. Miller.

President: Joseph L. Fisher
Vice President: Michael F. Brewer
Secretary-Treasurer: John E. Herbert

Resources for the Future is a non-profit corporation for research and education in the development, conservation, and use of natural resources. It was established in 1952 with the co-operation of the Ford Foundation and its activities since then have been financed by grants from that Foundation. Part of the work of Resources for the Future is carried out by its resident staff, part supported by grants to universities and other non-profit organizations. Unless otherwise stated, interpretations and conclusions in RFF publications are those of the authors; the organization takes responsibility for the selection of significant subjects for study, the competence of the researchers, and their freedom of inquiry.

This book is one of RFF's studies in water resources, which are directed by Allen V. Kneese. John V. Krutilla is senior research associate with Resources for the Future.

Director of RFF publications, Henry Jarrett; *editor*, Vera W. Dodds; *associate editor*, Nora E. Roots.

Copyright © 1967 by The Johns Hopkins Press, Baltimore, Maryland 21218
Printed in the United States of America
Library of Congress Catalogue Card Number 67–16037

Foreword

~~~~~~~~~~~~~~~~~~~~~~~~~~~

Formal approval of the Columbia River Treaty in 1964 brought to a conclusion two decades of study and negotiation by the United States and Canada for joint development of the Columbia River Basin. The Treaty provides the framework for one of the most far-reaching water development efforts in North America. Through its terms, the United States acquires large quantities of Canadian storage to meet certain power and flood control objectives, and Canada receives a share of the increase in power produced at U.S. generating plants plus payment for its storage contribution toward flood damage reduction within U.S. borders. The terms also provide for a transboundary storage project, the dam site of which will be situated in the United States and the reservoir headwaters extending into British Columbia. The Treaty thus represents an outstanding example of international co-operation in river basin development.

The engineering and economic studies made in preparation for international agreement on so complex an undertaking as the Columbia were concerned with the selection of sites, the timing of project construction, and the division of costs and benefits between the upstream and downstream countries. The negotiations were protracted. The issues involved not only the interests of the United States and Canada, but also those of British Columbia which, as a province of Canada, constitutionally retains jurisdiction over its own natural rescources. Also, in the course of two decades changing technological, economic, and political conditions in both countries were factors complicating final decisions.

In this book, John V. Krutilla reviews the process by which the Treaty came into being and analyzes the economic implications of the terms. Long known for his economic analyses of river basin development—especially noteworthy in his and Otto Eckstein's book *Multiple Purpose River Development*—Mr. Krutilla began his study of the Columbia Treaty six years before its final ratification, systematically examining official studies and making his own evaluations of the economic consequences of the terms. Special mention should be made of the encouragement and critical review provided by Irving K. Fox while the study was in preparation. The book is important not only as an independent economic appraisal of a major undertaking in international river development; it is also a case study of value to future international development efforts, and a contribution to deeper understanding of the economics of water management.

JOSEPH L. FISHER

February, 1967   Resources for the Future, Inc.

Preface

Work on this study was begun during the spring of 1958 when I undertook a preliminary reconnaissance to evaluate the availability of data required for its undertaking and the feasibility of the research project in other respects. That the evaluation might have been overly optimistic is reflected in the publication date of this volume. Since work on this study was performed intermittently over a period of almost a decade, and since I failed to anticipate the need for keeping a log, I have neither an accurate nor a comprehensive list of individuals who at one time or another assisted me with data, background briefings, political and technical understanding of the problem, and in various other ways large and small. To those whose assistance I have inadvertently failed to acknowledge I apologize, and trust they will appreciate that my gratitude has been no less genuine despite the omission of their contribution.

A study such as this could not have been undertaken successfully without a great deal of co-operation from public officials both in Canada and the United States. I am indebted to the late Governor Douglass MacKay, chairman of the U.S. Section, International Joint Commission United States and Canada, and to his opposite number the late Honorable A. G. L. McNaughton, for their interest, co-operation, and general encouragement. Equally, my great debt to Mr. Eugene Weber, member, U.S. Section, and Mr. Donald Stephens, member, Canadian section of the International Joint Commission, for numerous lengthy and informative discussions, critical review of various manuscript materials, and for other courtesies, is gratefully acknowledged.

I am indebted also to the Honorable Elmer Bennett, formerly Under Secretary of the U.S. Department of the Interior and chief of the United States negotiating delegation, for his assistance in briefings and interpretation of events associated with results of the

Treaty negotiations, and to his principal staff assistant, Mr. Morgan Dubrow, whose assistance in many ways was especially great.

Public officials in Canada were no less helpful; I must mention especially the Honorable Alvin Hamilton, formerly Minister of Northern Affairs and National Resources, and Mr. Gordon Robertson, formerly Deputy Minister and member of the Canadian negotiating delegation, as much for their interest and encouragement as for the opportunities to discuss at length issues involved in the Columbia undertaking and the critical distinction between the Canadian and United States points of view. Along with these, I must include the Honorable Ray Williston, Minister of Lands, Forests and Water Resources, and his Deputy Ministers, Messrs. E. W. Basset, also member of the Canadian negotiating delegation, and A. F. Paget, formerly Comptroller of Water Rights, Province of British Columbia, who at one time or another over many years were helpful in a number of ways. I am also grateful to the co-chairmen of the British Columbia Hydro and Power Authority— Dr. Hugh L. Keenleyside for his many courtesies, and Dr. G. M. Shrum for his co-operation in providing technical materials on the Peace River project.

But it is largely the technical personnel of both countries to whom I owe what knowledge I have gained about power systems and the intricacies of the interdependencies which loom as unsuspecting hydras at almost every turn. I am particularly indebted to Mr. David Lewis, U.S. Corps of Engineers, Portland, Oregon; and to Messrs. Henderson McIntyre, Chester Mohler, and Carl Blake of the Bonneville Power Administration; to Messrs. Gordon J. A. Kidd, Bill Fisher, and David Tanner, all of the Province of British Columbia; to Mr. T. M. Patterson, Director, Water Resources Branch, Department of Northern Affairs and National Resources, and to members of his staff—particularly Messrs. Gordon Mac-Nabb and Ralph Purcell, the latter more recently chief engineer with the British Columbia Energy Board. I have also relied heavily on the orientation obtained early from Mr. Ross Brudenell, Office of Power, Tennessee Valley Authority, especially in connection with the change in the role of storage facilities as systems develop from predominantly hydro systems into mixed hydro-thermal systems.

I should like to mention also the great assistance rendered me by Dr. Herschell F. Jones and Mr. Lyle Dunstan of H. Zinder and Associates, in overseeing the simulation studies required in Chapters 7 and 9; and to Mr. Pat Cawood for programing assistance in connection with implementing the Northwest-Southwest intertie model in Chapter 9.

To Dr. Kristjan Kristjanson, formerly secretary to the Water Policy Coordination Committee, Department of Northern Affairs and National Resources, I owe an especially large debt. Not only did we engage in many provocative discussions from which I learned a great deal, but also he was extremely helpful in making arrangements for my meeting virtually everyone in Canada who could be of assistance in the conduct of the study.

Many members of the academic community also fell victim to their courtesy and had their fortitude tested in reviewing the manuscript. These have been: Professors Gilbert F. White and W. R. Derrick Sewell, University of Chicago (the latter formerly with the Department of Northern Affairs and National Resources, Vancouver Office); Professors A. D. Scott and Peter Pearse of the University of British Columbia; Professor Neil Swainson, Victoria University; Professor Richard E. Caves, Harvard University; Professor Aaron Wildavsky, University of California; and Professor Michael Brewer, George Washington University.

There have been others as well who have been helpful in reviewing the manuscript, including Mr. R. Deane of Rossland, British Columbia, and Mr. Larrat Higgins of Toronto.

Brigadier General P. C. Hyzer, Division Engineer, Division North Pacific, and his staff should be mentioned especially for the vigorous and constructively critical review of the manuscript. Not all of their suggestions have been incorporated, but all demanded careful consideration; those I have felt unable to accept within the framework of my analysis have been noted in the text. The manuscript was submitted, incidentally, to all the water resource development agencies involved in the Columbia River project in both countries for similar review and comment.

To Dr. Kristjanson and Professor Scott I owe the opportunity to discuss the issues with Canadian academic and governmental personnel through several seminars arranged for my benefit. These exchanges always were of the utmost value in helping me to perceive aspects of the problem through Canadian eyes. Although I should not claim to have obtained much expertise in this department, I feel my progress in this respect was a function of the skill and vigor with which many ideas (entirely outside the scope of my unaided perception) were pressed by various members at one or another of the several meetings. In the same vein, I should acknowledge the informative discussions I have had with Mr. Paddy Sherman, editor of *The Vancouver Province*, Professor Swainson, and

Professor Vincent Ostrom, the latter on the faculty at Indiana University, all of whom helped me to acquire my limited education in politics and public administration.

My special gratitude goes to Irving K. Fox who, as director of the water resources program at Resources for the Future, gave me continuing encouragement and counsel in the course of the research for this study. Valuable to me also has been the willingness of my colleagues at Resources for the Future to review the manuscript at various stages and to offer suggestions with respect to its improvement. Chief among these have been Charles Howe, Henry Jarrett, and Allen Kneese, who gave unsparingly of themselves in an effort to make the manuscript "available" to a non-technical readership. Had I been better able to implement their suggestions in this respect, the objective would have been better met. But what was accomplished in this regard, I suspect, must be attributed more to Vera Dodds who edited the manuscript, than to my ability to respond effectively to my colleagues' exhortations.

While I owe much to many individuals and organizations, it would be inaccurate to leave an impression that the approach adopted in this study, and its conclusions, enjoy universal endorsement. As a matter of fact, while almost everybody will find some things in the study with which he can agree, almost nobody will subscribe to all. Differences from the viewpoint shared by some public officials, their supporting staffs, and some reviewers may to some extent derive from the varying degrees of significance attached by different people to the same event, and this in turn is connected with personal involvement or differing interpretation of information. Of even greater moment may be the differences in viewpoint among the various disciplines involved in so multi-faceted an undertaking as the Columbia. Economists, engineers, political scientists, and public administrators do not always see eye to eye in a given situation. The divergence between my view of an economic system to deal with flood losses on the lower Columbia and Kootenay rivers, for example, and that of professional members of the Corps of Engineers stems largely from variations in approach and perception of the problem which, in turn, are determined largely by professional backgrounds.

With these caveats, it is superfluous to say that while my debt to many is enormous, my acknowledgement of their assistance does not imply endorsement of the results nor responsibility for any remaining errors of analysis or judgment.

August, 1966   John V. Krutilla

Contents

~~~~~~~~~~~~~~~~~~~~~~~~~~

LIST OF TABLES

LIST OF FIGURES

PART I

Development of
International Rivers

Chapter 1

Introduction

~~~~~~~~~~~~~~~~~~~~~~~~

In recent years, notably during the postwar period, the field of water resources development has been enriched by examples of co-operative planning for the development of international rivers. The St. Lawrence, Indus, Nile, Jordan, Columbia, and Mekong are familiar cases of international streams the development of which requires a measure of mutual accommodation among the riparian countries involved. That mutual accommodation is required is not difficult to perceive. A river system is a hydrologic unit. The volume of discharge at its mouth is systematically related to the flow of its tributaries and run-off from its headwater catchments. And the water environment in its upstream reaches may not be independent of the way the natural conditions in its downstream portions are modified. Thus, the substantial efforts devoted to working out mutual accommodations for the development of international streams have tended to reinforce the belief that co-ordinated development of international streams brings results for the co-operating parties which are in some sense superior to those which each could have achieved acting unilaterally.

There are several ways in which co-operative international river development offers possibilities for mutual gain. An upstream riparian may wish to undertake measures on the domestic reaches of the stream in order to reduce the variability of streamflows and thus provide some protection from flood hazards and some improvement of streamflows during the season of low runoff. Such an undertaking will also affect the hydrologic variability downstream in the reaches of a riparian neighbor, so that the value of the measures in question, even their scale and method of operation, may be substantially altered if account is taken of the consequent hydrological modifications downstream. Co-operative participation

3

in design and scale, and mutually planned sharing of costs and attendant benefits, are likely to lead to more effective exploitation of the river's potential in such an undertaking than if each party were to take an independent course of action, ignoring off-site effects. Similarly, a downstream riparian may wish to construct locks and dams at the fall line of a river within its own reaches—a project which can provide a navigable channel to the sea for a previously landlocked upstream riparian. Here again, a co-operative venture by both riparians can achieve more efficient use of the stream than can an independently planned project. In general, then, where interdependencies exist, pooling the resource potential of an entire river system offers a wider range of technically feasible alternatives and, by avoiding duplication, an opportunity to select the most economical combination of sites and measures for attaining mutually desired objectives.

Even when the objectives of riparians differ, it is still possible that mutual accommodation can be a means of improving the economics of an international water resource undertaking, provided the co-operation is sustained. Consider the case in which an upstream consumptive use would inflict a cost on a downstream riparian in excess of the domestic benefits to the upstream country. Theoretically, through a co-operative accommodation the downstream riparian could compensate the upstream country for returns it would forego by abstaining from the planned development, and this payment would be less than the cost the downstream country would suffer in the absence of the accommodation. Or, alternatively, one can assume the understanding among riparians to be such that one country may undertake no action relating to its reach of an international stream which adversely affects another riparian, without compensating the latter for damages suffered. In that event, it is clear that the upstream measure referred to above would not be undertaken, despite the benefits realizable domestically, if the external liability exceeds the on-site benefits. Whichever party is liable for absorbing the external costs—a matter that is not settled *in general*—a co-operative accommodation presents the possibility of maximizing joint returns or minimizing the opportunity returns foregone.

Given the apparent advantages inherent in a co-operative approach to the development of an international stream, why have such undertakings not always proceeded smoothly and to an expeditious completion? There are many reasons.

One of them, completely consistent with a co-operative spirit on the part of both riparians, is the technical complexity of such undertakings and the difficult task of sorting out the repercussion of the interrelationships within a system of works on large streams and tributary systems. These repercussions are not likely to be confined to different locations and projects along the stream course under initial conditions; they also may have implications of an intertemporal nature, a problem that will be discussed in some detail in later chapters. Economic consequences are difficult to evaluate with precision under the best of circumstances, and when these occur in an international context, in a dynamic or intertemporal setting, the task is immensely complicated.

Another reason for the protracted negotiations and absence of ready agreement among riparians contemplating the co-operative use of a river system is the ill-defined rights and responsibilities vis-à-vis other riparians with respect to assumption of liability or provision of compensation for off-site effects. In the illustration above in which actions of the upstream country would have adverse implications for a downstream riparian, the consequences for an efficient design of the water resource system would not vary regardless of which country assumed the obligation for external liabilities. But the outcome for the two countries would certainly differ; the relative gains of each would depend upon which country was required to absorb the cost of the off-site liability. Thus, although a community of interest may exist with respect to the most efficient way of exploiting the potentials of a stream, there is a conflict regarding the assumption of off-site costs or recognition of off-site benefits. In the resolution of this problem the gain to one country comes at the expense of the other, and a lively controversy can be anticipated in coming to an accommodation on such issues.

A third reason for difficulties in negotiating mutually acceptable agreements may be the existence of differing goals that cannot be represented by a simple balance sheet of costs and gains to the countries concerned. In the brief representation of the inherent advantages of co-operative undertakings noted above, it has been assumed that benefits and costs ultimately could be reduced to monetary equivalents in such a way that the side payments agreed upon would render any riparian indifferent as to a choice among mutually exclusive locations in which a development project may be undertaken. If this should not be the case, however, side payments in monetary terms will not suffice to resolve differences of opinion that arise from incompatible objectives. This need not necessarily imply that co-operative development of the river in question will be impossible. There is always the possibility in negotiations between neighboring states that reciprocity on the point at issue—in this case water resource development—can be reached through concessions in an unrelated area of mutual concern.

Finally, we need to recognize a set of conditions in which our earlier assumption of a sense of mutual responsibility among riparians is relaxed. In such circumstances one can imagine that the countries might not be content with an outcome representing an absolute gain as compared with one achievable by independent action neglecting external effects. For example, should a spirited rivalry exist between two riparians, the objective of each may be to realize a gain relative to the other rather than to maximize the joint gain for mutual sharing with unacceptable relative shares. With motivations of this nature, there will be little prospect of agreement unless each country considers the probable economic consequences to be in its own favor.

Or the traditional relationship between riparians may be one of undisguised hostility, in which case any joint undertaking, if in fact conceivable, could be motivated by the objective not of maximizing joint gains but of minimizing the risk of adverse effects from actions taken in the reaches of the riparian neighbor. In this event, there might be more interest during negotiations in monitoring the actions of the neighboring country and stalemating development than in achieving positive results in the conventional sense. And in this event, also, development of an international stream would be out of the question if the rival countries were left to their own devices. It is possible, of course, that in such circumstances the hazard of open hostility might seem to the world at large to warrant intercession by intermediaries (e.g., international agencies) who could organize a wider range of compensatory measures than would be available to the riparians. An arrangement of this kind might effectively resolve the conflict over the development of an international stream.

We should recognize from this brief discussion of conditions ranging from the ultimate in co-operation to active hostility, that the role of research and analysis in the development of an international river system will vary directly with the degree of the disposition toward co-operation. Economic analysis, which is required to evaluate the costs and gains of alternative courses of development, is based upon a rationality postulate that is consistent with co-operative behavior directed toward maximizing joint gain for mutual sharing. Moreover, it postulates that if the achievement of objectives can be expressed in monetary equivalents, the resources of one riparian can be developed at least partially for the use of another in exchange for appropriate compensation payable in monetary units.

In this study I shall assume as a point of departure that there are cases in which mutual benefits derive from co-operative development of international streams. This implies that the yields from such a venture will exceed in the aggregate the sum of the yields from purely domestic possibilities developed by each riparian independently and without regard to external effects. In this respect, there is a community of interest among riparians in which the more closely an economically efficient system design is approximated, the greater will be the joint gains for mutual sharing. Such a community of interest, however, depends upon one or another of two conditions: (a) absolute mutual confidence that each country will refrain from exploiting an opportunity, should it arise, in which a larger share of a reduced total net gain might accrue to its advantage, or (b) a precommitment by all parties to the principle that economic criteria will govern the selection of sites for development as well as the design of the system in such a way that no element is included or excluded which prevents the maximum economies in meeting a mutually desired objective.

To be feasible in practice, assurance must be provided that no participant will be jeopardized by such a commitment. This can be accomplished by a corollary commitment concerning the division of the gains, through which each participating nation in the co-operative venture is guaranteed: first, an allocation out of the co-operatively achieved gains that will leave the participant in a position not inferior to that which could have been achieved independently; and second, an allocation of the remaining gains through a mutually agreeable standard which ensures for each participant a position superior to one that could have resulted from an independent course of development.

It must be acknowledged that while these precommitments appear reasonable in principle, in practice the measurements to be made and the relationships to be quantified in order to implement the approach may be quite subtle. It is even possible that the relationships and methods for their quantification may be too elusive to command widespread understanding, perhaps even among the principals to whom the negotiation of the arrangements have been entrusted. This may pose further difficulties if the agreements that are reached require broad public support before they can be implemented by each riparian domestically.

.   .   .

In the light of political and social as well as economic factors, and of the effectiveness of present methods of analysis, what are the potentialities and limitations of international co-operation in river basin development? Perhaps the best way of seeking answers is to study an actual case. That is the purpose of this analysis of the Columbia River Treaty and the circumstances surrounding it.

In taking the Columbia as an example of international river development (as well as an inquiry of substantial interest *per se*) it must be remembered that conditions here were highly favorable as compared with many of the world's other great river basins. Yet the negotiations were protracted and the results perhaps fell short of some expectations.

Several circumstances were favorable. The Columbia River is shared by two countries that have been at peace traditionally; between the peoples of the United States and Canada there exists a spirit of amity and trust as great as any to be found. In both countries capital and technical expertise are available, and there are similarities between their political ideologies. Superficially, at least, the further development of the Columbia appears to be free from the difficult problems that arise when large consumptive uses of water needed by one riparian can be attained only by reducing the water supplies of a neighboring riparian. In contrast, the objectives of a co-operative undertaking on the Columbia appear to be fairly simple ones involving headwater storage in the upstream country not only for its direct use, but also for use in the downstream country which benefits from the storage in two ways: increased flows during periods of natural low flow can increase production of hydroelectric power at head plants downstream; and modification of the peak discharge during the season of high runoff can reduce flood hazard in exposed reaches of the downstream floodplain. From the conditions of the case, it would seem that there can be only mutual benefits from such an undertaking, with incentives present for compensation payable by the downstream country to encourage development by the upstream neighbor.

Doubtless motivated by the possibility that joint endeavor would have mutually beneficial results, the governments of the United States and Canada in 1944 referred the task of assessing the possibilities for co-operative development of the Columbia River to the

International Joint Commission (IJC).[1] Fifteen years later the International Columbia River Engineering Board (ICREB), established by the IJC to undertake the necessary engineering investigations, submitted its technical findings. Within the year the IJC, at the request of the two governments,[2] began to formulate a set of principles by which to determine the benefits to be realized from the co-operative undertaking and to guide their division between the two countries. Shortly following submission of the IJC's recommendations in this regard,[3] the two governments appointed delegations to begin negotiations in February of 1960 looking toward an agreement between the two countries for the co-operative development of the Columbia. The agreement, known as the Columbia River Treaty of 17 January 1961, was reached following close to a year of negotiations.

In broad outline, the Treaty provides for the construction in Canada of storage projects to provide 15.5 million acre-feet of Canadian storage to be used largely for power and flood control objectives in the downstream reaches in the United States. In exchange, Canada received a share of the increase in power produced by U.S. generating plants benefiting from Canadian stream regulations, and also a sum intended to represent one-half the value of the flood damage reduction the reservoirs would achieve for the critical floodplain area in the United States. In addition, a transboundary storage project was agreed to, with the dam site in the United States and the reservoir headwaters extending 42 miles into the Province of British Columbia in Canada. For the latter project, each country agreed to bear the cost associated with the construction of the facility in its own country in exchange for the benefits which accrued within its own reaches of the river.

Although the Treaty was signed early in 1961 and ratified by the United States Senate within months, the Treaty's implementation was delayed for three years pending the definition of responsibilities between the Federal Government of Canada and the Province of British Columbia, and the negotiation of a revised or supplemental

[1] Reference submitted to the International Joint Commission by the Governments of Canada and the United States, March 9, 1944.

[2] Reference submitted to the International Joint Commission from the Governments of Canada and the United States, January 28–29, 1959.

[3] *Report of the International Joint Commission United States and Canada, on Principles for Determining and Apportioning Benefits from Cooperative Use of Storage Waters and Electrical Interconnection within the Columbia River System*, December 29, 1959.

agreement between the two national governments [4] preparatory to ratification by the Government of Canada. When the ratifications were exchanged in September 1964, two decades had elapsed between initiation and consummation of all steps preparatory to implementing the co-operative international river development.

Viewed in the larger perspective, the accomplishments of the Columbia River Treaty are not inconsiderable. In today's world it is no mean achievement for two riparians to come to an amicable understanding regarding a course of action when confronted by a highly complex hydrologic, economic, and political problem. In the course of the continuing dialogue we observe the evolution of an acceptance of the principle that compensation is due one riparian whose activities on his reach of the stream benefit his downstream neighbor. It may even be suggested that the results are completely consistent with the concept (which received considerable attention in the dialogue) that when the action of one riparian adversely affects another, compensation is due not only to the extent of covering the costs of damages suffered, but also to permit participation in the net yields of the undertaking which depends upon both countries' resources. And finally we witness a willingness on the part of the larger country with greater technological and economic resources to accommodate the smaller when difficulties are encountered by reason of the size of undertaking.

Although these achievements are considerable, we may not be able to learn much of practical value for future undertakings by viewing the significance of the Treaty in the broader perspective. A close and critical look at the conduct and consequences of the Columbia experience is essential if we are to appreciate fully the technical achievements that are possible and the pitfalls that should be circumvented in any similar undertaking.

Viewed in closer detail, the Columbia experience reveals shortcomings as well as accomplishments. The principles formulated to guide decisions regarding the development options marked notable advances, but they were not rigorous enough to result in the most economical system of works or to maximize the co-operative gain for mutual sharing. The temptation to exploit the foibles of the negotiating opposite number in order to obtain a larger share of a diminished joint gain proved to be overpowering. As a consequence, the Treaty system exhibits some awkward elements of such deficiencies. I believe also that the analysis in the following chapters

[4] *Annex to Exchange of Notes Dated January 22, 1964 between the Governments of Canada and the United States Regarding the Columbia River Treaty.*

will show results which cannot claim to represent an advantage to both countries when compared with alternatives available domestically to achieve equivalent flood control and power supply objectives. Doubtless, higher goals were being served. Nevertheless, while one riparian clearly advanced to a position superior to that which it could have achieved independently, the other emerged with a position inferior to one attainable had it chosen to rely exclusively on its domestic resources. This outcome was not related to the technical conditions of the matter. It came about because the United States and Canada departed from a strict adherence to one of the principles formulated by the two sections of the International Joint Commission.

The economic analysis which is the heart of this study is subject to the constraints peculiar to the circumstances of the negotiations as they developed over time. It will be recalled that some five years were spent in more or less active negotiations looking directly toward the resulting international agreement. In the interim, the government in Canada changed three times, and so did the administration in the United States. With these changes came fundamental shifts in policies which had relevance for the negotiation of the international agreement for the co-operative development of the Columbia. Meantime, also, significant technological changes took place which considerably altered the range of technical alternatives available to the two countries. As a consequence, in evaluating the economics of the international undertaking many of the "constants" of conventional economic analysis were subject to parametric shifts or, in fact, in some cases took on values of the opposite sign.

Thus, in reviewing options available to the negotiators, it is necessary to accept the policy, informational, and technological constraints within which the principals worked at that juncture in the development of the agreement which dominated the decision of the moment. This is significant because the arrangements for the Columbia tended to emerge not with a single agreement at one point in time, but rather at two junctures characterized by terms reflected in the Treaty of 1961 and the Protocol Note and related documents of January 1964.

Briefly, the problems can be posed as follows: Analysis of the technical details shows that the superior sites for storage reservoirs exist on the Canadian reaches of the Columbia and its Kootenay tributary. Funding these projects could be accomplished more economically by utilizing the superior financial resources of the

United States. Under the circumstances, an obvious approach to the problem might well have been for the United States to advance capital to Canada for the construction of storage projects of value to the United States, in exchange for the consequent increase in power and savings in flood damages.[5] However, Canadian energy policy, prior to 1963, forbade the export of energy and, according to the interpretation of the day, required that the Canadian share of the downstream power gains be repatriated. As an additional factor, during the period preceding the opening of negotiations, it was the Canadian government's policy to reduce reliance on American capital and commerce.

There were problems of policy also in the United States. There, from 1953 to 1961 the administration was hostile to federal development and operation of hydroelectric projects, among which were those contemplated on the Columbia River. Preference for licensing the development of hydroelectric resources was, therefore, given to nonfederal entities, and funds for this type of development as a federal undertaking were severely restricted under the so-called "Partnership Policy." In fact, considerable pressure was exerted to obtain power requirements in the Pacific Northwest by means other than expenditures out of the U.S. federal treasury. As a consequence, the development of storage sites lagged appreciably. A critical reason lay in the provisions of the Federal Power Act, which discouraged development of storage by nonfederal entities under the circumstances peculiar to the "Partnership" approach.[6] Similarly, little executive branch leadership was exerted on behalf of meeting power demands in the Pacific Northwest by means of, say, the Hanford nuclear reactor, or on behalf of the extra-high voltage interconnection between the Pacific Northwest and Southwest in the United States. The latter could provide a considerable amount of additional usable power from the pooled resources of the two regions operating in co-ordination. In short, under the policies of the administration in office during this period, there was little enthusiasm for any of the alternatives to obtaining power through storage projects in Canada. This attitude conditioned to an appreciable extent the selection of projects for co-operative development and the value of the international agreement itself.

[5] G. L. Reuber and R. J. Wonnacott, *The Cost of Capital in Canada, with Special Reference to Public Development of the Columbia River* (Washington: Resources for the Future, Inc., 1961), p. 84.

[6] John V. Krutilla and Otto Eckstein, *Multiple Purpose River Development* (Baltimore: The Johns Hopkins Press for Resources for the Future, Inc., 1958), Chapter V.

Following the signing of the Treaty in 1961, however, changes in government, both in Ottawa and Washington, produced a marked shift in the policies of relevance to the negotiations for the Columbia Treaty. In Canada, the Province of British Columbia asserted independent goals, which were found to be incompatible with the terms of the Treaty—specifically with respect to repatriation of the Canadian share of the jointly produced power and the rejection of American capital for the construction of Canadian storage projects on the Columbia River in Canada. In the United States, prospects improved for the development of domestic resources. A federal storage project was authorized and construction began; prospects for construction of another were promising; and a license was issued for private development of a third project. The Hanford New Production Reactor became a valid alternative for producing thermal power, and prospects were bright for developing a large-scale extra-high voltage transmission facility which would interconnect the Pacific Northwest with California and the Pacific Southwest. Accordingly, many of the critical "givens" during the period in which the Treaty of 1961 was negotiated were altered before the final negotiations started which would lead to the ultimate terms of the 1964 agreement.

In view of the foregoing, it is clear that an analysis of the economics of the Treaty results must guard against hindsight. To view the outcome from the standpoint of the present time might well cast light on the wisdom of the policies as they evolved, but would not faithfully reflect the options open to the planners and negotiators at any one point in time. Therefore, I do not choose to evaluate the terms of the Treaty of 1961 on the basis of the subsequent relaxation of policy constraints and the accumulation of additional information not available to the decision makers during their earlier discussions. Nor, in considering the outcome of later negotiations and the final terms of the international agreement, do I wish to ignore the commitments which, for all practical purposes, had been frozen into the agreement by circumstances governing the earlier periods. To take a different course might reveal much that is significant, but would incur resources of planning and engineering equivalent to those available to the governments concerned which, of course, are utterly beyond the resources at the disposal of an individual scholar or a modest research institution.

In this study, therefore, I shall attempt to review the data that were available at the time each decision juncture was reached and to recognize the policy constraints that bounded the range of feasible alternatives open to the principals negotiating the agreement. Enough can be learned from the exercise, I believe, to attain a better understanding of the circumstances in which decisions of this sort are likely to occur. In addition, analysis of the experience in these terms may provide lessons of considerable transfer value for the planning and negotiation of other international agreements for co-operative undertakings around the globe.

Chapter 2

The Columbia River: Its Physiography and State of Development

The Columbia River system drains a watershed of about a quarter of a million square miles and has a mean annual discharge of close to 250,000 cubic feet per second (cfs). Its volume of flow is exceeded only by the Mississippi's, the MacKenzie's, and the St. Lawrence's on the continent of North America, and is almost four times as great as the Tennessee's, perhaps the world's best known power stream. In addition to its volume of discharge, the Columbia and its tributaries rise at high elevations in mountainous terrain with numerous sites along the stream course where the fall of the river can be utilized effectively for the generation of hydroelectricity. The Columbia also supports an anadromous fishery, supplies water in the arid portion of its basin for irrigation agriculture, and is used as an artery of commerce from its mouth inland over 350 river miles as well as upon isolated reaches upstream. As a resource of considerable economic potential, it has long commanded attention for development and exploitation.

The Columbia River Basin consists of all of Montana lying west of the Continental Divide, the bulk of Idaho, eastern Washington and Oregon, relatively small portions of northern Nevada, Utah, and western Wyoming in the United States, and southeastern British Columbia (see Figure 1). Extending some 270 miles north into British Columbia, it occupies about 39,000 square miles of Canadian territory, equivalent to about 11 per cent of the land area of British Columbia. Its southern extension into Nevada and Utah lies some 550 miles south of the international boundary, and its widest portion from Astoria, Oregon, to the headwaters of the Snake River measures about 730 miles. The total area of the basin in the United States is about 220,000 square miles. The Columbia's

15

watershed lies generally between the principal chain of the Rocky Mountains and the Cascade Range, with the Puget Trough, a sub-basin lying between the Cascades and the Coastal ranges of Washington and Oregon, making up the relatively small portion of the basin which lies west of the Cascades.

The Columbia River has its origin in British Columbia, emerging from Columbia Lake at an elevation of 2,654 feet. It flows north-westerly in the Rocky Mountain Trench around the northern extensions of the Purcell and Selkirk mountains, turning sharply around the latter in the Big Bend to proceed southerly down the

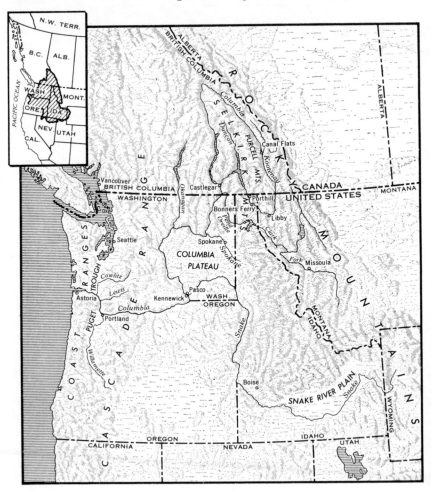

Figure 1.   The Columbia River Basin.

Selkirk Trench to its confluence first with the Kootenay (Kootenai, U.S. spelling) and next with the Pend Oreille (Pend d'Oreille, Canadian spelling) just prior to its entering the United States. Over this course it descends 1,366 feet and at the international boundary the flow is about 40 per cent of the Columbia's ultimate discharge. The mainstem accounts for about 17 per cent of the flow at the border; the Kootenay, about 12 per cent; and the Pend Oreille, about 11 per cent.

In the United States the Columbia continues its course for approximately 100 river miles to its confluence with the Spokane River, a lesser tributary of the Columbia. Thereupon it changes direction abruptly toward the west, flowing into the Grand Coulee and St. Joseph reservoir areas, and beyond to its confluence with the Okanogan (Okanagan, Canadian spelling). Turning south beyond this point it flows in a southerly direction to its confluence with the Snake, the largest tributary of the system. Below the Snake it proceeds generally in a westerly direction through a series of reservoirs from McNary to Bonneville, emerging into the Puget Trough through Columbia Gorge, a gap in the Cascade Range. At Portland, Oregon, it is joined by the Willamette, the largest of the Puget Trough tributaries. Beyond Portland it picks up the flows of the Lewis and Cowlitz tributaries before discharging into the Pacific Ocean at Astoria, Oregon.

The tributary of major concern in a co-operative effort for development of the upper Columbia Basin resources is the Kootenay. This tributary rises in the Rocky Mountains approximately 40 miles west across the Continental Divide from Banff, at an elevation of 4,150 feet. Its flows parallel the Columbia's in the opposite direction for approximately 80 miles, after which the Kootenay cuts westerly to enter the Rocky Mountain Trench, converging on Columbia Lake where it passes within a mile and a half of the Columbia's source in the vicinity of Canal Flats. It then proceeds generally southward across the international boundary to a point beyond Libby, Montana. Downstream from Libby it swings northward along the Purcell Trench to re-enter Canada 47 miles downstream from Bonners Ferry, Idaho, near Porthill. It then proceeds another 28 miles into British Columbia before discharging into Kootenay Lake. The Duncan River, rising in the Purcell Trench and flowing southward, joins the Kootenay in this vicinity, and the combined flows proceed downstream another 23 miles to their confluence with the Columbia River near Castlegar, British Columbia.

Climatically, the Columbia Basin is affected by a combination of maritime and continental meteorological factors. West of the Cascades, the maritime influence predominates. East of the Cascades, the winter season is relatively more affected by the maritime influences, whereas the continental weather patterns predominate during the summer season. Precipitation tends to vary greatly between the Puget Trough and the principal portion of the Columbia lying east of the Cascades (see Figure 2). Annual precipi-

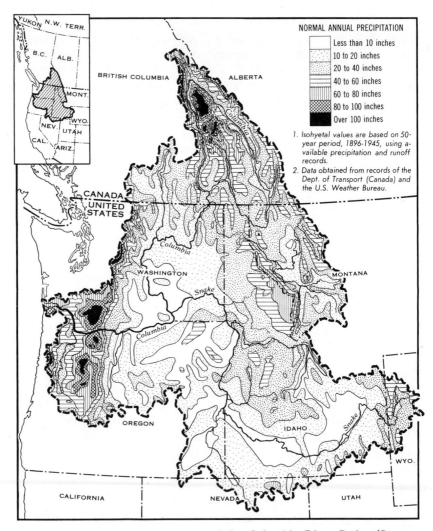

Figure 2. Climatic characteristics of the Columbia River Basin. (Source: *Columbia River and Tributaries*, Vol. I, H.D. No. 403, 87th Cong., 2nd Sess., Plate 5.)

tation of 150 inches is known along the summits of the Coastal Range, whereas the mean in the Kennewick-Pasco area of south central Washington is only about 7 inches. More typically, the precipitation ranges from 40 to 80 inches in various localities in the Puget Trough, to 10–15 inches in much of the arid portions of the Snake Basin, and 15–25 inches more generally in the Columbia Plateau areas. Along the slopes of the Rockies and in the upper reaches of the Columbia watershed in the Monashee, Purcell, and Selkirk mountains, large areas receive precipitation in the 60–80 inch range with some receiving in excess of 100 inches.

Atmospheric moisture precipitates in the form of rain in the warmer climes of the areas west of the Cascades, predominantly in the winter months. Peak runoff occurs during the period of peak precipitations. By contrast, the eastern slopes of the Cascades, the Columbia Plateau, and the western slopes of the Rockies receive their precipitation mostly in the form of snow during a long winter season. A large part of the moisture is immobilized in the snowpack, accumulating until spring when thaws, sometimes accompanied by warm rains, release the accumulated moisture generally at a rapid rate. The peak runoff occurs during the months of May, June, and July at the height of the snowmelt, while low flows occur during the winter months of January and February. Since about three quarters of the discharge of the Columbia originates in the watersheds east of the Cascades (see Figure 3), the hydrologic variation on the mainstem of the Columbia is dominated by the seasonal pattern, reflecting gradual accumulation of the snowpack followed by the relatively abrupt releases of moisture with the onset of warm spring and summer temperatures. The variation in the rate of runoff, accordingly, is quite large, with the mean monthly discharge during the highest flows of record exceeding the lowest flows by 30 to 35 times along the mainstem of the Columbia (see Figure 4).

Such hydrologic variability represents a serious limitation, under natural conditions, on the potential contribution of the water resources to the welfare of the region's inhabitants. The volume of discharge during the late spring and early summer under the more extreme conditions is capable of reaching flood stages of damaging proportions. Similarly, low flows occurring during the winter months of peak power demand adversely affect the generation of power in relation to its seasonal demand in the absence of storage development to achieve stream regulation.

The major area of general flood hazard is in the floodplain of the lower Columbia in a reach of about 140 miles downstream from

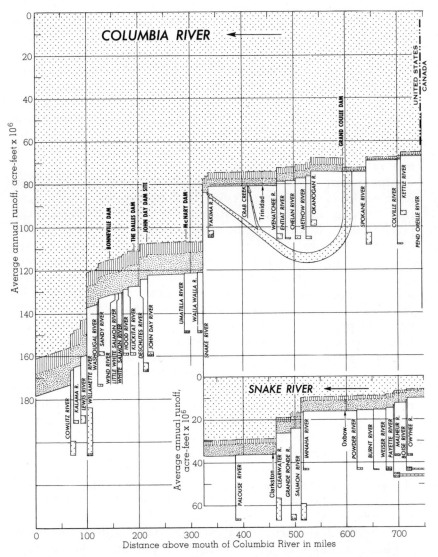

Figure 3. Watershed area and runoff diagram of the Columbia River and its tributaries. (Source: *Columbia River and Tributaries*, Vol. I, H.D. No. 403, 87th Cong., 2nd Sess., Plate 7.)

Bonneville Dam. Here, because of the relatively dense settlement, high-valued agricultural pursuits, and the urban-industrial developments along the floodplain, the damage potential is large, amounting to roughly 90 per cent of the estimated total throughout

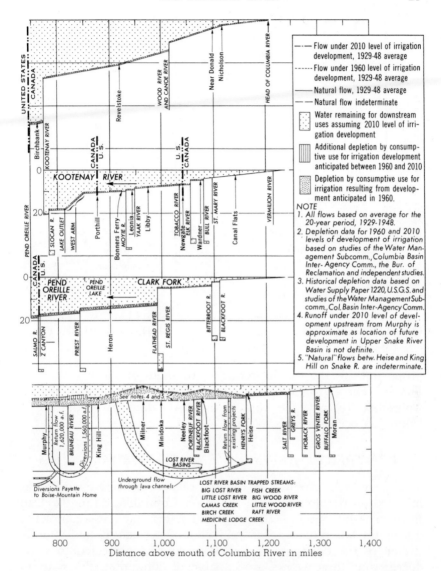

Distance above mouth of Columbia River in miles

the Columbia Basin.[1] In the upper Columbia and related sub-basins the potential flood damage is of a different order, occurring often in response to localized weather and runoff conditions which do not necessarily contribute to peak discharges on the lower Columbia. On the Kootenay, a persistent problem of significant

[1] *Columbia River and Tributaries, Northwest United States*, Vol. I, H.D. No. 531, 81st Cong., 2nd Sess., March 1950, p. 119.

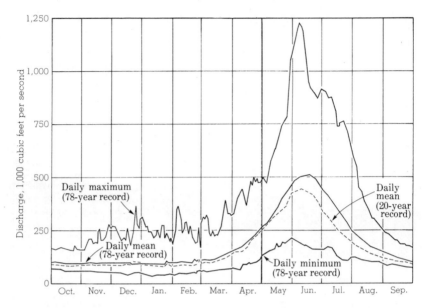

Figure 4. Summary hydrographs of the Columbia River near The Dalles, Oregon. (Source: *Columbia River and Tributaries*, Vol. I, H.D. No. 403, 87th Cong., 2nd Sess., Plate 8.)

proportions occurs with a frequency of about one in five years at Bonners Ferry, Idaho, and in the Creston Flats area of British Columbia. In fact, the bulk of the flood damage in the upper Columbia occurs at this locality.

PRE-TREATY DEVELOPMENT OF THE COLUMBIA

An extensive system of levees and related protective works was initiated on the floodplain of the lower Columbia, dating back to the turn of the century. The major part of this system was completed during the late nineteen thirties. About 60 per cent of the 140-mile stretch of the floodplain below Bonneville is protected to some degree and these works are capable of containing flows up to 800,000 cfs as measured at The Dalles, the focal point for the flood management operations on the lower Columbia. Such flood walls reduce annual damage potential by an estimated 35 per cent. [2]

Over the years since the mid-nineteen thirties, the United States has built and planned multiple-purpose projects on its reach of the

[2] "Determination of Annual Average Damage" (worksheet), NPP Form 285, U.S. Army Engineer Division, North Pacific, Portland District, March 21, 1958.

Columbia. By 1959—the year in which the International Columbia River Engineering Board completed its investigation of the possibilities for joint development of the river by the United States and Canada—existing storage projects and those well under construction aggregated about 10.5 million acre-feet of potentially usable storage. But, owing to difficulties in utilizing the bottom tier of outlets at Grand Coulee without additional storage upstream to eliminate involuntary filling during flood-routing operations, only about 8 million acre-feet could be used. This complement of storage, in conjunction with irrigation diversion during the flood period, could reduce a natural peak discharge at The Dalles of 1,240,000 cfs, characteristic of the 1894 flood of record, to 1,030,000 cfs. Control such as this would reduce the total damage potential in the lower Columbia by an additional 44 per cent,[3] leaving the floodplain subject to about 21 per cent of the total damage potential. Reduction of the damage potential further depends on additional flood control storage along with additional local flood protection measures.

Associated with the program of multiple-purpose project development, about 1,121 feet of the 1,288-foot drop between the international boundary and the mouth of the river were either developed, under construction, or under active consideration in 1960, at the time serious negotiations leading to the Columbia Treaty were initiated (see Figure 5). Only the Ben Franklin site between McNary Dam and Priest Rapids remained for active consideration to complete a continuous development of the head between Bonneville Dam and the boundary. Upon completion of the projects then under way, the mainstem below the boundary would have about 9.8 million kilowatts of installed capacity and about 5.7 million acre-feet of storage usable for power production. The mainstem development of multiple-purpose projects will represent an investment of about $2.7 billion when projects are completed. Another 3 million kilowatts and about 8 million acre-feet of storage—approximating in capacity the TVA hydro system—were distributed on the Clark Fork–Pend Oreille and Snake rivers.

Although the British Columbia portion of the Columbia system has a large hydroelectric potential, only limited development has taken place, none of which is on the mainstem of the Columbia River. About 364 feet of head on the lower Kootenay in the 23-mile reach below Kootenay Lake and the river's mouth have been

[3] *Ibid.*

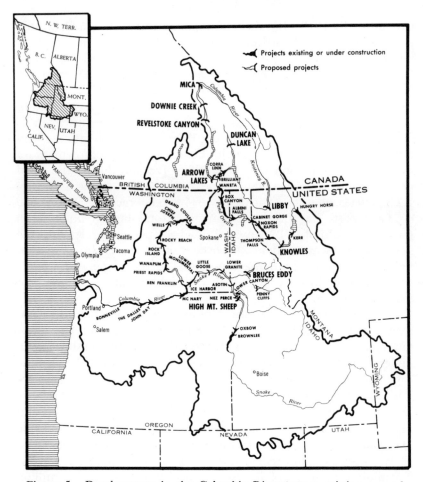

Figure 5.   Developments in the Columbia River system existing or under construction in 1960, and those proposed during Treaty negotiations. (Sources: *Columbia River and Tributaries*, Vol. I, H.D. No. 403, 87th Cong., 2nd Sess., Plate 1; and International Columbia River Engineering Board, *Water Resources of the Columbia River Basin*, Report to the International Joint Commission United States and Canada, 1959, p. 67.)

developed with about 271,000 kilowatts of installed generator capacity. One facility, operating in conjunction with outlet improvements on Kootenay Lake, provides about 800,000 acre-feet of controlled storage. Another 181,000 [4] kilowatts of capacity have

---

[4] A third unit was installed at Waneta in 1964 and a fourth was in progress for operation in 1966, for a total of 360,000 kw. Letter from Mr. Richard Deane, August 24, 1965.

been installed at Waneta on the lower Pend d'Oreille, in British Columbia. Major hydroelectric developments on the mainstem over the 1,366 feet of head remain to be developed along with storage possibilities on the upper Kootenay.

Table 1 gives a breakdown of the major hydroelectric developments on the reaches of the Columbia and tributary system, of interest in this study. In spite of the substantial investment, hydroelectric development there has been uneven. Moreover, in an

TABLE 1

Major Power Projects on the Columbia and Major Tributaries East of Cascades, 1959

Projects	Gross head (feet)	Installed capacity (kilowatts)	Storage (acre-feet)
Kootenay River			
Corra Linn	53	40,500	817,000
Upper Bonnington	70	54,700	Pondage
Lower Bonnington	70	47,250	Pondage
South Slocan	70	47,250	Pondage
Brilliant	93	81,600	Pondage
Clark Fork–Pend Oreille			
Hungry Horse	477	285,000	2,980,000
Kerr	187	168,000	1,219,000
Thompson Falls	47–60	30,000	Pondage
Noxon Rapids	154	336,000	Pondage
Cabinet Gorge	97	200,000	Pondage
Albeni Falls	28	42,600	1,155,000
Box Canyon	28–42	60,000	Pondage
Waneta	210	144,000	Pondage
Snake River and Tributaries			
Palisades	245	114,000	1,202,000
American Falls	48	27,500	—
Upper Salmon	45	34,500	Pondage
Lower Salmon	59	60,000	Pondage
Anderson Ranch	326	27,000	423,200
Brownlee	272	360,400	1,000,034
Oxbow	122	190,000	Pondage
Little Goose	100	405,000	Pondage
Lower Monumental	100	405,000	Pondage
Ice Harbor	100	270,000	Pondage
Columbia River (Mainstem)			
Grand Coulee	341	1,944,999	5,072,000
Chief Joseph	171	1,024,000	Pondage
Wells	68	490,000	Pondage
Rocky Reach	95	712,000	Pondage
Rock Island	49	206,400	Pondage
Wanapum	80	831,000	500,000
Priest Rapids	80	788,000	170,000
McNary	78	980,000	Pondage
John Day	104	1,200,000	500,000
The Dalles	86	1,119,000	Pondage
Bonneville	59	518,400	Pondage

Source: International Columbia River Engineering Board, Water Resources of the Columbia River Basin, report to the International Joint Commission United States and Canada, 1959.

COLORADO MOUNTAIN COLLEGE
LRC---WEST CAMPUS
Glenwood Springs, Colo. 81601

economic sense the development represents an imbalance, with a preponderance of investment in run-of-the-river plants and a deficiency of storage. This situation had developed largely in response to the federal "Partnership Policy" during the decade of the nineteen fifties which, as has been mentioned in Chapter 1, had a wholly unintended result of discouraging development of storage facilities. [5] To illustrate the relation between storage and prime power production, the system existing as of 1959 could produce but 2,972 megawatts (mw) of prime power in the absence of stream regulation. With the storage then existing, used for stream regulation, the prime power production increased to 5,310 mw an increase of almost 80 per cent. Without further development of head, an additional $5\frac{1}{2}$ million acre-feet of storage in the reaches upstream from Grand Coulee, usable for power operations, would increase prime power production another 1,000 mw.

Thus, given the relationship between hydrologic variability and both the potential flood damages and power losses, the construction of storage projects was a prime objective of further development of the Columbia system when the Columbia Treaty negotiations began. Nevertheless, other objectives of multiple-purpose river development influenced the selection of the reaches in which storage was marked for development, and the volume of storage, in turn, has implications of a somewhat more limited sort for their realization. Because these secondary objectives will not be dealt with explicitly in the detailed analysis of the Columbia Treaty which follows in later chapters, they are mentioned here to give some indication of the side effects which had to be considered during the negotiations.

CONSEQUENCES OF THE TREATY FOR EARLIER OBJECTIVES

The Columbia Basin Project, initiated in the mid-thirties, developed hydroelectric and irrigation facilities on the Grand Coulee, which created an obstacle to migrating Pacific salmon above this point and thus eliminated the salmon fishery in the upper Columbia. [6] Further developments upstream from Grand Coulee could not further damage the Columbia salmon fishery, whereas storage projects on some tributaries of the Snake, for

[5] See p. 12.

[6] Save for a species of landlocked salmon popularly referred to as Kokanee.

example, might substantially impair the quality of the fishery in spite of fish ladder facilities and related measures to help the fish in their migrations. Development of projects upstream from Grand Coulee was looked upon, therefore, as a rational way to "buy time" for the Salmon and other tributaries of the Middle Snake. But for anadromous fish the obstacles posed by hydroelectric facilities are not confined to the upstream migration of spawning adults. Equally difficult for them is the return migration to the open sea, when the young fry can be destroyed if they are unable to avoid the turbines. With the volume of storage contemplated by the Treaty, a succession of below-normal runoff years will require all the stream flow to pass through the turbines. Consequently, the fry will be unable to use the spillway as a means of escape, a present possibility with the less completely controlled hydrologic regime. While this problem represents an unconsidered consequence of the Treaty storage and has not been thoroughly evaluated, it remains basically a domestic problem for the United States and is not related to the co-operative use of Treaty storage. [7]

Similarly, irrigation development remains predominantly a local matter without significant implications for international co-operative efforts. In the United States portion of the basin major irrigation development, planned by the U.S. Bureau of Reclamation, has occurred since the turn of the century; save for the Columbia Basin Project (in association with Grand Coulee) and the Yakima and Snake River projects, most of it was completed by 1928. In the Canadian portion of the basin the limited amount of irrigation there occurred prior to 1928.

While irrigation development has been a principal undertaking in the multiple-purpose development of rivers in the United States, it cannot everywhere be regarded as an economic venture. [8] Further irrigation development, therefore, is largely dependent on public policy which must judge the extent to which such development should be subsidized to realize some strongly entrenched social objectives—objectives which appear anachronistic in the last

[7] Canadian storage by itself will not eliminate summer spills; thus, if annual spilling is required to preserve the anadromous fishery, further storage development on the U.S. reaches of the Columbia system could be halted. This does raise an interesting "displacement" problem which will be developed fully in Chapter 3.

[8] Rudolph Ulrich, "Relative Costs and Benefits of Land Reclamation in the Humid Southeast and the Semi-Arid West," *Journal of Farm Economics*, Vol. XXXV, No. 1 (February, 1953), pp. 62–73.

half of the twentieth century. Whether scarce water supplies should be dedicated to uneconomic agricultural pursuits is a matter attracting increasing attention in the United States and is likely to come under review in the foreseeable future. The prospect for future irrigation development in the arid west is therefore uncertain. In the Canadian portion of the Columbia Basin, potentially irrigable land is quite scarce so that, regardless of the policy issue, depletion of streamflows for agricultural purposes is unlikely to be a significant factor there. Thus, except for possible depletion of flows (diversion less the subterranean return of a portion of diverted flows), irrigation development in the separate portions of the basin remains largely a domestic consideration with only limited significance for the planning of co-operative development of the Columbia. [9]

There is one respect, however, in which the storage secured by the Treaty raises questions about the operation of the Columbia Basin Project. Since it began operating, this irrigation project has used dump power (generated during the season of peak runoff), for which there was no alternative productive use, to pump water out of the Grand Coulee reservoir into a retention basin above the Coulee. With the volume of storage secured by the Treaty, however, the conversion of such power into firm power will permit its use in much higher-valued alternative applications; thus, the real costs of the Columbia Basin Project operation will be substantially increased.

Another objective of pre-Treaty development on the Columbia in the United States has been the provision of an inland waterway. The Columbia is navigable from its mouth to the McNary pool, and the means for its extension into the lower reaches of the Snake and upward to Rock Island Dam have been provided for in the facilities built in those reaches. Unlike some other purposes for which development has been undertaken, navigation upstream is not dependent on additional flows made available from storage operations during periods of low runoff, but rather upon the relation between the anticipated volume of traffic, the cost of alternative means of transportation, and the cost of channel maintenance and lock installations in existing dams. For navigation, the one implication of the Columbia River Treaty stems from the related Northwest-Southwest intertie, a development which advances the

[9] The Treaty permits diversion from the Columbia for consumption uses but the likelihood of significant diversions in Canada appears negligible. See *Minutes of Proceedings and Evidence*, No. 3, Standing Committee on External Affairs, House of Commons, Twenty-Sixth Parliament, Second Session, April 9, 1964, p. 140 ff.

date at which the Columbia's generating capacity will be used essentially for diurnal peaking, with attendant surges of water in the vicinity of the power houses that may complicate the movement of barge traffic on the waterway.

Finally, there is the question, often raised as an adjunct to a regional water quality management program, of the need for storage to provide low-flow augmentation for municipal, industrial, and general non-irrigation water supplies. In the case of the Columbia Basin, this need appears to be amply met by a storage capacity considerably less than that proposed under the terms of the Treaty to take care of flood management and power operations. Studies made by the Senate Select Committee on National Water Resources indicate that storage for municipal and industrial water supply and waste dilution on the Columbia, projected to the year 2000, will require little more storage than presently exists and greatly less than the storage in prospect, especially that set aside for power operations. [10]

Having reviewed the characteristics of the Columbia River system and the state of development existing there prior to the Columbia River Treaty, it is understandable why the Treaty negotiators found the provision of storage and its co-operative use to be the area in which a co-operative effort appeared most promising. It will be shown in succeeding chapters that the storage that can be employed usefully in the Columbia is governed predominantly by the stream regulation requirements for an efficient power-generating program. To a somewhat lesser extent, additional storage is required for meeting flood management objectives in the lower Columbia and, also to an extent, the flood hazard problems in the Bonners Ferry, Idaho, area. Since the prospect is slight in either country that domestic undertakings will involve large-scale consumptive diversions for irrigation agriculture, with consequent reduced river flow across the international boundary, the negotiations appeared to offer no problem of the sort encountered when one riparian's consumptive use of a resource adversely affects the quantity or quality of a neighboring riparian's water supplies.

The avoidance of a difficult pre-emption problem, however, is more apparent than real. When one riparian provides storage services for another under given circumstances, certain attributes

[10] *Water Resource Activities in the United States: Water Supply and Demand*, Select Committee on National Water Resources, United States Senate, 86th Cong., 2nd Sess., Committee Print No. 32, p. 9, Table 4.

of the problem bear a close correspondence to the pre-emption of a scarce resource. In this instance, as will be shown, the outcome has the effect of pre-empting not the resource in question, but the returns that can be obtained from resources in the neighboring country. In order to understand the mechanism by which this result occurs, a careful review of some basic storage relationships must be undertaken. This task is addressed in Chapter 3 preparatory to analyzing the specifics of the Columbia River Treaty.

Chapter 3

Some Economic Attributes
of Storage for Flood Management
and Power Production

~~~~~~~~~~~~~~~~~~~~~~~~~~~~~~~

In Chapter 2 it was asserted that the most productive sector on which to focus for the co-ordinated planning and operation of the Columbia system related to the use of storage principally for the production of power, and, to a lesser extent, to meet flood management objectives on the lower Columbia. This, in fact, was the substance of the Columbia River Treaty and related documents. The matter of determining which storage sites best met the needs of the system and the question of an equitable division of the resulting benefits were deliberated by the two countries over a period of five years after the technical possibilities had been identified through engineering investigations. The great amount of effort expended in resolving the issues was due at least partly to the complexity of the problem of evaluating the ultimate effects of storage projects—of understanding the subtle relationships involved and how these could change in response to the growth of the regional power system over time. This chapter will explore, first, the complementary (additive) and substitutive (displacement) effects of storage in a hydrologic system to illustrate the problem in its simplest—i.e., static—form. In addition, it will consider how these relationships, in the case of storage used in power operations, will change as the regional power market grows to the point at which the hydro-electric potential of the region is exceeded and thermal sources of energy are required to meet the region's power demands. The principles established, while illustrated with examples drawn from the Columbia case, have general applicability.

31

THE STATIC CASE

STORAGE AS VIEWED IN ITS COMPLEMENTARY ASPECTS

Power production. In the United States, power is sold a consumer with the expectation that it will be available on demand at the convenience of the consumer irrespective of the time of day or season of the year. Since most uses of electricity to power motors, provide illumination, and produce heat tend to be intermittent, greater capacity is needed to meet the demand than would be the case if the electricity were consumed at a uniform rate through time. In thermal electric systems it is customary to install sufficient capacity (along with reserves) to meet the coincident peak demands on the system. This capacity represents the firm load-carrying capability of the system and is referred to as "dependable capacity." The capacity is operated at whatever fraction of the time it is required by the time distribution of the system's load. [1]

In the Pacific Northwest, because of the large hydroelectric potential in relation to past and present regional power demands, the region's loads have been met almost exclusively with hydroelectricity. Unlike thermal systems, however, the amount of capacity installed does not necessarily represent the firm load-carrying capability of a hydro system, or its dependable capacity. The production of power is ultimately related to the flow of water over a given head, and the dependable capacity is limited by the availability of water during the most adverse streamflow conditions.

The use of streamflows for the production of power usually takes account of the variability of the instantaneous demand by providing pondage at the hydroelectric dam to enable varying the rate of energy supplied to conform to the diurnal or weekly variation in the load. However, if the entire power supply were provided by such hydroelectric installations alone, it is estimated that because of the hydrologic variability of the stream only about 20 to 25 per cent of the theoretically possible energy from a stream such as the Columbia River could be relied upon as a source of firm power. [2]

[1] The intermittent demands for power in residential and commercial activities give rise to what is called a "load duration curve." This curve describes the relation between the amount of power demanded and the percentage of the time each amount is required ordered from the highest or peak demand, to the minimum required. The average demand during an interval divided by the peak demand of the interval represents the system load factor for the interval.

[2] B. E. Torpen, *Storage for Power, Columbia River Basin*, U. S. Army Engineer Division, North Pacific, Portland District, August 1945.

For example, consider the prospective power dams at Downie Creek and Revelstoke Canyon on the upper Columbia in Canada. Relying only on the natural flows on the mainstem of the Columbia at these points, the amount of power which could be supplied under the most adverse streamflow conditions at each site would be, respectively, 45 mw and 36 mw. With storage upstream at the Mica site of roughly 11 million acre-feet, the amount of power that could be generated under similar streamflow conditions would be increased respectively to 481 mw and 339 mw. In this respect there is evidence of significant complementarity between run-of-the-river head plants and storage projects. The way inflows in excess of requirements of the moment are stored for release during adverse streamflow conditions is illustrated graphically in Figure 6.

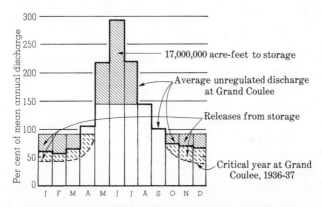

Figure 6.   Storage release cycle of the Columbia River at Grand Coulee. (Source: B.E. Torpen, *Storage for Power, Columbia River Basin*, U.S. Army Engineer Division, North Pacific, Portland District, August 1945.)

Here it is observed that during the months of May, June, and July, during the peak discharge season, excess flows are retained in storage reservoirs to be released during the seven months when energy requirements exceed streamflows.

The production of hydroelectricity is the product of the volume of flow and the drop, or head, over which the water falls. [3] Accordingly, it is usually most economic to locate the storage capacity as high in the headwaters of a river system as feasible (subject to there

[3] The relationship between power in kilowatts and the flow and head, under assumed conditions of 90 per cent turbine and 94.5 per cent generator efficiency can be shown approximately as $KW = 0.072 (Q \times H)$, where Q is the flow in cubic feet per second and H the head in feet.

being sufficient flow to utilize the storage capacity). With this arrangement of storage and run-of-the-river plants, the loss of head at storage projects occasioned by drafting the reservoir to augment low flows can be more than compensated by the larger amount of developed head downstream over which the improved streamflow passes.

Given these relationships, it is understandable that for reasons of economy a fine balance should exist between the head to be developed and the amount of storage to be associated with it. Because the preponderance of the investment in hydroelectric plants on the Columbia went into head plants during the decade of the nineteen fifties, the addition of some storage could be expected to show disproportionate returns, as in fact it will.

Flood management. A substantial portion of the floodplain in the lower Columbia benefits from a system of levees capable of containing flood crests up to 800,000 cfs at The Dalles, the focal point for the flood management operations on the lower Columbia. The U.S. Army Corps of Engineers estimates that it is desirable to extend the levee system to afford protection against flows of up to 940,000 cfs, but that it is impracticable to go beyond this level.[4] To reduce the flood damage potential further will require either complementary non-structural measures,[5] or storage facilities upstream to impound the peak of the discharges exceeding 940,000 cfs.

Figures 7a and 7b illustrate the effects of storage operations in achieving a crest reduction to 800,000 cfs to complement the levee system. Assuming a flood with characteristics comparable to the record flood of 1894, Figure 7a shows schematically the effect of using 9.5 million acre-feet of storage located above Grand Coulee in comparison with the unregulated hydrograph at that site.

[4] *Columbia River and Tributaries,* Vol. I, H.D. No. 403, 87th Cong., 2nd Sess., containing "Review of H.D. 531, 81st Cong., 2nd Sess., Water Resources Development of the Columbia River Basin," p. 30.

[5] For a discussion of non-structural measures in reducing flood damage, see the important work of Gilbert F. White and colleagues, University of Chicago, Department of Geography Research Papers Nos. 56, 57, 65, 70, 75, 78, and 93. In fact, whether or not levees capable of containing flows up to 940,000 cfs and/or additional storage are warranted economically is not independent of the potential for flood damage reduction of such non-structural measures. Analyses of the kind suggested by White and colleagues were not performed in connection with the floodplain studies on the lower Columbia and thus, whether there is a lower cost alternative to the program advanced by the Corps of Engineers is not known.

Figure 7b shows the effects of the Grand Coulee and similar controlled storage operations, and surcharge storage through changes
in levels of natural lakes, on the hydrograph at The Dalles. The
reduction of the crest from 1,240,000 cfs to 790,000 cfs is accomplished by approximately 7.5 million acre-feet of usable storage
additional to that available in 1959.

Storage can be utilized with maximum effectiveness if located
near the floodplain to be protected. Control of the peak discharge
of the 1894 flood to 800,000 cfs at The Dalles, Oregon, in fact,
could be achieved with only 6.5 million acre-feet of storage additional to that available in the existing system, if it were located
immediately upstream from the floodplain for which the flood-
routing operations are undertaken. However, in view of the
multiple-purpose nature of the Columbia River projects—their
joint use, especially in the production of hydroelectricity—it is

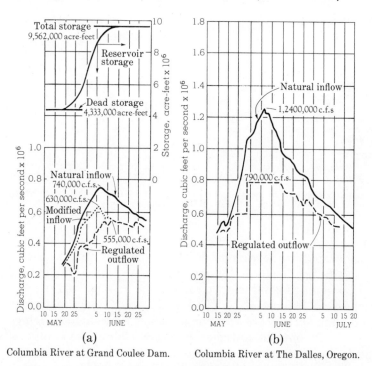

(a)   (b)

Columbia River at Grand Coulee Dam.   Columbia River at The Dalles, Oregon.

Figure 7.   Natural and regulated hydrographs in flood management
operations for the Columbia River System at Grand Coulee Dam and
The Dalles. (Source: *Columbia River and Tributaries*, Vol. I, H.D. No.
403, 87th Cong., 2nd Sess., Plates 11 and 12.)

neither feasible nor economic to locate flood management storage in the lower reaches, where the largest flood hazard is encountered. Storage in the upper reaches of the mainstem and tributaries, while most efficient from the standpoint of producing power and protecting exposed reaches of the floodplain at isolated locations along the tributary reaches of the system, can be utilized with only diminished effectiveness for flood control on the lower Columbia. For this reason, a larger absolute amount of flood control storage than the theoretical minimum is required and will be used with diminished effectiveness to provide the equivalent of the 6.5 million acre-feet of flood control storage at The Dalles. Table 2 gives the amount of flood control storage in the Columbia system as of 1959 with its associated effectiveness factor.

TABLE 2

Columbia River Flood Control Storage and Effectiveness Factors, 1959

Projects	Usable flood control storage for 1894 flood (acre-feet)	Estimated per cent[1] effectiveness for controlled discharge to 800,000 cfs
Grand Coulee	5,230,000[2]	99
Hungry Horse	1,830,000	74
Palisades	1,150,000	91
Boise River projects	240,000	94
Payette River projects	420,000	87
Brownlee	1,000,000	100
TOTAL	9,870,000	

[1] Columbia River and Tributaries, Vol. II, H.D. No. 403, 87th Cong., 2nd Sess., Appendix A, Table 4.
[2] Requires sixty outlets operating, only forty of which were effective as of 1959. This also assumes additional storage upstream of Grand Coulee in order to permit effective operation of the lower tier of twenty outlets.

In a real sense, then, since the flood control storage cannot be concentrated in the vicinity of The Dalles but must be distributed among the headwater streams, storages distributed among the upper reaches tend to complement each other in achieving a controlled discharge of 800,000 cfs at The Dalles. And the fact that more than 6.5 million acre-feet of additional storage is required to achieve the 800,000 cfs controlled discharge at The Dalles is of comparatively minor significance, as the amount of storage to be incorporated into an efficient Columbia system will be dominated by the demand for storage capacity associated with the production of power. To state the matter somewhat differently, when all the storage that can be justified for hydroelectric power production has been included, wherever located in the system, the storage available for flood management operations will be ample, given the relative power and flood management storage demands. This being the case, the analysis in this study is concerned primarily with the power production aspects. However, since matters related to flood management figured in the design of the Treaty system and in the division of the co-operative gains, a brief discussion of the flood management aspect is required before the matter can be dismissed.

STORAGE AS VIEWED IN ITS SUBSTITUTIVE ASPECTS

There is little question that storage in a hydroelectric or in a flood management system complements other elements in such systems to achieve most economically the objectives of flood damage reduction and power production. This, in fact, is the relation which tends to dominate thinking when consideration of storage is at issue, usually to the exclusion of the substitution relationships which, in an internationally co-operative venture, are especially important. That a substitution relationship exists is due to the diminishing incremental yield of storage for power production and/or the diminishing incremental reduction of peak discharge in flood management operations, as more storage is added to the system beyond a certain point. Such relationships are quite important and have been at the root of much of the controversy preceding a resolution of the issues on the Columbia River. They should, therefore, be given careful consideration here, despite their essentially elementary nature.

SUBSTITUTION OR DISPLACEMENT EFFECTS IN FLOOD MANAGEMENT

The U.S. Army Corps of Engineers tends to treat the value of storage for flood management purposes as a discontinuous function of the volume of storage provided. Largely because of the levee system which is effective for considerable reaches on the lower Columbia floodplain in containing flood crests up to 800,000 cfs at The Dalles, the "primary flood control objective" as stated by the Corps is a storage system capable of reducing the peak discharge of a flood of the characteristics of the 1894 flood of record to 800,000 cfs measured at The Dalles. Each acre-foot of the 17 million acre-feet of effective storage is regarded as making an equal contribution toward meeting the flood management objective and in the planning and analysis is credited with an equal value, namely, $1.34 per acre-foot irrespective of the sequence in which the various storage projects making up the total are introduced into the system. A secondary objective is that of providing additional storage sufficient to reduce the peak discharge further to 600,000 cfs as measured at The Dalles. Again, a uniform value of $0.11 per acre-foot is applied to all storage components of the system irrespective of their sequence of addition to the system. This procedure was also adopted by the International Columbia River Engineering Board. [6] Implicit in the procedure is a recognition of the diminishing marginal utility of storage since the average value per acre-foot drops from $1.34 to $0.11 between the two levels of storage in the Corps calculations although the diminishing marginal utility within blocks is neglected. We shall go through the exercise by steps which will demonstrate the diminishing marginal value of storage and contribute to an understanding of how storage for flood management objectives may bear a substitution relationship with other storage in the system.

Let us first consider the hydrograph at The Dalles giving the flows during the flood of 1894 (Figure 8a). The ordinate of the hydrograph gives the discharge in cubic feet per second. The abscissa gives the duration in days (units of 8,640 seconds each). The discharge in cubic feet per second at any time multiplied by the duration gives the volume of discharge, and this summed over the total duration of the flood period gives the total volume of runoff and is represented by the area under the hydrograph. Similarly, if we wish to know the volume represented only by the discharge above a given level we measure the ordinates from that level to the hydrograph's upper boundary, multiply by the duration, and sum for each time unit under the curve to give the volume discharged above the given level. Actually we can closely approximate such volumes by superimposing an equilateral triangle upon the hydrograph and readily computing the area within segments of the altitude. From familiar properties of equilateral triangles we know that the area represented by equal intercepts along the altitude ordered from the apex to the base is given by the expression $V_n = V_1 (2n - 1)$. [7] Computing the volume in this manner and con-

[6] International Columbia River Engineering Board, *Water Resources of the Columbia River Basin*, report to the International Joint Commission United States and Canada, 1959, Appendix VI, p. 6.

[7] Where V_1 is the triangle formed by the first intercept on the altitude with $V_2, V_3 \cdots\cdots V_n$, the trapazoids formed by the remaining intercepts.

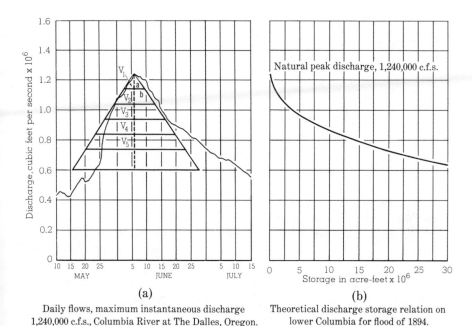

(a)

Daily flows, maximum instantaneous discharge
1,240,000 c.f.s., Columbia River at The Dalles, Oregon.

(b)

Theoretical discharge storage relation on
lower Columbia for flood of 1894.

Figure 8.   Estimating the theoretical storage-discharge relation.

verting to acre-feet (43,560 cubic feet per acre-foot) we can depict
the storage-discharge relation shown in Figure 8b. It is readily
perceived that equal successive discharge decrements can be accomplished only with increasing amounts of storage. For example, a
reduction of the controlled discharge from 940,000 cfs to 840,000
cfs requires approximately seven times as much storage capacity
as a reduction from 1,240,000 cfs to 1,140,000 cfs.

Such a relation holds closely for storage situated ideally with
respect to the floodplain for which storage operations are undertaken. However, because of the need to locate storage in the
Columbia system primarily with the objective of most efficient
power operations, the theoretical discharge-storage relation is
modified to an extent as shown in Figure 9. Here we represent the
storage-discharge relation as a band rather than a locus of points,
since some variation in the relationship is possible depending on the
sequence and distribution among the headwater areas of storage
project construction. Despite this factor, the general diminishing
incremental effectiveness, as measured by discharge reduction, is
clearly revealed in the empirical relation as well. In value terms the
same relation will hold. That is, if we consider a case of, say, a
single-purpose flood control system in which the cost per acre-foot

of additional storage remains constant, the cost of providing storage for successive equal decrements of controlled discharge will rise, other things being equal.

Reinforcing the diminishing incremental returns to storage, as measured by peak discharge reduction, is a companion relationship between the incremental damage reduction (benefits) and successive equal decrements of discharge. The empirical relation between discharge and damage for the lower Columbia is illustrated in Figure 10. Here again, we need to represent the relation as a band within which some variation is possible, depending on the location of individual storage projects among the several tributaries and their sequence of construction. It is obvious from the discharge-damage reduction relation that successive equal decrements of discharge are attended by diminishing incremental benefits.

The diminishing marginal benefits to storage in flood management operations gives rise to the substitution effect among storage projects. To illustrate the substitution effects, it is convenient to combine the data of the storage-discharge and discharge-damage reduction relations into a storage-damage reduction relation. This storage-benefit relation is illustrated in Figure 11, giving flood control benefits as a cumulative function of storage. It can be observed that the amount of flood control benefits derived from

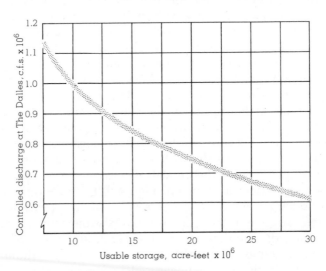

Figure 9. Empirical discharge-storage relation on the lower Columbia River. (Source: U.S. Army Engineer Division, North Pacific, Portland District, work sheets.)

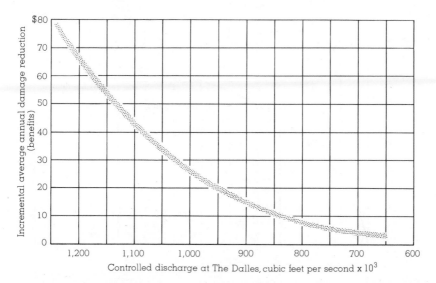

Figure 10. Incremental discharge-damage reduction relation for the lower Columbia floodplain. (Source: U.S. Army Engineer Division, North Pacific, Portland District, work sheets.)

storage capacity in the system rises from zero (with absence of storage) to approximately $16 million as an average annual expectation, with 30 million acre-feet of storage in the system. [8] Note that the change in vertical height per unit of storage (incremental flood control benefit) progressively decreases as equal increments of storage are added. To illustrate the substitution effects, consider the addition of 7 million acre-feet of storage to the existing 10.5 million acre-feet of the system. A flood control benefit of $3.5 million as an average annual expected value is associated with such storage. Consider duplicating the addition of storage as a second increment. Seven million acre-feet of storage as second-added is associated with only a $1.5 million average annual expected value. Should the two blocks of storage be located in separate countries we can observe that the benefit from the second block will be adversely affected by

[8] Actually the average annual expected benefits are greater at every level of storage by approximately $9 million as a result of the existing levee system. To have illustrated this on the diagram would have required moving the origin of the storage-damage reduction relation to $9 million on the ordinate. This in no way alters the relation between storage and expected average annual benefits in the diagram, but would illustrate the invariant complementarity between storage and levees.

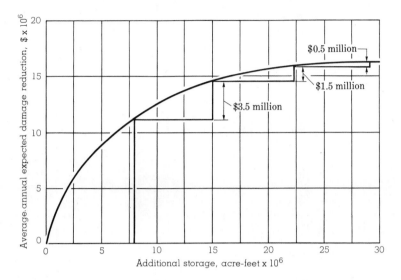

Figure 11. Empirical storage-benefit relation for the lower Columbia floodplain. (Source: U.S. Army Engineer Division, North Pacific, Portland District, work sheets.)

the substitution of the first in its place. [9] Now, given the empirical circumstances in this particular case, if the upstream riparian provides a 7 million acre-foot block of storage in exchange for what equity is sometimes thought to require—i.e., one-half the gross value of the average annual expected damage reduction—the return to the downstream riparian on his subsequent investment in the domestic block of 7 million acre-feet of storage ($1.5 million average annual) added to the benefits of the damage reduction secured through the upstream riparian's block reduced to a half to account for the payment ($1.75 million average annual) will fall short of the benefit he would realize ($3.5 million average annual) by proceeding independently without benefit of the upstream riparian's storage. This, of course, would be subject to severe qualification if insufficient storage possibilities existed in the reaches of the stream in the downstream country. However, since in the case at hand roughly 14 million acre-feet of storage can be provided by the downstream riparian through development of domestic sites, the returns on all of the investment are correspondingly affected. In

[9] The displacement effect, it should be noted, is not unlike that illustrated by P. O. Steiner in his article "Choosing Among Alternative Public Investments in the Water Resources Field," *American Economic Review*, Vol. 49, No. 5 (December, 1959), p. 906 ff.

short, all but approximately $500,000 average annual benefits can be obtained by construction of domestic storage in the reaches of the downstream riparian, restricting the additional flood control benefit to it from the upstream riparian's block of storage to this level. [10]

Accordingly, the sharing of half the benefit of the 7 million acre-foot block of storage, evaluated as first-added, represents compensation equivalent to three times the value of the additional benefit. This latter observation, while accurate within the context of discussion of the static case, will require qualification if it is recognized that some difference in the time distribution of the storage in question is possible, and thus something in excess of the $500,000 as an average annual net gain is a possibility. This possibility will be considered in the final evaluation of the Columbia Treaty in Part III. At the moment, however, the exercise above has been undertaken merely to illustrate the possibility inherent for the displacement of resource values in one country by virtue of the provision of storage by the other, when the effect of the sequence of project addition on the valuation of the additional benefit is not taken into consideration explicitly.

SUBSTITUTION OR DISPLACEMENT EFFECTS IN POWER PRODUCTION

The diminishing incremental effectiveness of storage in flood management operations as storage capacity is increased, other things being equal, has a counterpart in the production of power.

Electricity surplus to the power demands at any moment cannot itself be stored or accumulated for later distribution out of inventories. In hydroelectric systems, however, the potential energy of falling water can be stored in reservoirs for release at times during which the required discharge through the turbines exceeds the streamflows into the reservoirs. The period between the beginning of storage reservoir drafting from full pool elevations to the completion of the refilling operation is referred to as the "critical period." The average generation over the critical period fixes the prime power capability of the system. Power which can be generated during times at which the cumulative inflow to the reservoirs will exceed storage capacity and firm load requirements is referred to

---

[10] The limited additional protection of the second block of storage suggests that management measures other than storage for flood damage reduction should be considered. See the work of Gilbert White and colleagues, of the University of Chicago, *op. cit.*

as secondary energy and may be sold as "interruptible power" on an "if and as available" basis, provided a market exists for it.

The increase of prime power associated with additions of storage capacity tends to be constant, other things such as developed head below the storage and comparable factors remaining equal, so long as the amount of storage in the system does not lengthen the critical period. When sufficient storage is added to the system to lengthen this period, however, the incremental prime power gain per unit of storage diminishes with each change in the length of the critical period. Perhaps this can be made clear heuristically.

When the critical period is short—as, for example, when storage is sufficient only for seasonal regulation—the reservoir capacity is fully utilized (i.e., fully drafted and refilled) each year. As the storage increases to provide regulation "over the year," or cyclical regulation, the critical period is lengthened and the incremental capacity may not be fully used except over many more months or even a matter of years. Now assume the energy content of a reservoir to be 8,760,000 kilowatt-hours (8,760 kwh = production from one kilowatt over one year). A kilowatt-hour being the output of a kilowatt of capacity operating for one hour, the amount of prime power which such energy in storage can produce will depend on the number of hours during which it is released. That is, if 8,760,000 kwh are drafted during a six-month period each year, the amount of prime power they would provide will be 2 mw. If the critical period is extended, say, to twenty-four months, the prime power gain from drafting 8,760,000 kwh from storage will be only 8,760,000/2(8,760,000) or only 0.5 mw. The storage capacity in the present hydroelectric system on the Columbia is associated with only a seven-month critical period. With the addition of Treaty storage and domestic storage development, the critical period will ultimately be extended by a factor of six, or to forty-three months. Accordingly, the incremental prime power gain from equal increments of storage from the present to the projected levels will be characterized by marked diminishing returns. Figure 12 depicts graphically the diminishing incremental power gain as a function of storage, other things being equal.[11] The pre-emption of resource values, or displacement effects, follow from this relation as in the case of flood management storage; thus we need not repeat the exercise demonstrating the effect at this point.

[11] Figure 12a gives the relation between prime power or average generation over the critical period and storage. Figure 12b gives the relation between dependable capacity (prime power divided by the load factor) and storage and average annual energy (prime and secondary) and storage.

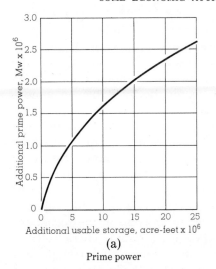

(a)
Prime power

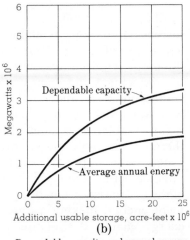

(b)
Dependable capacity and annual energy.

Figure 12.   Empirical storage–prime power relation for the Columbia River
hydroelectric system. [(a) Based on graph, "Effects of Canadian and Libby
Storage on U.S. Base system Prime Power," Bonneville Power Administration,
Branch of System Operations and Power Resources, 1960. (b) Based on Plate 9
in *The Columbia River Treaty and Protocol*, Departments of External Affairs and
Northern Affairs and National Resources, Ottawa, April 1964.]

While the diminishing marginal productivity of storage for power
purposes gives rise to displacement of resource values of subsequently added storage, similar to the case involving flood management operations, the underlying determinants of this displacement
result have comparable implications for displacement effects as
between storage in a hydro system and interconnection with a
thermal system. This is possible, for example, by means of long-
distance, extra-high-voltage transmission facilities interconnecting
the Pacific Northwest with the Pacific Southwest in the United
States. Again, a heuristic approach to illustrating this phenomenon
may be useful.

Since there is substantial variation in streamflows on a river such
as the Columbia, the firm load carrying capability is limited by the
average critical period generation. A great deal of additional, or
secondary, energy can be generated at all times other than during
the most adverse streamflow conditions. If we were to take the
energy represented by the runoff and array it in decreasing order
of the proportion of the time it is available, we would have a
diagram as shown in Figure 13. A given proportion would be
available under the most adverse conditions of streamflow and
would be represented as prime power. Additional to the power

available continuously, or 100 per cent of the time, there will be increasing amounts available a decreasing proportion of the time. The object of storage operations is to impound flows in excess of the discharge required to meet the demands of the moment for releases to supplement the energy which would be available on a non-continuous basis under natural streamflow conditions. This tends both to increase the firm load carrying capability of the system and makes usable, or salable, otherwise secondary energy for which there may be no market. Interconnecting a predominantly hydro system with a predominantly thermal system may achieve the same or better results. First, secondary energy surplus to the needs of the hydro region can be sold in the thermal region as fuel replacement energy, making a much larger proportion of the secondary energy salable. But, of equal significance, economy energy off the diurnal peak in the thermal system can be imported during periods of adverse streamflows to serve the market in the hydro region, and

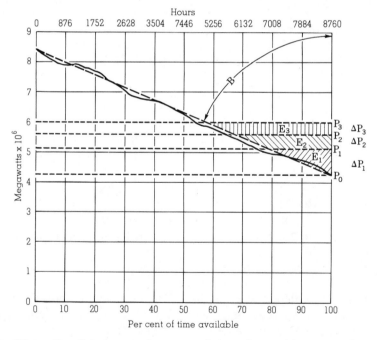

Figure 13.   Prime power increments for equal energy increments in storage, given the energy duration curve for Columbia hydroelectric system, 1968–69 system conditions. (Adapted from graph, Bonneville Power Administration, System Operations and Power Resources Branch, March 10, 1959.)

thus conserve energy in storage. The operation can be conceived, in fact, as a gigantic interregional pumped storage operation in which economy thermal energy is used in the off-peak hours to permit equivalent accumulation of energy in storage which otherwise would need to be drafted.

How the displacement effects between storage and intertie transactions are experienced can be readily appreciated from Figure 13. Reading from the lower right corner, increments of power are available a decreasing proportion of the time, the exact relation being suggested by the energy duration curve, in turn derived from the hydrology of the river system and its power installations. To firm up power which is available 80 per cent of the time would require either stored or imported energy of an amount equal to about 10 per cent of the firm energy from the prime power gain, the remainder being provided by secondary energy available 80 per cent of the time and between 80 and 100 per cent of the time. This is shown as the difference between P_0 and P_1 in the diagram. However, if the identical amount of stored energy or imported economy energy were to be used to firm up an additional block of secondary energy, a smaller amount of prime power would be provided, as such energy would have to be spread more thinly over a higher proportion of the time. In the illustration, $E_1 = E_2 = E_3$, representing the firming energy, but $\Delta P_1 > \Delta P_2 > \Delta P_3$, representing the diminishing incremental prime power gain with equal increments of firming energy.[12]

Accordingly, insofar as firm load carrying capability is concerned, either storage or intertie economy energy may be used as substitutes for achieving the same purpose. If both are used, the returns from the employment of each will not be independent of the sequence in which they are introduced into the system. Again, if storage from an upstream riparian is to be used by the neighboring downstream country and compensation paid for the service provided, the opportunity returns foregone from domestic alternatives to such power-firming facilities must be regarded as a cost to the downstream riparian for the services received. Unless these dis-

---

[12] More generally $Pn = \sqrt{nK} - \sqrt{(n-1)K}$ where $K = 2E/\tan \angle B$. The algebraic expression gives only illustrative results as the model implicitly assumes a continuously replicating annual streamflow pattern. In this respect, however, it does not differ in principle from established engineering procedures in power systems planning which take a hydrologic trace of some years' duration for use to approximate the solution in deterministic form of a problem inherently probabilistic in character.

placement effects are taken explicitly into account in a co-operative undertaking, the division of the apparent gains from the upstream riparian's storage can result in a net loss to the downstream riparian. That such a consequence can readily occur if the subtle relationships are not properly evaluated will be demonstrated in Chapter 7.

THE CASE INVOLVING GROWTH OF THE POWER SYSTEM: THE THERMAL COMPONENT

The diminishing marginal productivity of storage can be readily appreciated by inspection of storage-yield and storage-discharge relations for hydrologic systems. There is also an aspect of diminishing marginal productivity of storage that is not related to the volume of storage provided, but rather to the growth of a power system over time. Abstracting initially from the case in which a hydro and a thermal power system can be interconnected, the phenomenon of diminishing marginal productivity of storage is related to the growth of a thermal component in the regional power system as the regional power demands increasingly exceed the hydroelectric potential of the region. As greater amounts of thermal power are added to the system, increasingly all the hydro energy that can be generated at any time becomes usable in the power system to replace fuel consumption at the thermal plants. If the hydro secondary energy is used in this way, less storage will be needed to regulate the generation of hydro energy at specific seasons of the year.

Moreover, as the thermal component grows in response to developing loads, more hydro turbines and generators will be installed in the hydroelectric plants in order to peak the load. The use of hydro plants for peaking is related to their ability to respond almost instantaneously to surges in the load without appreciable efficiency loss. This is not the case with thermal plants; hence they tend to be used in the base of the load to be operated as close to 100 per cent plant factor as is feasible to achieve maximum economy. With expansion of capacity in the hydro plants, a higher proportion of the streamflows can be run through the turbines and generators as such flows occur, thus reducing further the dependence on storage for stream regulation in power operations.

Finally, in time, the thermal component of the system will be sufficiently large so that use of hydro for meeting critical period generation will no longer be required. Prime power will therefore no longer be a measure of storage benefits, and the utility of storage will be further reduced. After all three conditions obtain, the benefits of storage will have diminished to only the value of the energy represented by the water which would be spilled in the absence of storage.[13] The quantitative implications of the change in the value of storage as the role of the hydro component in the regional power system changes to accommodate the growth of the thermal component is illustrated in Figure 14, with estimates drawn from the Columbia case.

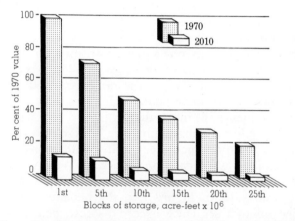

Figure 14.   Diminishing value of storage under initial (1970) and terminal (2010) conditions for storage operations.

With the marked ultimate reduction of the value of storage in a mixed hydro-thermal operation dominated by thermal power production, there is a premium on the construction of joint head-storage projects—i.e., projects in which the reservoir is utilized for storage purposes so long as it is of economic advantage, but with the technical option remaining of conversion to operation as a head plant, and ultimately as the peaking complement to the thermal base load operation.

[13] Actually this represents an oversimplification because some amount of storage continues to be useful to complement thermal operations so as to permit maximum plant factor on the more efficient thermal plants in the system and minimize use of the less efficient thermal plants. See Ross N. Brudenell and Jack H. Gilbreath, "Economic Complementary Operations of Hydro Storage and Steam Power in the Integrated TVA System," paper presented at the AIEE Summer Meetings, Buffalo, New York, 1958.

CONCLUDING OBSERVATIONS

Two prescriptive conclusions emerge from the analysis of the storage-return relationship in water resource systems. One involves a matter of substance, the other a matter of analytic procedure.

Given the diminishing marginal yield of storage and the associated displacement effects among project possibilities, significant implications emerge both with respect to the design of water resource systems and to the division of co-operative gains in connection with international ventures. To illustrate the first point, let us consider four storage projects that are identical in every respect (inflow, capacity, developed head downstream, etc.) except for cost of the projects. Under the conditions posited, the gross benefits, B, are identical if any one site is substituted for any other site in any specified sequence of developments, say, first-added as illustrated in Figure 15a. Any of the projects added subsequently in the sequence has an incremental value less than preceding elements in the sequence, as illustrated in Figure 15b, whenever such storage has the effect of lengthening the storage drawdown period. Next, assume that the four projects differ with respect to cost per acre-foot of storage as indicated in Figure 16. We can now consider two alternative sequences of project construction as shown in Figure 17a and 17b. In Figure 17a, the benefits associated with each project in that sequence exceed its cost, hence the average benefit of the block of storage exceeds the average cost. [14] On the

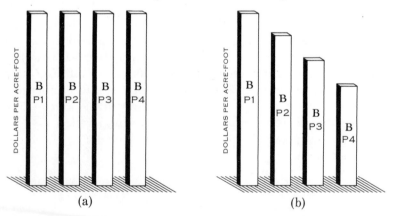

Figure 15.   Alternative relationship among storage benefits.

[14] This is not unlike the procedure implicit in the ICREB report, nor the conception of the Corps of Engineers flood control objective evaluation.

other hand, the benefits associated with each project ordered in the least-cost sequence reveals that the incremental cost of the fourth block of storage exceeds the benefits it can realize, thus reducing the net return to the investment in storage. Accordingly, if the objective of an international co-operative venture is to maximize the net gain for mutual sharing, it is important to introduce projects in their most economical sequence for two reasons:

First, if this is not done, it is possible to include storage projects whose benefits exceed their cost on a first-added basis only because they pre-empt some part of the surplus benefits of the economic storages projected for subsequent addition to the system. Such procedure will result in a larger *gross* gain, the last increment of which, however, has a value which is less than the cost involved in obtaining it. The *net* gain consequently will be reduced.

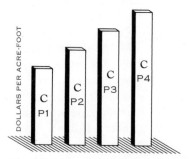

Figure 16.   Assumed relation among project costs.

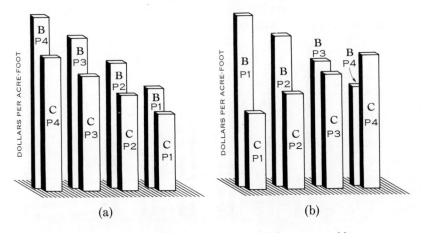

Figure 17.   An illustration of the consequence of failure to consider sequence in project construction.

Second, although some test designed to evaluate the comparative benefits and costs of the last increment of a block of projected storage may be devised to screen out any project which would appear warranted only because it pre-empts a part of the surplus benefits of an economic project, there will be no assurance that the economic projects will not be added in an *uneconomic* sequence. In this event, higher costs will be incurred earlier in time than necessary and will result in a diminished present value of the total *net* gain compared with construction of projects in economic sequence.

Now consider the implications of the displacement effects for the sharing of co-operatively achieved gains. Figure 18 illustrates a case in which equal increments of storage added at the same stage in the sequence of development would produce equal gross benefits, as before, but each added successively will realize a diminished gross benefit. Further assume that the two most economic storages, C_1 and C_2, are located in the reaches of the upstream riparian (Country X), and the four less economic, $C_3 \ldots C_6$, are alternative storage possibilities in the lower riparian (Country Y). Assume that the relative costs and benefits are such that only the four least costly storages added incrementally will produce benefits exceeding costs as shown. In an economic system, abstracting from the distribution of resource ownership between the riparians, only the four least costly storages would qualify for development.

Let us assume further, however, that the upstream riparian provides the storage services in exchange for one-half the gross benefits realized in the reaches of the downstream riparian evaluated as first added to the system. Under these circumstances we would have results as shown in Option I of Table 3.

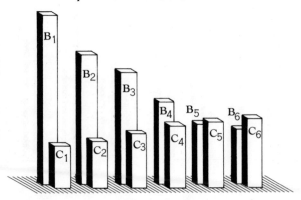

Figure 18.   Benefits and costs of Country Y's projects 5 and 6 when displacement effects are present.

TABLE 3
Relative Costs and Benefits of Alternative Options for
Downstream Riparian (Country Y)

Projects	Option I for Country Y		Option II for Country Y	
	Y's costs	Y's benefits	Y's costs	Y's benefits
1 (X)	0	20	—	—
2 (X)	0	15	—	—
3 (Y)	12	27	12	40
4 (Y)	14	18	14	30
5 (Y)	—	—	16	27
6 (Y)	—	—	17	18
Country Y's Totals	26	80	59	115

Net gain (benefits minus costs)....54...............................56
Country Y's net advantage from Option II....2

Should the downstream riparian (Y) elect to proceed with his own
four most economic projects instead of the co-operative undertaking,
however, we would have a distribution of the costs and benefits as
shown under Option II. Under the circumstances characterized by
the two options, the downstream riparian relying on his higher cost
projects which, in the absence of upstream storage, show benefits
in excess of costs (see Figure 19), achieves a position superior to that
realizable through a co-operative undertaking.

Of course, there is nothing immutable about the so-called
"50-50" share rule. There will be some share of the downstream
gains from the upstream riparian's storage services which would not
penalize the downstream riparian for co-operating: namely, a share
which would leave the downstream riparian indifferent as between
co-operation and independent action. And, of course, there is some
share which would move him from the margin of indifference to a
position superior to one he could achieve acting independently.

Figure 19.   Benefits and costs of Country Y's projects 5 and 6 when displacement effects are absent.

Does it follow that such a modified share of the gross gains—say, a 65-35 per cent split for the downstream and upstream riparians respectively—will leave the upstream riparian an incentive to enter into a co-operative venture rather than proceeding independently? If there are economies inherent in developing the hydrologic unit as an integrated undertaking due to the interdependencies involved, there will be some share that is advantageous to both riparians. But, of course, it does not necessarily follow that a net gain will result from uneconomic ventures simply because they are undertaken co-operatively.

Even should the venture be undertaken economically with respect to the resources of the river basin in question, there may be circumstances in which the upstream riparian can integrate his reach of the river with other hydrologic units in his territory, and the lower riparian integrate his facilities on the river with other hydrologic units and/or power systems, so that independent development is more advantageous to each than any share of the co-operative gains. Such a possibility should always be considered until demonstrated to the contrary, in order that two riparians committed to an investigation of possibilities for mutually advantageous co-operative development of a river system need not feel committed to the co-operative development itself, unless the engineering and economic studies provide a case for doing so.

Let us now consider the implications of the diminishing marginal productivity of storage for questions of analytic procedure. We have observed that the value of storage declines both as a function of the volume of storage added and as a function of the growth in regional loads exceeding the hydro potential of the region. How then is the value of storage added at any particular time and sequence of construction to be evaluated?

First, we have a test devised by the Army Corps of Engineers for the case of diminishing marginal productivity of storage as a function of the amount of storage in the system, when such addition causes a lengthening of the critical period. The procedure of the Corps on the Columbia River was to scan several alternative combinations of projects which were viewed as representing the "ultimate system." That alternative combinations were required followed from the fact that some projects in each combination were mutually exclusive possibilities with projects in other combinations. For each potential "ultimate system," the system regulation was simulated for an intermediate point in time between the initiation of the first project and the fifty-year terminal date used for depreciation purposes. The systems' outputs were noted, and then iteratively one after another of the storage projects were omitted and the reduction in system benefits was compared with the reduction in system costs occasioned by the elimination of the storage project. If the reduction in costs exceeded the reduction in benefits, the project in question failed the "last-added" test. That is, the incremental value of the project to the system's output was less than the incremental cost, and thus the project in question was not deemed justified. Each of the storage projects in each of the mutually exclusive systems was tested in this manner to determine whether any given project in some early point in the sequence was justified only because of the pre-emption of surplus benefits of other projects added subsequently.

This is not a bad test if the value of storage remains invariant with respect to time. However, as the role of storage in a hydro system changes in response to load growth over time, a spot check of a net benefit for individual projects at one stage in the system's evolution becomes a substantially inadequate test of the justification of storage projects. There is, in addition, no formal criterion indicating the sequence in which elements of the total block of projected storage should be added to the system to maximize the present value of the system.

A better procedure is to simulate the evolution of the system over time, introducing storage projects in each combination in the various possible permutations and comparing the present value of the net benefit of each. The combination of projects in that sequence which provides the greatest present worth of net benefits will be the system which is superior, on economic criteria, to all of the others. What may be the practical outcome or difference that may result from such a procedure? Perhaps the most significant if not obvious result may be the elimination of an exclusive storage project which appears quite economic as an early increment, but which, having no head development for conversion to peaking, may have a zero value at some subsequent time in the future, and may have a true present worth evaluated in this manner which is less than its present cost, yet which might nevertheless pass the alternative so-called "last-added test."

Use of system simulation takes on an added significance in cases where storage services are provided one riparian by another and benefit-sharing issues must be considered. Only by simulating the "treaty" system over time for comparison with an alternative "domestic" system can the implications of the location of the storage-head facility in one country or the other be revealed. Unless the storage-service receiving riparian is granted a first option on the at-site generation of the upstream storage-head facility equal in amount and at cost equivalent to that which would obtain from the lower riparian's displaced domestic resources, the downstream riparian will receive either a smaller amount of power from the hydro system, or possibly, if an equal amount, [15] receive it at higher real costs than would be required by using independent alternatives.

The implications for analytic procedures, then, are clear. First, in order not to saddle the system with duplicating facilities and un-necessarily high-cost elements, the elements of the most economic water resource system should be identified, abstracting initially from the distribution of resources among riparians. This will provide a system from which the joint gains for mutual sharing will be a maximum. Second, after such a system, as well as the sequence of all its elements, has been identified, each of the participating riparians should conduct a similar set of simulations for its reach of the river based on the associated domestic resources available to each. If the sum of the net gains from independent individual ac-tions is less than that of the joint gains from co-operative action, there is prima facie evidence for the utility of a co-operative venture. The difference between the sum of the individually achieved net benefits and that of the jointly achieved benefits is the measure of the gain from co-operation. It is this sum that should serve as the basis for division. Whether it is agreed that one of the participants will receive all of the net gain from co-operation or that the gain is to be shared, both riparians will be assured of a result leaving each in a position not inferior to one that could have been achieved independently. Unless the analysis is conducted along these lines, there is a strong probability that one or both of the parties to the agreement will have no informed conception whether an economi-cally superior position has been achieved.

This will be demonstrated in Chapters 7 and 9, where these basic concepts will be applied to an analysis of the economics of the Columbia Treaty results.

---

[15] If the storage site values which are pre-empted by the upstream riparian's first-added storage projects are not sufficient to eliminate any of the lower ripar-ian's storage-head potential (which is not likely to be true in the general case), the same amount of at-site generation may still be available to the lower riparian, but at a cost which may be greater depending on the extent to which the displace-ment effects are taken into account explicitly in the sharing of the benefits.

PART II

The Columbia River Treaty, 1960-61

Chapter 4

The IJC Principles:
Background for Analysis

The problems of identifying the most economic storage projects for co-operative use of a river system, and of measuring the gains realizable are not trivial, as the discussion in Chapter 3 has demonstrated. To deal with these matters, the governments of the United States and Canada in January 1959 requested the International Joint Commission to make recommendations on the principles that should be applied in determining:

    a) the benefits which will result from the co-operative use of storage of waters and electrical interconnection with the Columbia River System; and

    b) the apportionment between the two countries of such benefits more particularly in regard to electrical generation and flood control. [1]

The IJC grappled with the problem for eleven months—a period as long as was to be required to negotiate the Treaty of 1961. During this time conflicting interests were pressed by a dominant member of each of the two national sections of the IJC. Two storage sites were at issue. One, the Libby site in the United States, was known to all to be economically inferior to mutually exclusive Canadian sites; provision for it in the general principles governing the ultimate arrangements with Canada was bound to create difficulties; yet favor for such a provision persisted in the U.S. section. The other disputed site, the "High" Arrow Lakes storage site in British

---

[1] Letters to the United States and Canadian Sections of the International Joint Commission, dated January 28, 1959 and January 29, 1959 from the Secretary of State of the United States and the Secretary of State for External Affairs for Canada, respectively.

Columbia, was a project of some economic merit, but its development in an international undertaking was vigorously opposed by
some interests in Canada. Accordingly, the task of formulating
principles governing the ultimate arrangements was greatly complicated by incompatible objectives: those of providing a set of
principles which would stand critical scrutiny, yet would also allow
latitude for the inclusion of an uneconomic project and the exclusion of an economic project.

The dilemma was resolved by constructing a rather straightforward statement of principle and following it with an explanation
which permitted the principle to be interpreted flexibly. To give
a flavor of the guiding rule, we have:

> If projects are developed successively to meet the growing needs for
> power production and to provide flood protection, the most efficient
> projects for those purposes should generally be developed first in
> order to maximize the net benefits to each country.[2]

This prefatory statement is followed by General Principle No. 1:

> Cooperative development of the water resources of Columbia River
> Basin, designed to provide optimum benefits to each country, re-
> quires that the storage facilities and downstream power production
> facilities proposed by the respective countries will, to the extent it is
> practicable and feasible to do so, be added in the order of the most
> favorable benefit-cost ratio.[3]

Again, in the interpretive discussion we have:

> The phrase "to the extent that it is practicable and feasible to do so"
> is included in recognition of the fact that it will not always be possible
> to adopt a project wholly on the basis of its benefit-cost ratio, as com-
> pared to other projects in the river basin. There may be important
> non-monetary factors, not reflected in the benefit-cost ratio, which
> may require consideration and which may be of compelling influence
> in choosing projects for construction.[4]

[2] "Report of the International Joint Commission on Principles for Determining
and Apportioning Benefits from Cooperative Use of Storage of Waters and Electri-
cal Interconnection within the Columbia River System," December 29, 1959.
Reprinted in *The Columbia River Treaty, Protocol and Related Documents* (Ottawa:
Departments of External Affairs, and Northern Affairs and National Resources,
February 1964).

[3] *Ibid.*, p. 41.

[4] *Ibid.*, pp. 41–42.

Then, following a general discussion related to recognized constraints on development of particular sites owing to conflicts with
fishery interests, financial constraints, etc., we find a specific statement which is designed to take care of the Libby project:

> . . . an urgent need to provide for such purposes as local or regional
> flood control, navigation, irrigation, or exceptional increases in
> power requirements may determine the order of project construction
> rather than the ratio of benefits to costs, [5]

and one to take care of High Arrow Lakes:

> . . . the attitude of affected interests on the flooding of lands and im-
> provements or to the effect of a project on other uses of the water
> resources may require postponement or abandonment of construction
> of projects that are the most attractive when viewed solely from the
> standpoint of their benefit-cost ratio. [6]

Two observations on General Principle No. 1 and related commentary bear making. First, the principle advanced to guide the
selection of projects in the most efficient manner, including their
sequence as well as their individual returns, is correct if the objective
is to maximize the gain for mutual sharing. However, the wording
does not escape imprecision, and in the prefatory remark, where
there is allusion to maximizing net benefits *to each country*, is capable
of leading to an impasse. For example, one can conceive of circumstances wherein maximizing the net gain to one riparian may
require the construction of a project in the neighboring riparian's
reach of the river, while maximizing the net gain for the latter may
require the construction of a mutually exclusive project in the
former's reach. In such special circumstances, the statement is not
rigorous enough to serve as a guide to the selection of projects.

Second, the principle in spirit reflects a criterion that would, if
applied conscientiously, result in the most economic projects being
built in their most economic sequence—a procedure shown in
Chapter 3 to be necessary if net gains for mutual sharing are to be
maximized. The wording of the statement itself, however—"most
favorable benefit-cost ratio"—contradicts the intent. Proper opti-
mizing procedure does not require that the highest benefit-cost
ratio govern, for this would doubtless lead to the design of systems in
which a substantial share of the supramarginal increments would be

[5] *Ibid.*, p. 42.
[6] *Ibid.*, p. 42.

eliminated.[7] Instead, the intent of the optimal plan, I believe, is to ensure that the positive difference between benefits and costs be a maximum—i.e., the *incremental* benefit-cost ratio be unity—or that the project scale be extended (either directly or through a larger mutually exclusive alternative project) so long as the added benefits exceed the added costs.

When the primary statement of General Principle No. 1 and its interpretive comments are looked at together, it is clear that the ideal of benefit maximization was not the sole aim of the phrase finders. The general sense represents a qualified statement looking toward the achievement of a commendable objective. On the other hand, since the wording provides the greatest latitude with respect to the selection of projects, the statement can be interpreted as justifying several different sets of projects regardless of their consistency with maximizing the joint gains for mutual sharing. Justification for several projects dubious on purely economic grounds was, in fact, sought as General Principle No. 1 was debated in the Treaty negotiations.

In the detailed discussion of the Columbia Treaty undertaking, which follows this chapter, I have restricted my analysis to purely economic considerations, believing that if net benefit maximization had been the aim of the Treaty makers, the arguments and comparisons I make are applicable. In doing so, I have corrected for the inconsistencies which could result from the imprecise phraseology in the two instances mentioned above.

Let us assume that there is mutual agreement regarding the selection of projects and their order of construction in the system. What then will be the measure of benefits from storage projects and how are they to be divided? Several points of view on this aspect were advanced by interested parties in both countries prior to the IJC recommendation of General Principle No. 2.

In some quarters there was advanced a naive net-benefit division rule holding that the gross value of the increment of power and flood damage reduction each project provided, evaluated in the sequence of its projected construction, should first be corrected for the costs incident on each riparian before the "net" gain was

---

[7] For example, a project with benefits having a present worth of $150 million and present costs of $75 million would have a more favorable benefit-cost ratio (2:1) than a mutually exclusive alternative with benefits having a present value of $300 million and present costs of $175 million (1.7:1). The increment in scale, comparing the two projects, results in a greater addition to benefits than to costs, thus increasing the *net benefit* by $50 million for the system in question.

divided equally. On the Canadian side, a variant of this view was put forward to the effect that the total cost of storage in Canada and the nominal costs of processing the more highly regulated streamflow through existing U.S. head plants should be taken into account, and that the division of the gains should be such as to reflect the disproportionate outlays for the two countries. Since a substantial amount of excess turbine and generator capacity had been installed in the U.S. head plants in anticipation of additional storage upstream, this rule would result in Canada's receiving a vastly preponderant share of the gross gains in output.

An equally persuasive case was made by interested parties in the United States to the effect that since over $2 billion had been invested in head plants and related works in the United States, without which the more highly regulated flows provided by Canadian storage would be valueless (for power production), the division of the downstream gains should be proportional to historic as well as expected costs of treaty projects in the United States and the substantially lesser Treaty costs incurred by Canada. Curiously, the identical general rule pursued with equal rigor had opposite implications for the benefit shares when advanced from the viewpoint of the United States. I think perhaps both riparians suspected the premises, if not the rigor, of the naive net benefit-sharing argument.

Another approach was developed by the technical personnel of the U.S. Army Corps of Engineers. Here it was proposed that Canada's entitlement to the increment in system output incident upon its storage should be based on the increment evaluated as of the time or sequence of its construction. This was to be enjoyed by Canada so long as no additional U.S. storage projects were built. Upon the completion of U.S. projects, however, these would receive precedence, and Canadian storage benefit credits would be re-evaluated as though they were added subsequently. The procedure recommended thus was sensitive to the displacement effects demonstrated in Chapter 3. It would preclude the pre-emption by Canadian storage of any of the net benefits of U.S. projects subsequently added; on the other hand, so long as the U.S. storage projects were delayed, full first-added benefits would be credited to Canadian storage in evaluating its incremental gain to system output.

The proposal ran into considerable opposition in both countries. In Canada there was at that time no general understanding of displacement effects, and thus the procedure appeared highly suspect. In the United States, too, displacement effects were not generally understood and, in addition, there was skepticism in some quarters because the procedure not only protected supramarginal projects against pre-emption of yields by Canadian storage, but also admitted the construction of inframarginal projects the benefits from which *appeared* to exceed their cost only because claim could be laid to a part of the surplus benefits of Canadian projects. Such a procedure, in effect, would have permitted the construction of uneconomic storage projects which would have displaced stream regulation already provided by economic Canadian projects in the system. The U.S. reach of the Columbia, therefore, could expect to be developed as though Canadian Treaty projects had no influence on the performance or design of the system in the United States. Consequently, the potential economy from co-operative development would be sacrificed.

A third advocated approach followed in outline the practice used by electric utility systems when faced with an option to meet projected loads by proceeding independently or in collaboration with an adjacent fiscally independent utility. Here, the procedure is no different from that already implied in Chapter 3, where the net gain from co-operation for mutual sharing was determined as follows: once there is mutual agreement with respect to the most economical way to achieve power and flood control objectives through co-operative development, each country should evaluate the cost of meeting comparable objectives by the least-cost alternative means available domestically. The difference between the cost of meeting objectives by co-operative endeavor and the sum of the costs of meeting comparable objectives by independent alternatives constitutes the relevant net gain, or savings in costs, from co-operation. Observe that this procedure does not consider historic or sunk costs, nor, in fact, the relative costs incurred by each riparian specifically in connection with the co-operative projects.

Now that we have surveyed the various approaches to benefit sharing which formed part of the IJC deliberations, let us examine the Commission's ultimate recommendation on this matter.

General Principle No. 2 reads:

Cooperative development of the water resources of the Columbia River Basin should result in advantages in power supply, flood control, or other benefits, or savings in costs to each country as compared with alternatives available to that country. [8]

[8] *The Columbia River Treaty, Protocol and Related Documents, op. cit.*, p. 45.

The statement of principle is consistent with sharing the net gains in such a way that both countries can achieve a position superior to one each could attain independently. However, we need to consider the specific recommendations to appreciate how this is contemplated. The procedure in question is given in Power Principle No. 6 as follows:

> The power benefit determined to result in the downstream country from regulation of flow by storage in the upstream country should be shared on a basis such that the benefit, in power, to each country will be substantially equal, provided that such sharing would result in an advantage to each country as compared with alternatives available to that country, as contemplated in General Principle No. 2. Each country should assume responsibility for providing that part of the facilities needed for the cooperative development that is located within its own territory. Where such sharing would not result in an advantage to each country as contemplated in General Principle No. 2, there should be negotiated and agreed upon such other division of benefits or adjustments as would make the cooperative development feasible. [9]

And to complete the principles for the division of benefits relevant to our purposes, Flood Control Principle Nos. 3 and 4 read:

> The monetary value of flood control benefit to be assigned to the upstream storage should be the estimated average annual value of the flood damage prevented by such storage. [10]

> The upstream country should be paid one-half of the benefits as measured in Flood Control Principle No. 3, i.e., one-half of the value of the damages prevented. [11]

If General Principle No. 1 were applied strictly, I believe the provisions of the principles dealing with the division of power and flood control benefits—half the power gains and half the value of the flood damage reduction—would be wholly incompatible with General Principle No. 2, bearing in mind the displacement effects of first-added storage. Consequently, it would appear that the controlling provisions are those portions of the primary statements which qualify the rule, namely:

> Where such sharing should not result in an advantage to each country . . . there should be negotiated and agreed upon such other division

[9] *Ibid.*, pp. 549–50.
[10] *Ibid.*, p. 53.
[11] *Ibid.*, p. 53.

of benefits or other adjustments as would be equitable to both countries and would make the cooperative development feasible. [12]

In effect, then, the IJC principles provided little guidance for the
negotiators as to how the benefits should be divided. Similarly, if
strict adherence to the spirit of General Principle No. 1 were not
observed, a selection of projects could be agreed to under the
qualifications supplementing this principle, which, while perhaps
producing an equal amount of power for each riparian, would do so
only at the sacrifice of the economies inherent in co-operative
development.

The conclusion is inescapable that no clear-cut agreement was
reached by the two sections of the IJC concerning how the principles they had formulated should be applied. The final document
preserved as much latitude for negotiation as would have been
available without the IJC principles. Observe, for example, the
equivocal wording of General Principle No. 3:

> With respect to trans-boundary projects in the Columbia Basin,
> which are subject to the provisions of Article IV of the Boundary
> Waters Treaty of 1909, the entitlement of each country to participate
> in the development and to share in the downstream benefits resulting
> from storage, and in power generation at site, should be determined
> by crediting to each country such portion of the storage capacity and
> head potential of the project as may be mutually agreed. [13]

Equipped with a set of principles meaning all things to all men,
how did the economics of the selection of projects included in the
co-operative venture operate, and how closely did the Treaty
system approximate one that could have been selected if the spirit
of General Principle No. 1 had been conscientiously applied to the
Columbia River? These questions will be addressed in Chapter 5.
In subsequent chapters, the related question—How faithfully did
the distribution of the benefits from the co-operative undertaking
correspond to the intent of General Principle No. 2—will be
investigated.

As far as possible the discussion will be conducted within the
context of information, policy, and related constraints applying at
the time the negotiating teams were establishing the terms of the
Treaty of 1961. In Chapters 8 and 9 comparable analysis will be
made reflecting the additional information that became available

[12] *Ibid.*, pp. 40–50.
[13] *Ibid.*, p. 43.

and the changes in policy and related parameters that occurred between the agreements of 1961 and the later agreements of 1964.

Before concluding this discussion of the IJC principles, it should be emphasized that despite shortcomings in terms of precision, the work of the International Joint Commission in this regard represents a contribution of substance. General Principles 1 and 2 in concept and spirit provide the fundamentals for guiding an efficient and equitable co-operative development of an international river. At this general level, the IJC principles articulate an advanced understanding of the economic and equity considerations confronting such a co-operative undertaking. Whether the qualifications and reservations appearing in the supplementary commentary represent necessary concessions to political reality and wisdom on the one hand, or to expediency on the other, cannot be assessed in a study of this kind. One might conclude, however, that even were the IJC principles prepared ultimately to preserve the maximum latitude for the negotiators, this might have been done without articulating in the first instance the general rules essential for an economic and equitable development. To this extent the general principles formulated by the International Joint Commission represent a level of sophistication and an advance in concepts applicable to co-operative undertakings.

Chapter 5

The Economics of the Columbia
Treaty Projects Selection

~~~~~~~~~~~~~~~~~~~~~~

What set of projects, developed in what sequence, would most economically meet the flood control and power objectives in the Columbia Basin? Since, in 1960, existing development on the Columbia was known to be deficient in storage capacity, projects with storage were of most immediate concern to the negotiators of the Columbia River Treaty. Also, since development of storage in the reaches of the Columbia above Grand Coulee had been postponed pending agreement between the United States and Canada, it is reasonable to suppose that storage first in that area would seem to offer the most efficient addition to the system provided that adequate sites were available for development.

THE TECHNICAL OPTIONS

The International Columbia River Engineering Board identified several good sites: Arrow Lakes, Mica Creek, Dorr, Luxor, Bull River, and Duncan, all in British Columbia; and Libby, in Montana, but with headwaters extending into British Columbia. These projects are in part mutually exclusive; that is, they can be grouped into alternative complexes, each complex containing at least one or part of one project that is excluded from the others because of physical incompatibility. The ICREB report identified three complexes with an explanatory statement indicating that each alternative "achieves about the same degree of water resource development,"[1] providing, that is, from 27 million to 29 million acre-feet

[1] International Columbia River Engineering Board, *Water Resources of the Columbia River Basin*, report to the International Joint Commission, 1959, p. 65.

of additional storage on the main stem of the Columbia and on the Kootenay River (see Figure 20).

Basically, there were two mutually exclusive schemes of development with some variation within each. The "non-diversion" plan would allow all streams to flow in their natural channels, with storage provided in each watershed to regulate flows in the associated streams. Such a scheme would involve the Arrow Lakes storage a short distance above the international boundary on the Columbia, development of the Mica Creek site near the Big Bend of the Columbia, and storage on the upper Kootenay either in the Libby transboundary reservoir or by an alternative complex consisting of the Dorr and Bull River sites, both to regulate flows on the lower Kootenay and Columbia.

The alternative basic plan, also with possibility of variation, would involve a system of works in which the flows of the upper Kootenay would be diverted into the headwaters of the Columbia near the vicinity of Canal Flats (8,000 cfs out of the total 11,000 cfs that crosses the international boundary under natural conditions). This would be accomplished by diversion works developed in the

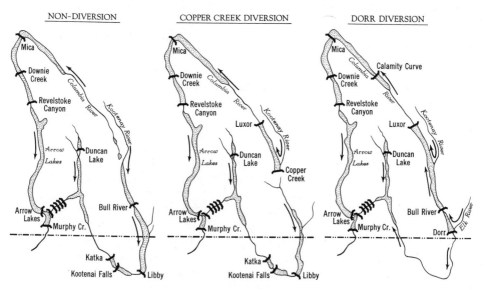

Figure 20. Alternative possibilities considered by the International Joint Commission for development of the upper Columbia River. (Source: International Columbia River Engineering Board, *Water Resources of the Columbia River Basin*, Report to the International Joint Commission United States and Canada, 1959, p. 67.)

Dorr, Bull River, and Luxor complex, and pumping facilities to provide the lift from the Dorr into the Bull River–Luxor reservoir, thereby reversing the natural flow of the Elk tributary of the Kootenay from the latter into the Columbia. A storage project on the Duncan tributary of the Kootenay would be developed, in part to aid in regulating streamflows over head plants in the lower Kootenay, in British Columbia. [2]

In addition to these two basic plans, there was a third, and intermediate, possibility—the Copper Creek diversion—which would have the result of diverting about 3,600 cfs of the Kootenay's flow into the Columbia in the vicinity of Canal Flats, permitting the remainder to flow in the natural channel of the Kootenay into the United States.

The storage sites and volume for each alternative set are tabulated in Table 4.

TABLE 4
Projects and Storage Capacity in Columbia-Kootenay Alternatives
(thousand acre-feet)

Storage site	Dorr diversion	Copper Creek diversion	Non-diversion
Dorr	881	—	—
Bull River	—	—	2,794
Bull River–Luxor	3,996	—	—
Copper Creek–Luxor	—	2,275	—
Mica	11,685	11,685	11,685
Arrow Lakes	5,165	5,165	5,165
Murphy Creek	2,834	2,834	2,834
Libby	—	4,045	4,045
Long Meadows	400	400	400
Kootenay Lake	1,028	1,028	1,028
Duncan Lake	1,400	1,000	1,000
Total upper Columbia and Kootenay	27,389	28,432	28,951

Source: International Columbia River Engineering Board, *Water Resources in the Columbia River Basin*, report to the International Joint Commission, 1959, pp. 69–71.

Mention should be made of a potential extension of the Kootenay diversion plans, which was not within the compass of the two governments' 1944 reference to the International Joint Commission. The diversion of the Kootenay into the Columbia could be followed by a similar diversion from the Columbia into the Fraser, in British Columbia, at one of at least two possible locations where

[2] An independent scheme, investigated by Crippen Wright Engineering, Ltd., engaged by the Province of British Columbia, proposed a combination consisting of a high dam at Calamity Curve, works in the vicinity of Canal Flats to divert the Kootenay at that point, and a diversion tunnel from Findlay Creek, a tributary of the upper Kootenay, directly into Columbia Lake with power facilities to utilize the drop.

the headwaters of the Fraser, or one of its tributaries, are nearest the Columbia.

Under the basic diversion scheme, the Libby project would be rendered inoperative owing to reduced flows on the upper Kootenay resulting from diversion; also, the Downie Creek and Revelstoke Canyon head plants might be significantly affected, depending on the point at which the Fraser was led out of the Columbia system.

No really comprehensive analysis of the potential Fraser diversion is available on which to base a proper evaluation of the alternatives it offers, but several observations can be made in passing. First, certain legal issues would require satisfactory resolution with respect to the rights and obligations of the diverting upstream country: there are questions, for example, concerning its potential liability for damages to the downstream country in connection with existing power operations. Second, diversion into the Fraser would not be meaningful unless a fairly high head were developed on the Fraser in Canada, with consequent ill effects for the fishing industry. Engineering analysis of a combination involving a series of low-head plants to permit passage of anadromous fish, in conjunction with a diversion from the Columbia, indicates that the costs would be prohibitive, even if one does not consider the inevitable losses occasioned by existing developed head in the natural channel of the Columbia.[3] If, on the other hand, the Fraser were developed by means of the most economical high head and related storage facilities (ignoring the fisheries), diversion of the Columbia into the Fraser would have to be justified largely by the gain in energy alone, as the Fraser would have provided the capacity and realized most of the capacity benefits.[4] Moreover, as indicated on page 27, so high a head, entailing large-scale obstructions in the stream, would create difficulties for the salmon fisheries, part of which might involve the question of U.S. equity in the fisheries.

For these reasons, the relevance of the Fraser diversion as an immediate alternative complementary development linking the Columbia and Fraser rivers appears sufficiently remote[5] to justify

[3] "An Investigation of Columbia to Fraser River Diversion Project, 1956," summary of report by B. C. Engineering Company Ltd., in *The Columbia River Treaty, Protocol and Related Documents* (Ottawa: Departments of External Affairs, and Northern Affairs and National Resources, February 1964). Hereafter referred to as *White Paper*.

[4] I owe this point to Ralph Purcell, Engineer, British Columbia Energy Board.

[5] *The Columbia River Treaty and Protocol: A Presentation* (Ottawa: Departments of External Affairs, and Northern Affairs and National Resources, April 1964), p. 51. See also W. R. Derrick Sewell, *Water Management and Floods in the Fraser River Basin* (Chicago: University of Chicago Press, 1965), especially Chapter V.

omitting it from systematic analysis in considering an optimal system for the development of the Columbia and tributary system.

With respect to the Kootenay diversion, excluding further diversion into the Fraser, it is important to distinguish between the comparative contribution of the alternatives to the system considered as an interdependent hydrologic unit, and the locus of occurrences of this contribution. The obvious consequence of the Kootenay diversion is the shift in the relative amount of power originating at head developments in the two countries from the United States to the Canadian side of the boundary, rather than the achievement of any significant gain in system output. Tabulated below (Table 5) is the relative head over which the quantum of water in question would fall under the alternative plans.

TABLE 5

Comparative Gross Heads and Country Distribution of Head, Diversion vs. Non-Diversion

I. Comparative amount of head over which diverted water would fall:

	Non-Diversion (feet)		Diversion (feet)
Bull River	201	Dorr (pumping)	−240
Libby	340	Bull River–Luxor	90
Kootenai Falls	160	Calamity Curve	120
Katka	100	Mica Creek	566
Lower Kootenay plants	353	Downie Creek	257
		Revelstoke Canyon	169
Totals	1,154		962

II. Comparative distribution of head over which potentially diverted water would fall:

	Canada (feet)	United States (feet)		Canada (feet)	United States (feet)
Bull River	201	—	Dorr (pumping)	−240	—
Libby	—	340	Bull River–Luxor	90	—
Kootenai Falls	—	160	Calamity Curve	120	—
Katka	—	100	Mica Creek	566	—
Lower Kootenay plants	353	—	Downie Creek	257	—
			Revelstoke Canyon	169	—
Totals	554	600		962	0

Source: International Columbia River Engineering Board, Water Resources of the Columbia River Basin, report to the International Joint Commission, 1959.

The tabulation refers to head associated only with the volume of water involved in the diversion, but the degree to which other flows —those additional to the diverted quantities—would be utilized should also be considered. The reduced volume of Kootenay flow

below the point of the Dorr diversion would be insufficient to
warrant development of any head between the point of diversion
and present developments on the lower Kootenay, and insufficient also for extension of the development in the lower reaches of
the Kootenay. In short, the power loss would be related not only
to the decrement in head over which the diverted waters would
fall, but also to the loss of potential energy of the residual flows in
the Kootenay below the point of diversion. Somewhat similar
effects apply to the head in the Luxor and Calamity Curve sites,
the warrant for developing these possibilities being problematical
in the absence of augmented flows in that reach of the Columbia.
A final consideration concerns the compensatory reduction in
storage in the Arrow Lakes site that is incorporated into one variation of the Dorr diversion plan. This is the so-called "Sequence
IXa" plan associated with the late General A. G. L. McNaughton,
who in 1959 was chairman of the Canadian section of the IJC. This
contemplated the substitution of a somewhat enlarged capacity at
the Murphy Creek site for the High Arrow structure, with the
intention partly of molifying local objections to the flooding associated with the High Arrow structure, and partly of retaining a
measure of flexibility compatible with a subsequent diversion of
part of the flow of the Columbia into the Fraser.[6] The combined
effect of the Dorr diversion and reduced regulation on the lower
Columbia reduces total system output marginally. While increasing
output within the Canadian reach of the river, it does so at the
expense of substantial reduction at the sites of potential U.S.
projects, mainly on the Kootenai.[7]

It must be cautioned that the above data represent physical indi-
cators only and have no ultimate reliability with respect to the
relative economy of the two alternatives. A comprehensive analysis
involving a comparison of the difference in present worth of the
value of power contributed by *only the economic projects* participating
in each of the alternatives was not undertaken by the International
Columbia River Engineering Board. In the absence of more accurate studies, however, we must rely on the data of the ICREB
report to provide a suggestion of the relative economy of the basic
alternatives and their variations. Given below (Table 6) are some
comparative data on the various plans, designated also by the
"sequence" numerals by which they became known to those
interested in the upper Columbia development.

[6] Personal interview with General A. G. L. McNaughton, Fall, 1959.
[7] *White Paper, op. cit.*, pp. 151–52, plans 1 and 6.

TABLE 6

Comparative Data on Range of Upper Kootenay Diversion Alternatives

Project investment	Sequence VII Non-Diversion	Sequence VIII Copper Creek	Sequence IX Dorr with High Arrow	Sequence IXa Dorr Diversion with Low Arrow
	($000)	($000)	($000)	($000)
Bull River (B.C.)	83,632	—	—	—
Dorr (B.C.)	—	—	35,840	35,840
Libby (U.S.)	342,800	312,800	—	—
Kootenai Falls (U.S.)	98,000	92,500	—	—
Katka (U.S.)	97,500	90,674	—	—
Duncan Lake (B.C.)	—	—	24,807	24,807
Kootenay River plants (B.C.)	40,756	40,756	2,399	2,399
Bull River–Luxor (B.C.)	—	—	110,023	110,023
Copper Creek–Luxor (B.C.)	—	54,390	—	—
Calamity Curve (B.C.)	—	32,972	38,223	38,223
Mica Creek (B.C.)	302,442	314,805	327,167	327,167
Downie Creek (B.C.)	123,463	138,914	146,640	146,640
Revelstoke Canyon (B.C.)	104,379	116,904	123,168	123,168
Arrow Lakes (B.C.)	66,400	66,400	66,400	—
Murphy Creek (B.C.)	94,883	94,883	94,883	103,501
Total investment	1,336,255	1,355,998	969,550	911,768
Total power				
Prime power (mw)	9,118	9,220	9,150	8,960
Average energy (mw)	8,038	8,168	8,058	7,862
Canada:				
Investment ($000)	815,955	860,024	969,550	911,768
Prime power (mw)	2,549	2,785	2,986	2,962
Average energy (mw)	2,441	2,682	2,852	2,852
United States:				
Investment ($000)	520,300	495,974	—	—
Prime power (mw)	6,569	6,435	6,161	5,998
Average energy (mw)	5,597	5,486	5,206	5,010

Sources: International Columbia River Engineering Board, Water Resources of the Columbia River Basin, Appendix VI, Economic Studies, report to the International Joint Commission, 1959; and White Paper, pp. 151 ff.

Although the ICREB data are deficient insofar as their use in comparative evaluation is concerned,[8] they may be taken as *prima facie* evidence to support a number of observations the negotiating teams and supporting staff were likely to have made.

[8] The output associated with any particular project was estimated on the basis of the physical amount of storage provided and the head over which it regulated streamflows in combination with all of the other physically compatible projects in the total system. Accordingly, the uneconomic projects in the set were credited with values they would not realize in an efficient program, whereas the economic projects were not imputed a value commensurate with their contribution in an efficient system. Moreover, the imputation to the projects was made on the basis of the conditions estimated to prevail in the system during one year alone (1985) despite the fact that the form and quality of the contribution of the projects with storage will be subject to change during the period relevant to the evaluation as the system emerges from a predominantly hydro into a predominantly thermal system.

It is apparent that from a system standpoint, ignoring the relevance of the international boundary, neither the non-diversion scheme nor the Copper Creek diversion could be seriously entertained as economic elements in an optimal system, based on the data available to the parties at the time of negotiation. As compared with the Dorr diversion, the non-diversion alternative reflects a loss of 32 mw of power and 20 mw of energy, yet entails an increased outlay exceeding a third of a billion dollars. The Copper Creek alternative suffers equally by comparison. Although it is attended by a small increase of 70 mw of power and 110 mw of energy, the additional investment is increased to $386.4 million. In both instances, this is accounted for largely by the physical compatibility of the Libby, Kootenai Falls, and Katka sites in the United States' reach of the Kootenay, which are all expensive relative to their contribution to the system. Finally, as between the High Arrow and Low Arrow variants of the Dorr diversion, the former provides for an increase of 190 mw of power and 196 mw of energy with an increased investment of $57.9 million. Table 7 provides a basis for comparing the economics of the three schemes of development.

TABLE 7

Comparative Data on Various Alternatives in Relation to High Arrow–Dorr Diversion

	High Arrow–Dorr diversion vs. non-diversion	High Arrow–Dorr diversion vs. Copper Creek diversion	High vs. Low Arrow–Dorr diversion
Excess over Dorr diversion Investment ($000)	366,700	386,400	−57,800
Excess over Dorr diversion Annual Costs ($000)	17,240	19,786	−2,960
Excess over Dorr diversion Power (mw)	−32	70	−190
Energy (mw)	−20	110	−196
Thermal available for difference in cost Power (mw)	642	400	80
Energy (mw)	398	625	83
Net efficiency gain of High Arrow–Dorr diversion in terms of power units Power (mw)	674	330	110
Energy (mw)	418	515	133

Note: Annual cost of hydro taken as 4 per cent interest and 50-year amortization term plus 10 per cent of interest and amortization liability for operation and maintenance and interim replacement. Thermal power equivalents assume investment in capacity of $150/kw installed, interest at 4 per cent and a thirty-five-year amortization term; energy values used assume a net heat rate of 9000 btu/kwh and fuel at 30 cents per million btu.

From the information contained in the ICREB report, inadequate as it may be, it is difficult to escape the conclusion that the Dorr diversion represents the most economical of the three possibilities for developing the upper Columbia, when viewed in the context of total (both Canadian and United States reaches) system development and operation.

SYSTEMATIC ANALYSIS OF SYSTEM COMPONENTS AND SEQUENCES

Since the principles formulated by the International Joint Commission were intended to provide a guide for the negotiation teams following completion of the International Columbia River Engineering Board's investigations, one would expect the negotiating teams and their work groups to have addressed themselves to the selection of the most economical configuration of projects. However, neither the work group reports nor staff memoranda and studies give any indication that the comparative economics of the diversion and non-diversion alternatives *operating in an internationally developed system* received systematic attention. [9] As a result, the additional data which were developed at the suggestion of the IJC and later of the negotiators, [10] and which supplemented the ICREB report, relate exclusively to a comparative analysis of the several upper Columbia and Kootenay sites, ignoring the diversion alternatives. It is, of course, beyond the capability of this study to undertake a comprehensive, independent analysis of the alternative possibilities. What can be done, however, is to use the available data on the non-diversion alternatives, supplementing them where necessary with independent estimates, to illustrate a systematic analysis of the economic alternatives in terms of selection both from among mutually exclusive alternatives and from among possible permutations of the selected set of projects.

[9] There is evidence of a substantial amount of work by the Canadian technical staffs (*Summary of Water Resources Branch Power Output Studies of the Columbia River*, Department of Northern Affairs and National Resources, Water Resources Branch, February 1964) and by the Provincial Water Rights Branch Staff in studies especially during the spring and summer of 1960, directed toward evaluating various degrees of Kootenay diversion, either in the context of Canadian independent development or as incident to strategy in bargaining for downstream benefit shares. But in no instance was a comprehensive analysis of the components of the system, which would maximize the net benefits of the international system for mutual sharing, undertaken by either country independently or by the International Work Groups.

[10] International Work Group Reports, June 24, 1959, May 1960.

Ideally, the analysis would proceed by estimating the demand curve for power over the entire period of the planning horizon with explicit consideration of future power rates and the elasticity of demand for power. However, because of the imponderables governing conditions over a period so far into the future, a cruder method is typically resorted to as a practicable alternative. Based on experience and judgment, a growth of power demand is projected for the area within which Columbia River power would be marketed. Known independent resources, such as expansion of facilities of independent utilities, are identified to the extent feasible and deducted from the area loads to provide the residual load requirements. The Columbia resources and related thermal capacity are then fitted to the deficiency in the most economic manner, giving the schedule of amounts of new energy resources projected as being required.

Since the effect of power rates and price elasticities on load growth cannot be taken into account explicitly in any meaningful manner, there is need to consider alternative growth rates. This is an essential step, because there are differences among projects in terms of the function they perform in the power system—whether it is exclusively stream regulation, as in the case of a storage project, or stream regulation in early stages plus peaking later, as in the case of a combined storage-head project which is designed to supplement the thermal base as the system evolves into a predominantly thermal system. The relative economy of a project is likely to be influenced, then, by the rate of load growth, since the value of storage progressively decreases with increasing amounts of thermal capacity operating in the system, whereas the value of head plants, with penstocks available for installation of additional generator capacity, will remain constant or even increase. On the other hand, a high rate of load growth implies the addition of electro-process loads and, as these have a high load factor, the shape of the load duration curve will be flattened, thus tending to prolong the period over which storage would perform a useful function. A lower growth rate correspondingly implies fewer high-load-factor industrial activities and more attenuated peaks. In short, the two effects tend to be offsetting. The net effect of these factors operating in combination would, however, require a systematic analysis beyond the scope of this study.

In the staff studies of the upper Columbia and Kootenay projects preceding the Treaty, a single growth rate and load shape was employed, doubtless due to the restricted time available to the staff. Accordingly, the data on which the following analysis is based are

relevant to a relatively high rate of load development and a uniform
load shape over time prepared by the Federal Power Commission
staff for the Columbia 308 Review Report.[11]

Given the indicated storage requirements for improving stream
regulation over head developments downstream, which among the
several projects would most economically satisfy this requirement,
and which sequence of construction would result in power production representing the highest present value net of costs? One consideration dominates the selection of the first storage project to be
added: The fact that the projected load growth indicated a deficiency in the later nineteen sixties means that this project should be
completed in time to meet the expected load. This consideration
would eliminate the Mica project from first-added consideration
as it is the largest and requires too long a construction period to
qualify. Among the projects that remain, there is a choice among
High Arrow, Duncan, Libby, and Dorr–Bull River—the latter considered as a substitute for Libby to be employed for regulating
streamflows within the Kootenay natural channel. Among these,
analyses were undertaken, predominantly with High Arrow and
Duncan functioning as a single storage unit. Table 8 gives relevant
data on the estimated power contribution of the projects, each
considered in turn as next-added to the existing Columbia system.
It will be seen that all three contenders provide approximately the
same amount of power in the early years and would be equally able
to meet the short-run load requirements. Since costs vary considerably among the three, however, it is necessary to compare the
present worth of the benefit streams over time with the corresponding costs for each project.[12] In computing benefits the value of

[11] *Columbia River and Tributaries*, Vol. III, H.D. No. 403, 87th Cong., 2nd Sess.'
Part 5, Appendix C.

[12] Basic cost information was taken from *Water Resources of the Columbia River
Basin, op. cit.;* House Doc. No. 403, *op. cit.;* and from correspondence with the
Department of Northern Affairs and National Resources, Canada. To construction costs were added interest accumulated during construction with rates alternatively taken at 4 per cent and 5.5 per cent. The 1970 worth of annual operation
maintenance and interim replacement costs discounted by corresponding factors
was deducted from the 1970 worth of gross benefits. The use of interest rates of
between 4 per cent and 5.5 per cent is suggested by studies addressing this question.
See, for example, G. L. Reuber and R. J. Wonnacott, *The Cost of Capital in Canada,
with Special Reference to Public Development of the Columbia River* (Washington:
Resources for the Future, Inc., 1961); and Maynard M. Hufschmidt, John
Krutilla, Julius Margolis, and Stephen A. Marglin, *Standards and Criteria for
Formulating and Evaluating Federal Water Resources Developments*, Report of Panel of
Consultants to the Bureau of the Budget, Washington, D.C., June 30, 1961,
Chapter II.

TABLE 8

Estimated Power Contribution of Selected Projects Substituted Alternatively into the U.S. Columbia Base System

Project	1970		1985		1995		2010	
	Dependable capacity (mw)	Annual usable energy (mw-years)	Dependable capacity (mw)	Annual energy (mw-years)	Dependable capacity (mw)	Annual energy (mw-years)	Dependable capacity (mw)	Annual energy (mw-years)
FIRST-ADDED TO BASE SYSTEM[1]								
High Arrow–Duncan Lakes								
At site	0	0	0	0	0	0	0	0
At W. Kootenay plants[2]	111	73	111	73	119	73	119	73
At U.S. base system plants	1,832	1,118	1,557	845	1,520	780	0	290
Total	1,943	1,191	1,668	918	1,639	853	119	363
Libby								
At site	258	188	258	188	320	188	791	228
At W. Kootenay plants[3]	344	212	344	212	451	212	451	212
At U.S. base system plants	1,380	860	1,040	750	1,000	755	0	200
Total	1,982	1,260	1,642	1,150	1,771	1,155	1,242	640
Bull River–Dorr								
At site	158	116	158	116	196	116	630	125
At W. Kootenay plants[3]	344	212	344	212	451	212	451	212
At U.S. base system plants	1,380	860	1,040	750	1,000	755	0	200
Total	1,882	1,188	1,542	1,078	1,647	1,083	1,081	537

[1] Projects appearing as "Base System" in Annex B, Columbia River Basin Treaty.
[2] Includes additional units at Brilliant and Waneta and integration benefits in the Canadian system.
[3] Includes additional units at Brilliant and Waneta and complete Canal plant.

power is taken as the cost of power for meeting demand from the most economical non-hydroelectric alternative, namely, thermal stations. The assumption here is that the projected load will be met in any event with or without the hydro projects; accordingly, the net benefit of the hydro cannot exceed the difference between hydro costs and the most economic competitive alternative.

To provide an estimate of value, then, certain assumptions must be made with respect to the determinants of cost for the thermal alternative. Since these cannot be predicted with accuracy, the approach will be to develop alternatives which will bracket the reasonable range within which thermal costs might be expected to fall. On the lower end of the scale, one can assume investment in capacity of about $130 per kilowatt installed, with interest on the investment at 4 per cent and a thirty-five-year estimated useful life. At the highest extreme, investment might be taken as $150 per kilowatt installed and interest at 5.5 per cent. Fuel costs, on the other hand, would doubtless be bracketed by 20 cents per million Btu at the lower end and 35 cents at the high extreme. A station heat rate of 9,000 Btu per kilowatt-hour can be taken as a reasonable approximation in both instances.

Given these magnitudes, the range of value for dependable capacity would run from $10.34 to $13.80 per kilowatt. Annual energy values would range from $15.77 to $27.59. These values, then, are imputed to the projects' capacity and energy estimates.

To make benefits and costs comparable with respect to time, both the stream of annual benefits and the operation and maintenance costs are discounted to a common time base, i.e., 1970. Since estimated output is given for only four points in time, each estimate is taken to represent the average value extending over the entire time period in which it occurs. For example, the 1970 estimates cover the decade of the seventies and those of 1985 extend over the period of the eighties.

When one follows the procedure outlined above, the comparative data for the three projects are as shown in Table 9. Here it is seen that the High Arrow–Duncan storage complex yields significantly greater net benefits and thus, under the criterion appropriate to maximizing system net benefits, qualifies for first addition to the base system.

Since benefits yielded by storage are subject to diminution with increased amounts of storage in the system, it is necessary to compare the benefits from Libby and Dorr–Bull River on a second-added basis when considering the choice of the next storage incre-

TABLE 9

Estimated Value of Power Output of Selected Projects Substituted Alternatively into the U.S. Columbia Base System

(million dollars)

Project	Estimated benefits		Estimated present costs	Estimated net benefits
	Capacity at.....	$10.34/kw		
	Energy at......	$13.80/kw		
		$15.77/kw		
		$27.59/kw		
High Arrow–Duncan				
Discount at 4%	630.8		112.2[1]	518.6
5.5%		810.3	111.3[1]	699.0
Libby				
Discount at 4%	756.3		415.2[2]	344.2
5.5%		944.7	421.7[2]	523.0
Dorr–Bull River				
Discount at 4%	702.2		219.6[2]	482.6
5.5%		880.0	220.5[2]	659.5

[1] Includes costs of additional units at Brilliant and Waneta plants.
[2] Includes additional units at Brilliant and Waneta, and complete new Canal plant.

ment to be added. In this instance, the Mica Creek project would also be a contender. The downstream run-of-the-river plants at Downie Creek and Revelstoke Canyon must be considered when evaluating the Mica project's contribution to the system because, being dependent on storage at Mica, the plants represent an interdependent complex. Expected to make their appearance in the system about the beginning of the eighties,[13] they are included in the 1985 estimate for Mica Creek. The relevant data on the three contending projects, second-added to the United States base system plus High Arrow–Duncan, are given in Table 10.

Given the estimated power output associated with each of the three projects added second to the system, an estimate of the present worth of benefits and costs is required to evaluate their comparative economics. In the case of the Mica–Downie–Revelstoke complex, the Mica benefits are assumed to begin in 1970 while the power benefits of the Downie and Revelstoke run-of-the-river projects are assumed to commence in 1980. In the latter instance, however, all time streams, benefits, and costs, are discounted to the 1970 base to render all projects comparable within the complex as well as between the Mica complex and the Libby and Dorr–Bull River contenders. The relevant data are shown in Table 11.

On the basis of the estimated costs and associated power output, it is clear that the Mica storage project (and interdependent head plants) qualify for second addition after the High Arrow–Duncan storage is added to the existing Columbia system.

Guides to the selection of the third storage to be added are to be found in the data already presented on Libby and Dorr–Bull River, for the relative economics of the two projects does not change whether they are evaluated iteratively as first-, second-, or third-added. However, with about 20 million acre-feet of additional storage represented by the High Arrow–Duncan and Mica Creek storages, it is essential to evaluate the contribution of the next 5 million acre-feet to determine whether the additional storage can be included economically. Table 12 gives the estimated power contribution of the two upper Kootenay projects when added iteratively after an additional 20 million acre-feet of storage has been provided for the system, and the estimated value of this last-added output.

[13] *Minutes of Proceedings and Evidence*, No. 6, Standing Committee on External Affairs, House of Commons, Twenty-Sixth Parliament, Second Session, April 14, 1964, p. 368.

TABLE 10

Estimated Power Contribution of Selected Projects Substituted Alternatively into the U.S. Columbia Base System Plus High Arrow–Duncan

Project	1970 Dependable capacity (mw)	1970 Annual usable energy (mw-years)	1985 Dependable capacity (mw)	1985 Annual energy (mw-years)	1995 Dependable capacity (mw)	1995 Annual energy (mw-years)	2010 Dependable capacity (mw)	2010 Annual energy (mw-years)
SECOND-ADDED AFTER HIGH ARROW–DUNCAN								
Mica								
At site	1,045	785	1,080	785	1,340	785	2,784	785
At Downie and Revelstoke plants[1]			1,125	838	1,704	838	1,704	838
At U.S. base system plants	1,168	600	1,175	360	980	295	0	160
Total	2,214	1,385	3,380	1,983	4,024	1,918	4,488	1,783
Libby								
At site	259	189	258	188	320	188	791	228
At W. Kootenay plants[2]	266	185	266	185	332	185	332	185
At U.S. base system plants	588	300	595	175	500	140	0	90
Total	1,113	674	1,119	548	1,152	513	1,123	503
Bull River–Dorr								
At site	158	116	158	116	196	116	630	125
At W. Kootenay plants[2]	266	185	266	185	332	185	332	185
At U.S. base system plants	588	300	595	175	500	140	0	90
Total	1,012	601	1,019	476	1,028	441	962	400

[1] Downie Creek and Revelstoke Canyon are not estimated to be operating until 1980; accordingly the benefits are to be considered lagged a decade behind the initial occurrence at site and at U.S. base system plants associated with the construction of Mica Creek.
[2] Includes additional units at Brilliant and Waneta and complete new Canal plant.

TABLE 11

Estimated Value of Power Output of Selected Projects Substituted Alternatively Second into the U.S. Columbia Base System plus High Arrow–Duncan

(million dollars)

Project	Estimated benefits		Estimated costs	Net benefits
Capacity at..... Energy at......	$10.34/kw $15.77/kw	$13.80/kw $27.59/kw		
Mica Creek Complex				
Discount at 4%	1,303.9	1,512.2	536.0[1]	767.9
5.5%			510.9[1]	1,001.3
Libby				
Discount at 4%	451.3	546.3	408.6[2]	42.4
5.5%			415.1[2]	131.1
Dorr–Bull River				
Discount at 4%	397.1	481.4	213.0[2]	184.1
5.5%			213.8[2]	267.6

[1] Includes discounted cost of Downie Creek and Revelstoke Canyon river plants.
[2] Includes cost of additional Brilliant and Waneta units and complete Canal plant.

TABLE 12

Estimated Power Contribution of Selected Projects Substituted Alternatively into the U.S. Columbia Base System Third after High Arrow–Duncan and Mica Creek Storage Projects

(megawatts)

Project	1970		1985		1995		2010	
	Dependable capacity	Annual energy	Dependable capacity	Annual energy	Dependable capacity	Annual energy	Dependable capacity	Annual energy
THIRD-ADDED AFTER MICA ARROW–DUNCAN AND MICA								
Libby								
At site	254	207	258	207	320	207	791	228
At W. Kootenay plants[1]	266	185	266	185	332	185	332	185
At U.S. base system plants	307	170	205	125	170	114	0	50
Total	827	562	729	517	822	506	1,123	463
Dorr–Bull River								
At site	154	128	158	128	196	128	630	125
At W. Kootenay plants[1]	266	185	266	185	332	185	332	185
At U.S. base system plants	307	170	205	125	170	114	0	50
Total	727	483	629	438	698	427	962	360

Estimated Value of Power Output of Libby and Dorr–Bull River Added Iteratively Third after High Arrow–Duncan and Mica Creek to the Existing Columbia System

(million dollars)

Project	Estimated benefits	Estimated costs	Net benefits
Libby			
Capacity at.....: $10.34/mw			
Energy at......: $15.77/mw			
Capacity at.....: $13.80/mw			
Energy at......: $27.59/mw			
Discount at 4%	367.5	408.6[1]	−41.1
5.5%	443.4	415.1[1]	28.3
Dorr–Bull River			
Discount at 4%	313.3	213.0[1]	100.3
5.5%	378.7	213.8[1]	164.9

[1] Includes cost of additional units at Brilliant and Waneta and complete Canal plant on lower Kootenay.

As expected, the Dorr–Bull River project is seen to be economically superior to the Libby alternative. The latter, if third-added after 20 million acre-feet, has a present cost in excess of present benefits when computed at the lower range of values for power. On the other hand, the Dorr–Bull River project remains economic as third-added whether the lower values or the higher values for power are used.

In summary, if the upper Kootenay storage projects were to be governed entirely by economic criteria, the Dorr–Bull River site, operating as a storage project to regulate flows down the Kootenay's natural channel, would be the economical supplement to the High Arrow–Duncan and Mica projects in Canada.

One question requires consideration before a final judgment can be made as to the selection of the entire complex of facilities in an efficient program: If 5 million acre-feet of storage are to be added on the upper Kootenay, along with the storages at High Arrow and Mica Creek on the Columbia, what value would the Duncan Lake storage have? Stream regulation on the lower Kootenay would be achieved by the upper Kootenay project with 5 million acre-feet of storage capacity, severely limiting the incremental contribution which the Duncan Lake storage project could make to the value of the regulation on the lower Kootenay. Similarly, with the volume of storage represented by the High Arrow, Mica, and upper Kootenay projects, the incremental value of the Duncan Lake storage for regulating streamflows over the downstream head plants in the United States is greatly diminished. Accordingly, without an explicit evaluation of the Duncan project as last-added to the system following close to 24 million acre-feet of new storage, it is not at all clear that the Duncan project should be included in an efficient program of development of the Columbia.[14]

A similar question might apply to the High Arrow project. In this case, however, the need both to re-regulate the Mica storage releases following the time when Mica generation will be undertaken to meet British Columbia loads, and to regulate the inflow

[14] I have addressed this question with a "last-added" analysis by reliance on crude estimating techniques, and find the Duncan project is difficult to justify economically when considering an integrated United States–Canadian system. While the shortfall is substantial, it must be acknowledged that it may fall within the margin of error of the estimating procedure and, therefore, although there is evidence which indicates the economics of the project is questionable, my analysis is not adequate to demonstrate this point conclusively. A further analysis of the decision to include Duncan Lake storage is made in Chapter 6.

between Mica Creek and the Arrow Lakes, appears to remove the High Arrow project from similar suspicion.[15]

THE OPTIMAL SYSTEM AND TREATY SYSTEM PROJECTS CONSIDERED

Given the data available at the time of negotiations leading to the 1961 Treaty, it appears that a faithful application of IJC General Principle No. 1 would have provided a system including High Arrow, Mica, and either of two alternatives: a diversion of the upper Kootenay into the Columbia (whether by the Dorr–Bull River–Luxor facility or an alternate High Calamity Curve scheme of Crippen Wright Engineering), or the Dorr–Bull River storage site in Canada used for purposes of stream regulation on the lower Kootenay without diversion. However, the result of the negotiations culminating in the Treaty included the High Arrow storage project with 7.1 million acre-feet, the Duncan project with 1.4 million acre-feet, Mica with but 7 million acre-feet devoted to stream regulation downstream in the United States, and an option for the Libby project with 5 million acre-feet of storage. (See Figure 21.) In addition, Canada obtained the right to divert the flows of the upper Kootenay to the extent of 1.5 million acre-feet (approximately one-fifth) annually after a lapse of twenty years following exchange of ratification, and from 70 per cent to 85 per cent of the Kootenay's flows progressively after the sixtieth and eightieth year following implementation of the Treaty.[16] Although Canada could provide 25 million acre-feet of storage, all of which appeared to qualify under the IJC principle relating to economic selection of projects and in the order of their economic merit, the final result of the negotiations provided for a Canadian contribution of 15.5 million acre-feet. The Libby project also is viewed as the third-added storage project following 15.5 million acre-feet of new storage. Assuming that the Mica storage potential will be restricted in use to the provision of only 7 million acre-feet for

[15] Comments on the Columbia River Treaty and Protocol (Montreal: Montreal Engineering Company Ltd., March 1964).

[16] *Treaty Between Canada and the United States of America Relating to Cooperative Development of the Water Resources of the Columbia River Basin,* signed at Washington, D.C., January 17, 1961, Article XIII, paragraphs 2, 3, and 4. (Hereafter cited as *Treaty.*)

regulation downstream,[17] the effect of this reduction in storage available for regulation downstream from the Mica reservoir will improve the returns to the Libby, or any other subsequently added alternative storage project. The effect of the redistribution of storage value from Mica to the Libby storage reservoir is illustrated in Table 13.

The redistribution of storage value will amount to a transfer of some $36 million to $48 million in favor of the Libby project.[18] While this is insufficient to qualify the project unambiguously on the basis of power value, the Libby storage, even after 15.5 million acre-feet of storage in the upper Columbia, would be effective for reducing the flood hazard in the Bonners Ferry area of Idaho. Prevention of average expected flood damage amounting to $815,000 annually would have a present value of $14 million to $18 million (discounted respectively at 5.5 and 4.0 per cent), thus passing the threshold of economic justification provided that neither the Kootenay diversion nor storage in the Dorr or Bull River sites represents a practical alternative.

However, one qualification should be made. While the upper Columbia portion of the system was deficient in storage prior to agreement on Canadian storage sites, with 15.5 million acre-feet of new storage in that reach of the river it is necessary to consider the next-added storage as being in competition with all of the available storage possibilities in the entire Columbia River system. It will be recalled that the Libby site was considered exclusively in terms of competitive sites on the upper Columbia and Kootenay prior to the existence of any appreciable storage in that reach of the river system. But with the procurement of 15.5 million acre-feet of new

---

[17] Presumably the remaining 4.7 million acre-feet could be used to increase the generation at the Mica site and over the Downie and Revelstoke Canyon head plants in British Columbia in meeting British Columbia loads. See Sir Alexander Gibb and Partners, Merz and McLellan, *Columbia and Peace River Power Projects: Report on Power Costs*, July 1961, where it is noted that a conflict may arise between maximum at-site generation on the Columbia in Canada and maximum system generation involving the downstream reach in the United States. With a fully integrated system, electrically, however, more power can be generated in Canada at-site by regulating Canadian storage for *maximum system benefits* than for maximum at-site generation in Canada, as higher flows are recorded in the Canadian reach during the system's critical period than during the critical period for an independent Canadian system. See *Columbia River Investigation*, Water Resources Branch, Department of Northern Affairs and National Resources, Ottawa, May 6, 1959; also explanatory letter from Mr. T. M. Patterson, Director, Water Resources Branch, April 28, 1960.

[18] Cf. Tables 12 and 13.

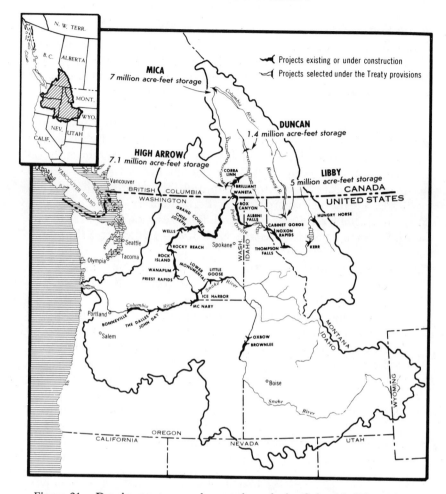

Figure 21. Developments agreed upon through the Columbia River Treaty, and those existing or under construction before 1960. (Sources: *Columbia River and Tributaries*, Vol. I, H.D. No. 403, 87th Cong., 2nd Sess., Plate 1; and International Columbia River Engineering Board, *Water Resources of the Columbia River Basin*, Report to the International Joint Commission United States and Canada, 1959, p. 67.)

storage for that portion of the system (which approximately doubles the total system capacity), the next storage capacity to be added must be considered in relation to alternative possibilities on the Pend Oreille and on the Snake River and its tributaries.

To short-cut the analysis of each possibility successively, as has been done earlier in this chapter, inferences can be drawn from an

TABLE 13

Estimated Contribution of Mica and Libby Storage Projects to Power Output in the Columbia Hydroelectric System (megawatts)

Project	1970 Dependable capacity	1970 Annual energy	1985 Dependable capacity	1985 Annual energy	1995 Dependable capacity	1995 Annual energy	2010 Dependable capacity	2010 Annual energy
MICA SECOND-ADDED WITH 7 MILLION ACRE-FEET								
At site	1,045	785	1,080	785	1,340	785	2,784	785
At d.s. Canadian plants	0	0	1,125	838	1,704	838	1,704	838
At d.s. U.S. plants	792	408	813	255	660	195	0	110
Total	1,837	1,193	3,018	1,878	3,704	1,818	4,488	1,733
LIBBY THIRD-ADDED AFTER 15.5 MILLION ACRE-FEET								
At site	268	215	272	214	320	214	791	228
At W. Kootenay plants	266	185	266	185	332	185	332	185
At d.s. U.S. plants	420	261	340	125	261	114	0	50
Total	954	661	878	524	913	513	1,123	463

Estimated Value of Added Power Output of Mica Storage (7 x 10⁶ acre-feet) Second-added and Libby (5 x 10⁶ acre-feet) Third-added after 8.5 x 10⁶ acre-feet of New Storage in the High Arrow Lakes and Duncan Lake Projects (million dollars)

Project	Estimated benefits — Capacity at $10.34/mw $13.80/mw; Energy at $15.77/mw $27.59/mw		Estimated costs	Net benefits
Mica Complex				
Discount at 4%	1,196.8	1,376.4	536.9[1]	659.9
Discount at 5.5%			510.9[1]	865.5
Libby				
Discount at 4%	403.7	490.9	408.6[2]	—4.9
Discount at 5.5%			415.1[2]	75.8

[1] Includes discounted cost of Downie Creek and Revelstoke Canyon plants.
[2] Includes cost of additional units at Brilliant, Waneta, and complete new Canal plant on lower Kootenay.

application of the last-added test developed by the U.S. Army Corps of Engineers.

For this purpose we shall consider 20 million acre-feet of new storage as a working hypothesis of the amount of new storage justified for the existing Columbia system, and shall consider, in addition to Libby, the Knowles project on the Clarks Fork–Pend Oreille, the Bruces Eddy (Dworshak) on the Clearwater in the Snake system, and the High Mountain Sheep project on the Middle Snake. These data are shown in Table 14.

Results of this last-added test confirm the belief that alternative sites require consideration following the addition of 15.5 million acre-feet of storage in the upper Columbia. The estimated values attributed to the selected projects suggest the desirability of adding a storage project on the Middle Snake in preference to additional projects on the upper Columbia. Moreover, after adding 15.5 million acre-feet of storage to the existing system, only the High Mountain Sheep project appears to be justified on the basis of power output. It is not at all clear that last-added flood control benefits would justify economically any of the other projects.

Between the conclusion of negotiations leading to the 1961 Treaty and completion of all arrangements for exchange of ratification in 1964, the Bruces Eddy (Dworshak) project was undertaken, which will add 2.0 million acre-feet of additional storage to the system.[19] The High Mountain Sheep project, with 2.2 million acre-feet of storage, would bring the new storage total to 19.7 million acre-feet. The question arises, therefore, whether or not the Libby project can be justified for addition to an economical system.

The data of Table 14 as they stand present an ambiguous situation. With power valued in the higher range of potential values, the Libby project, with the inclusion of local flood protection benefits, would just qualify. But this would not hold true at the lower range of power values. Since, however, it is a project which predominantly will involve U.S. costs, and the Treaty is permissive rather than mandatory with respect to the construction of Libby, it will be instructive to analyze the project in terms of U.S. benefits and U.S. costs. By terms of the Treaty,[20] the Libby project will be constructed at U.S. expense, save for the flowage costs associated

---

[19] The long delay in Canadian action on ratification of the Treaty impelled consideration of new storage in the United States, resulting in the initiation of construction on the Bruces Eddy project and the licensing for construction of the High Mountain Sheep project.

[20] *Treaty, op. cit.*, Article XII.

TABLE 14

Estimated Power Contribution of Projects Last-added Iteratively after 20 Million Acre-feet of New Storage in the Columbia System

(megawatts)

Project	1970		1985		1995		2010	
	Dependable capacity	Annual energy	Dependable capacity	Annual energy	Dependable capacity	Annual energy	Dependable capacity	Annual energy
Knowles	459	299	379	325	620	276	589	210
Bruces Eddy (Dworshak)	195	128	195	186	253	186	276	175
High Mountain Sheep	714	469	685	633	1,194	631	1,725	606
Libby								
At site	254	207	258	207	320	207	791	228
At W. Kootenay plants[1]	266	185	266	185	332	185	332	185
At U.S. plants	307	170	205	125	170	114	0	50
Libby Total	827	562	729	517	822	506	1,123	463

Estimated Value of Power Contribution of Selected Projects Added Iteratively after 20 Million Acre-feet New Storage

(million dollars)

Project	Estimated benefits	Estimated costs	Estimated net benefits
Capacity at......	$10.34/mw	$13.80/mw	
Energy at......	$15.77/mw	$27.59/mw	
Knowles			
Discount at 4%	205.5	288.2	−82.7
Discount at 5.5%	247.7	299.0	−51.3
Bruces Eddy (Dworshak)			
Discount at 4%	103.9	158.8	−52.9
Discount at 5.5%	124.4	158.1	−33.7
High Mountain Sheep			
Discount at 4%	410.1	304.6	105.5
Discount at 5.5%	474.7	304.4	170.3
Libby			
Discount at 4%	367.5	408.6[1]	−41.1
Discount at 5.5%	443.4	415.1[1]	27.3

[1] Includes cost of additional units at Brilliant and Waneta and complete new Canal plant on lower Kootenay.

with the Libby reservoir bottom which extends into British Columbia. In return, the Province of British Columbia retains all the benefits that accrue to it as a result of Libby regulation on the lower Kootenay at existing plants and extensions of development. By incurring the cost of project construction and land acquisition below the border, the United States retains all the benefits that accrue to it resulting from at-site power generation, improved regulation downstream over U.S. head plants, and residual flood protection. The comparative costs and benefits of the Libby project, when each country's shares are distinguished, are shown in Table 15.

TABLE 15

Estimated Distribution of Benefits and Costs of Libby Projects, and Net Benefits
(million dollars)

Project	Estimated benefits Capacity at.... $10.34/kw Energy at...... $15.77/kw	$13.80/kw $27.59/kw	Estimated costs		Net benefits
U.S. Libby B & C					
Discount at 4%	240.3		348.2		−107.9
Discount at 5.5%		290.3		356.2	−65.9
Canada Libby B & C					
Discount at 4%	127.1		60.4		+66.7
Discount at 5.5%		153.1		58.7	+94.4
United States benefit and cost of Libby:					
Power	240.3	290.3			
Flood control	17.5	13.8			
Total	257.8	304.1			
Benefit/cost	.7:1	.85:1			
Canada benefit/cost	2.1:1	2.6:1			

Viewing the project from a U.S. perspective, it is quite clear that Libby adds substantially more to U.S. cost than to the value of output accruing to the United States.[21] Accordingly, because of its ambiguity as a component of the system on economic grounds, the greatly biased distribution of costs and gains between the United States and Canada, and the Treaty terms which only permit but do not require the construction of Libby by the United States, it is obvious that if economic criteria alone were governing, the Libby project would be excluded from any U.S. plans for completion of development of the Columbia.

[21] An argument advanced in defense of the Libby project, that it is indispensable in managing the flood hazard in the Bonners Ferry area of Idaho, cannot be sustained, since an adequate and economical local flood control measure is available. See *Report on Survey for Flood Control of Kootenai River in Kootenai Flats Area, Idaho*, U.S. Army Engineer Division, North Pacific, Seattle District, December 1, 1958.

Since these observations are distinctly at variance with the U.S. Army Corps of Engineers' recommendations,[22] it may be well to probe the source of the discrepancy.

First, the submission of the Corps in support of the Libby project did not adhere to the customary practice of the Corps' North Pacific Division and subject Libby to a last-added test.[23] Libby's contribution to the Columbia hydro system was evaluated on a next-added basis following 15.5 million acre-feet of Canadian storage.

Second, the next-added evaluation was based on a single year out of the fifty-year period for which the project's discounted benefits must be shown to exceed present costs; its accuracy therefore depends on how closely the evaluation for that year approximates the weighted average annual value over the project's economic life-span.

Third, in the Corps' analysis a lower interest rate was imputed to the investment in the Libby project than is implicit in the estimate of the lowest cost non-hydro alternative source of power. Interest costs of 2.5 per cent were imputed to Libby, as against 3.85 per cent to the investment associated with the thermal alternative.[24]

Finally, there is the difference between imputed value of power used in the above analysis and that used by the Corps. A capacity value of $15.46 was selected from among alternatives prepared by the Federal Power Commission (FPC) in 1957. On the basis of information available even at that time, the estimate bears questioning. The FPC analysis of markets and power sources in the Pacific Northwest was based on statistical analyses of existing thermal plants and fuel costs. These facilities had been developed in earlier days on a scale appropriate to local (non-coordinated) system operations; thus, they were of diminutive scale and low efficiency. Viewed in the context of thermal plants appropriate to the size of the regional power system—based on the experience of large systems such as the American Gas and Electric, the Tennessee Valley Authority, and the Pacific Gas and Electric—the 100-mw units for the FPC computations are very inadequate. Units of 600, 750, and 900 mw are either in operation or being scheduled for installation, and options have been taken on units in excess of 1,000 mw. The difference in investment per kilowatt of capacity

[22] House Doc. No. 403, *op. cit.*
[23] *Ibid.*, p. 36.
[24] *Ibid.*, Volume II, Part II, Appendix C.

between such efficiently scaled units and the 100-mw units is substantial. The FPC estimates of $165–$175 per kilowatt of capacity used in hydro power evaluation studies may be compared with actual costs of between $95 and $120 for the large-scale units. The estimates of $130–$150 per kilowatt used in the present analysis appear quite conservative, therefore, in spite of their reduction from levels employed in the Columbia studies. The assumed heat rate of 10,000 Btu/kwh likewise appears excessive in comparison with the 8,750-Btu/kwh heat rate obtained in such performing units. Accordingly, our estimate of 9,000 Btu/kwh similarly appears conservative. This difference in heat rate would reflect a 10 per cent reduction in fuel costs/kwh for fuel at the same costs per million Btu.

When these factors are borne in mind, it is understandable that the conclusions of the present study and the conclusions of the Corps should vary considerably regarding Libby's worth to the United States.[25]

[25] A 1965 re-analysis of the Libby project conducted by the Corps of Engineers avoids some of the bases for difference between the conclusions of this study and the Corps of Engineers' findings regarding the economics of the Libby project. In the 1965 Corps study, Libby is subjected to a last-added test for purposes of evaluating power output but not, apparently, flood control. In addition, three representative points in time were selected which reflect three substantially different sets of conditions. The interest rate was raised from 2.5 per cent to 3.125 per cent, although it is not clear that a different (higher) interest rate was not imputed to the thermal alternative in deriving the value of dependable capacity. However, while the prime power attributed to the Libby project is somewhat less than I have used above, a lower system load factor is associated with this power than had hitherto been employed, and thus the dependable capacity attributed to the project exceeds the amount I have shown as well as the previous estimates made by the Corps of Engineers. A somewhat lower capacity value is employed by the Corps' 1965 study ($14.80) than previously ($15.46), as well as lower energy values ($23.65 as compared with $29.08). Even so, the energy values correspond to fuel costs of about 30 cents per million Btu—considerably in excess of the energy equivalents of nuclear plants following the Oyster Creek development in costs of nuclear power. Recreation benefits are attributed to the Libby project in this study, a factor not previously considered. With these changes, although the 1965 construction cost estimates for Libby have increased considerably over the 1960 estimates, and Libby's power output has been evaluated last-added after 20 million instead of 15 million acre-feet of additional storage, the benefit-cost ratio for Libby remains substantially unchanged by reason of the re-analysis.

On the other hand, if the flood control benefits were adjusted to reflect a last-added result, the energy values were considered to be bounded by the nuclear equivalent (thermal plants with fossil fuel using fuels at 25 cents/MMBtu) and the imputed interest rate increased minimally to 4 per cent, but accepting every other detail of the 1965 Corps' re-analysis, Libby's costs would still exceed its benefits to the United States.

CONCLUDING OBSERVATIONS

If we assume that the objective of the engineering investigation and planning effort relating to the international system was to provide an economical development of the Columbia Basin, then it must be acknowledged that the Treaty system represents a short-fall. The failure of both governments, independently or through joint work groups, to evaluate systematically the upper Kootenay diversion *within the context of an international system* precludes measuring the full extent of the shortfall. However, when one utilizes the data available on upper Kootenay storage sites for the regulation of flows downstream in the Kootenay's natural channel, it is seen that the inclusion of Libby in lieu of Dorr–Bull River results in a relative loss of net benefits amounting to between $135 million and $140 million at present value. A potential loss of this order, then, represents a comparable reduction in potential benefits available for mutual sharing between the United States and Canada. It should be added that exclusion of the Duncan project would probably result in a greater reduction in costs than in benefits.

Given these conclusions, it is evident that, IJC principles notwithstanding, the system resulting from the negotiations leading to co-operative development of the Columbia qualifies as economically suboptimal.

A word is needed about the accuracy of the information utilized in reaching these conclusions. Admittedly, the data on changes in the system output associated with changes in storage capacity have been obtained by relatively crude estimating procedures. Not all of the storage projects were regulated individually in the system by computer simulation. Rather, simulation studies of seven different levels of storage, representing actual projects in various combinations, were employed to fix points along a storage yield curve, with intermediate amounts of storage, corresponding to specific projects, often obtained by interpolation (see Figure 12). While this procedure can result in errors of estimate, the errors are likely to be of less consequence for comparing alternative projects than for determining absolute output associated with a particular project. Accordingly, the evaluation of the relative economics of mutually exclusive alternatives should be sufficiently accurate to warrant confidence. On the other hand, in connection with determining qualification for inclusion in the system, the margin of error in the estimates may be such as to leave inconclusive the evaluation of marginal projects. Where the differences are large, however, the error in the estimates appears to be well within the range to merit confidence in the conclusions reached.

Chapter 6

Determinants of the Treaty
Projects Selection

~~~~~~~~~~~~~~~~~~~~~~~~~~~~~~~~~~

The analysis of the previous chapter shows deficiencies in the selection of the Treaty system components if net benefit maximization for the system is taken as the objective. To review the conclusions reached: First, storage in the upper East Kootenay in British Columbia would meet the flood control and power objectives of the system more economically than the Libby project; thus, excess costs were incurred in the system projected by the Treaty of 1961. Second, assuming the unavailability of the upper East Kootenay storage sites in British Columbia—a matter that will be treated in this chapter—the Duncan Lake project is an anomaly given the sanction for development of 5 million acre-feet of storage upstream in the vicinity of Libby, Montana. Finally, considering the relative costs and benefits from the Libby project, and recognizing the relevance of an alternative local flood protection measure as a substitute for the Libby project, Libby is a dubious component in an efficient program of development for the Columbia. Were it not to be built, the justification for the Duncan project would be favorably affected.

To understand why the projects in the Columbia Treaty system were chosen, we need to go behind the results and examine the process by which they occurred. In this chapter, we address some of the considerations in addition to economics that ultimately were responsible for the projects secured by the Treaty.

OPENING STRATEGIES IN THE NEGOTIATIONS

When the negotiations began in February of 1960, the issues left unresolved by the International Joint Commission, regarding the formulation of principles to guide the selection of projects and division of gains, became the first order of business.

Taking IJC General Principle No. 1 in its unqualified sense, the position of Canada was to insist that in the first instance the projects for selection were to be consistent with the rule that only economic projects should be considered for inclusion in the Treaty system and that they should be added in an order prescribed by economic determinants. Since, from the standpoint of system economics, all of the upper Columbia and Kootenay storage possibilities in Canada were superior to any of the United States' storage possibilities, Canada could offer as much as 25 million acre-feet of storage in British Columbia before any storage projects in the United States would qualify for inclusion on economic grounds.

The United States resisted this interpretation of General Principle No. 1. Aware that all of the storage with a productive yield would be pre-empted by Canadian projects if this rule were to be followed and, further, that the specific power and flood control principles regarding the division of benefits called for an equal division of the gross gains evaluated on the basis of the sequence in which projects were constructed, the United States stressed the provisions of IJC General Principle No. 2 and the qualifying clauses in the specific power principles requiring that net benefits accrue to both parties to the agreement. Accordingly, as a means of qualifying for first-added benefits as well as for independent reasons, the U.S. negotiators pressed for early inclusion of the Libby project. This was defended on grounds that there was an immediate need for storage for power and flood control purposes; that the site investigations and advance planning on the Libby project would permit immediate construction and early completion; and that these reasons justified Libby also under the qualification embodied in General Principle No. 1, i.e., that the most economic projects should be added only "to the extent it is practicable and feasible to do so," taking account of considerations not reflected in the benefit-cost ratio. In part, the U.S. insistence on the Libby project stemmed from the apparently urgently felt need to provide storage on the upper Kootenay for flood control purposes in the Bonners Ferry, Idaho, reach of the river. Canada acknowledged the importance of this objective, but was explicit with respect to its ability and willingness to provide equivalent storage in an equivalent period of time at a lesser system cost.

Before the matter had progressed very far, however, a latent division of opinion between the provincial and federal authorities in

Canada emerged.[1] At the federal level, there was considerable support for an arrangement which would include Bull River–Dorr in association with assertion of the right to divert the Kootenay into the Columbia. Studies by the technical personnel held out the prospect of a more favorable over-all position for Canada in such a scheme of development if the terms of the Treaty should turn out to be favorable—a matter that could not, of course, be known in advance, particularly in the event that ultimately the division of the gains would not be independent of the choice of treaty projects.

The provincial authorities, however, were troubled by several considerations with respect to the East Kootenay storage. The amount of arable land in British Columbia is not great in spite of the size of the territory, and therefore the wisdom of inundating both the Arrow Lakes and East Kootenay areas was seriously questioned. In the latter case, the provincial authorities also attached considerable importance to the barrier to east-west transportation posed by a Dorr–Bull River or Dorr–Bull River–Luxor complex. Of perhaps equal concern to the provincial authorities was the potential burden of financing all the storages in the upper Columbia simultaneously, lacking sufficient domestic demand for the power they would produce. To support the British Columbia policy position, the technical personnel of the B.C. Water Rights Branch undertook a great deal of analysis comparing the financing of alternative system configurations. The results of the relevant study for this purpose are shown in Tables 16 and 17.[2]

In discussing the implications of their analyses, the technical personnel indicated a distinct preference for the Libby sequence, which substituted for the simultaneous construction of all three Canadian storages accelerated to meet the requirements of U.S. power and flood control objectives. This was asserted to be due mainly "to the development of High Arrow and Duncan as 'first added' followed by a project requiring little capital investment in Canada, that is to say, Libby."[3] The report further concluded that Canada should avoid projects requiring a high rate of investment in the initial stages (i.e., Mica and Dorr–Bull River) and that

---

[1] The province, in Canada, has the determining voice in relation to its own natural resources. National decisions concerning natural resources, therefore, are subject to negotiation between the government of a province and the federal government at Ottawa.

[2] *Supplement to the B.C. Paper entitled, "Economy of Mica or High Arrow Initial Sequence for Columbia River Development,"* March 1960.

[3] *Ibid.*

TABLE 16

Investment, Annual Cost, and Revenue; Sequence H—High Arrow, Dorr–Bull River,
Mica to Fit United States Load Growth

(million dollars)

Year	Projects under construction	Cumulative investment	Annual cost	Annual revenue	Cumulative surplus (+) or deficit (−)
1961	Mica (storage)	33.0	—	—	—
1962	Mica + Arrow + Bull River + Dorr	107.9	—	—	—
1963	Mica + Arrow + Bull River + Dorr	230.5	—	—	—
1964	Mica + Arrow + Bull River + Dorr	376.5	—	—	—
1965	Mica + Bull River + Dorr*	380.4	5.9	0.4	−5.5
1966	Mica + Bull River + Dorr*	413.9	4.3	3.4	−6.4
1967	Mica	440.7	15.1	7.8	−13.7
1968	– – –*	438.5	32.3	11.9	−34.1
1969	– – –	438.5	35.1	16.4	−52.8
1970	Kootenay plants	458.9	35.1	21.9	−66.0
1971	Kootenay plants + Waneta + Seven Mile	506.0	35.1	27.9	−74.0
1972	Waneta + Seven Mile	532.7	38.4	32.6	−79.8
1973	Seven Mile + Mica (power)	621.4	39.4	38.8	−80.4
1974	Mica (power)	699.3	43.9	45.4	−78.9
1975	Mica (power) + Downie	735.0	55.7	51.8	−82.8
1976	Mica (power) + Downie	785.3	56.5	58.8	−80.5
1977	Downie + Revelstoke	829.3	59.1	65.9	−73.7
1978	Downie + Revelstoke	890.1	59.1	73.7	−59.1
1979	Downie + Revelstoke	939.9	67.4	80.7	−45.8
1980	Revelstoke	969.7	69.0	88.5	−26.3
1981		—	77.4	96.9	−6.8

Note: When name of project in Column 2 is italicized, the corresponding date in Column 1 indicates year of completion.
* Flood control benefit payment assumed at this point, causing a reduction in costs.

development of High Arrow–Duncan as initial projects made it possible to achieve low-cost power throughout the full development of the Columbia in Canada. [4]

Near this juncture, the United States representatives, unaware of any difference of opinion within Canada regarding East Kootenay storage and wishing not to eliminate the possibility of including the Libby project in the Treaty system, categorized several possible outcomes: (1) inclusion of Libby following the High Arrow–Duncan complex, (2) pooling of the Mica and Libby projects for purposes of benefit crediting as second-added after High Arrow–Duncan, (3) including Libby third after High Arrow–Duncan and Mica, and (4) excluding Libby. Should all three storages—i.e., High Arrow–Duncan, Mica, and Dorr–Bull River—be provided by Canada, the United States would require an amount of power

[4] Ibid., p. 2.

TABLE 17

Investment, Annual Cost, and Revenue; Sequence D—High Arrow and Duncan
First-added Followed by Libby and Mica

(million dollars)

Year	Projects under construction	Cumulative invest- ment	Annual cost	Annual revenue	Cumulative surplus (+) or deficit (−)
1962	Libby + Arrow	20.0	—	—	—
1963	Libby + Arrow	66.1	—	—	—
1964	Libby + *Arrow*	135.6	—	—	—
1965	Libby + Duncan*	84.5	4.6	0.4	−4.2
1966	Libby + *Duncan* + Mica	158.3	5.9	3.4	−6.7
1967	*Libby* + Mica	211.9	18.5	7.8	−7.4
1968	Mica + Kootenay plants	279.3	11.3	11.9	−6.8
1969	Mica + *Kootenay* + Waneta + Seven Mile	372.5	11.3	16.4	−1.7
1970	Mica + Seven Mile + *Waneta*	447.9	14.6	21.9	+5.6
1971	Mica + *Seven Mile*	552.0	15.9	27.1	+16.8
1972	Mica	636.5	21.1	32.6	+28.3
1973	Mica + Downie	666.0	50.9	38.8	+16.2
1974	*Mica* + Downie	710.0	52.1	45.4	+9.5
1975	Downie	750.2	53.3	51.8	+8.0
1976	Downie + Revelstoke	822.3	53.3	58.8	+13.5
1977	*Downie* + Revelstoke	872.1	63.4	65.9	+16.0
1978	Revelstoke	901.9	65.0	73.7	+24.7
1979	*Revelstoke*	916.9	69.2	80.7	+36.2
1980		916.9	73.4	88.5	+51.3

Notes: When name of project in Column 2 is italicized, the corresponding date in Column 1 indicates year of completion.

For purposes of the above analyses the rate of growth of the British Columbia power load was assumed to be 8 per cent, costs were computed on the basis of interest at 6 per cent and amortization over fifty years, power sold at a rate of 4 mills per kilowatt-hour, and flood control benefits from the lower Columbia capitalized at 4.5 per cent.

* Flood control benefit payment assumed at this point, causing a reduction in costs.

equivalent to that which the United States would otherwise be able to obtain at-site from the construction of Libby (approximately 275 mw). The U.S. position was that it would prefer the first alternative, that the second would be difficult, the third infeasible; the fourth, however, would be entertained.

Following these representations, Canadian technical personnel analyzed the issues along the following lines:

If all three storages were to be provided by Canada with the accelerated construction required to meet U.S. requirements, they would provide downstream benefits the Canadian share of which would be surplus to Canada's needs. Thus, power would have to be sold to the United States to make the development economic. However, such power would be required to meet British Columbia loads prior to the expiration of the twenty-year term of sale which was the minimum required by the United States. Since the sale of power was contrary to existing Canadian energy policy, the policy would have to be changed if accelerated development were to be entertained.

Should an export policy be approved, the analysis continued, a suggested export of 275 mw under long term to the United States would leave Canada with less power, unless the Kootenay were fully diverted, than would result from a Libby development under favorable terms to Canada.[5] If the diversion were not undertaken, the sale price to the United States for the power would have to be at least 6 mills per kilowatt-hour in order to place Canada in as favorable a position as would the Libby plan. If the diversion were effected, the price would probably be reduced to about 4 mills per kilowatt-hour, and Canada would have a substantial block of power remaining (340 mw) in excess of that available from a scheme that included Libby.[6]

The analysis concluded that the Dorr–Bull River–Luxor diversion would mean a heavier financial burden in the initial stages, but would produce greater long-term power benefits at a unit cost competitive with the Libby plan. On the other hand, if the Libby plan were to be adopted, the financial burden on Canada would be reduced. It would also eliminate the need to decide whether or not to export power on a long-term basis.

The results of the technical analysis did not demonstrate a clear-cut superiority of one course of action over another. As it turned out, the provincial and the federal authorities tended to come down on opposite sides of the issue. Federal authorities believed that the option excluding Libby and providing power to the United States would be a profitable one to explore further with the United States. Such a course of action held out the possibility of securing first-added credit for all three Canadian storages, preserving the 50-50 division of downstream benefits, and could mean that, by selling a block of surplus power, substantial assistance could be secured to meet initial expenditures. This course the federal authorities believed to be consistent with the maximum long-term benefit to

[5] For purposes of analysis, it was assumed that Canada would forego claims to downstream benefits in the United States, resulting from stream regulation by means of Libby storage, but would retain the downstream benefits from Libby accruing in Canada, without contributing to the cost of the Libby project.

[6] Given the concessions which were subsequently required of Canada with respect to the terms for Libby, the power rates cited above would have been narrowed to approximately 5 mills without diversion and 3 mills in the event of diversion.

Canada. British Columbia's concern over the inundation of the East Kootenay valley persisted, however, as did its concern over financing the projects favored in the federal position. The division between British Columbia and Ottawa was not early resolved, and so an interim strategy was adopted in which the Canadian negotiators were only to explore implications of the alternative courses of the action with their United States counterparts.

THE CHANGE IN CANADIAN STRATEGY

In subsequent negotiations both the alternatives outlined above were explored with somewhat inconclusive results. The appearance of a stalemate developed concerning the price at which Canada would be willing to supply power and the price the United States would consider acceptable. And, in connection with the Libby alternatives, differences arose over the sequence in which Libby would be evaluated for credit purposes: Would it displace a portion of the supramarginality of the Canadian storages considered as earlier projects in the sequence?

At this juncture Canada appeared to be unprepared to offer three major storages with the export of 275 mw of power. Instead, Canada proposed that it would build High Arrow–Duncan and Mica as first- and second-added. If the United States considered Libby essential, the United States might build the project as third in the sequence on terms outside the IJC principles. In this event, the United States would absorb all the costs of the project and retain all at-site and downstream benefits in the United States resulting from Libby, and Canada would retain all downstream benefits on the lower Kootenay in British Columbia. Canada would expect the United States to absorb the cost of transmitting Canada's share of the downstream benefits to the Canadian border, and the share credited to Canada would not be computed so as to reflect loss of salable secondary energy by the United States, attributable to the improved stream regulation provided by Canadian storages.

The United States, stressing the difficulties of negotiating an agreement which would allow neither the construction of Libby as a feasible undertaking nor the securing of equivalent power from a Canadian alternative, proposed that High Arrow–Duncan and Mica could be added as first and second, and that the United States would take a five-year option to decide whether or not Libby could be built under these circumstances. Should the determination on

Libby prove negative, Canada would be required to build alternative storage in the East Kootenays immediately. Moreover, Canada would relinquish its rights to make a major diversion of the Kootenay into the Columbia. And, should the Dorr–Bull River storages be built, the United States would have no obligation to share downstream benefits at projects on the Kootenay, such as the Kootenai Falls head plant—this in exchange for withdrawing its requirement that power equivalent to the at-site generation of Libby be supplied by Canadian generation. However, the United States, under these circumstances, would require Canada to assume the cost of transmitting to itself its share of the downstream benefits. Moreover, the downstream benefits would be computed to reflect the offset occasioned by the reduction of salable secondary energy in the Columbia system incident on improved streamflows provided by Canadian storage.

The unresolved issue for policy consideration in Canada remained whether to adhere to its strict interpretation of General Principle No. 1, thereby increasing the amount of inundation in British Columbia and also the level of financial obligation (though the latter might be partially offset by sale of power to the United States), or whether to reverse its original position, in view of the prospect for a more favorable short-term outcome, given the restrictions on export of energy and receipt of financial aid from the United States.

In spite of the opposition of British Columbia to the inundation of the East Kootenay valley, federal authorities[7] continued to press the case for the desirability of retaining the right to a major diversion of the Kootenay River. It was argued that it would be necessary to develop storages in the East Kootenay compatible with such an ultimate diversion in order to maintain credibility for the Canadian claim. British Columbia, however, remained adamant. In this respect, the province may have obtained support from recommendations and conclusions drawn by the technical personnel of its Water Rights Branch based on their analyses of the sequence and timing of projects involving seven different possible contingencies.[8] A summary tabulation of the results of these analyses is given in Table 18.

[7] It is necessary here to distinguish between the federal authorities (policy level) and federal technical personnel whose analyses did not differ in substance from their British Columbia counterparts.

[8] Untitled British Columbia Water Rights Branch report, Victoria, May 1960. For purpose of analysis the power was assumed to be sold in Canada at 4 mills/

TABLE 18

Comparative Surplus or Deficits of Seven Alternative Sequences of
Upper Columbia–Kootenay Storage Development[1]

(million dollars)

Sequence	Cumulative investment by completion (1980)	Annual revenue on completion (1980)	Annual cost on completion (1980)	Surplus (+) or Deficit (−)	
				Equal annual increments (1980–2010)	Cumulative to date of completion (1980)
1) K-2	1,315.5	115.9	100.1	+15.8	+13.6
2) L-1	1,201.1	109.7	91.5	+18.2	+59.7
3) M-1	1,189.2	109.7	91.0	+18.7	+22.4
4) N-1	1,262.4	109.7	96.0	+13.7	− 1.0
5) N-2	1,262.4	115.9	96.0	+19.9	+63.1
6) P-3	1,111.4	106.7	85.2	+21.5	−41.0
7) Q-2	1,262.4	115.9	96.0	+19.9	− 2.5

1) Arrow, Dorr–Bull River, Duncan, and Mica with 275 mw export and accelerated to meet U.S. load growth.
2) Arrow and Duncan, followed by Libby and Mica pooled: to fit Canadian load growth.
3) Arrow, Duncan, Mica, and Libby, with Mica storage in two stages to precede Libby.
4) Duncan, Dorr–Bull River, and Arrow: to meet Canadian load growth.
5) Duncan, Dorr–Bull River and Arrow: with 275 mw export, accelerated to meet U.S. load.
6) Duncan, Dorr–Bull River, and Mica: accelerated to meet U.S. load growth.
7) Duncan, Dorr–Bull River, Arrow, and Mica: accelerated to meet U.S. load with 275 mw export.

[1] Untitled British Columbia Water Rights Branch report, Victoria, May 1960.

Inspection of the analyses shows only two of the possibilities (L-1 and N-2) to be of potential interest to British Columbia. The report discusses each of the seven contingencies, with the exception of N-2, observing for policy consideration that L-1 with High Arrow first-added, followed by Mica and Libby pooled, gave British Columbia the most satisfactory development from a financial point of view. When the details of the analyses are examined, however, it is possible to conclude that N-2 was at least as desirable and possibly slightly preferable, from both a financial and longer-run economic viewpoint. [9] An observation in the text

kwh. Power exported to the United States was assumed salable at 3.5 mills/kwh. The interest rate was assumed to be 5.5 per cent in Canada, and flood control benefits were assumed payable on storage up to 7.5 million acre-feet contributing to the primary flood control objective, and, thereafter contributing only to the augmented plan, capitalized at 5 per cent. Implicitly also the study assumed that the United States would bear the cost of transmitting the Canadian share of the downstream benefits to the border, as no cost entry was recorded in this particular.

[9] The present value of the difference in time streams between the L-1 and the N-2 sequences and project complexes is $23 million when capitalized at 5.5 per cent.

of the discussion alludes to the unlikelihood of being able "to afford to flood both the Arrow Lakes and East Kootenay valleys,"[10] and may account for the failure to consider the sequence. At any rate, British Columbia did not feel that proceeding with development of the East Kootenay storage reflected sufficient net advantage to the province to warrant this course of action.

The divergent positions resulted in Canada rejecting that feature of the U.S. proposal which would permit the United States an option to build Libby but would *require Canada to build the East Kootenay storages* should the United States decide not to take up its option. Concomitantly, Canada reverted to its previous position, namely, that High Arrow–Duncan be included with first-added benefits, and Mica second with a corresponding credit position, and that if Libby were an essential to the agreement, it could be added at U.S. expense third, with a credit position corresponding to its position in the sequence. Canada, however, was now prepared to make concessions with respect to assuming an obligation for the flowage costs of Libby in Canada; also to modify its previous requirements that the United States should pay the cost of transmitting Canada's share of the downstream power to the border and that energy releases from Canadian storages should be combined with salable secondary energy from existing U.S. system facilities in determining the power benefits that were to be shared equally.

The position finally adopted with respect to East Kootenay storage, accordingly, reflected the British Columbia viewpoint; and the original strategy of the Canadian delegation, based on an insistence that the Treaty projects be selected in a manner to maximize the benefit for mutual sharing consistent with General Principle No. 1, was abandoned. In its stead was substituted a narrower interpretation, namely, that the decision should be based on the maximum economic advantage to the Canadian system rather than to the Columbia as a whole.[11]

[10] Untitled British Columbia Water Rights Branch report, Victoria, May 1960.

[11] That such a position could be advanced is a result of the absence of rigor in the formulation of the IJC principles themselves. On the one hand, the principles called for the most economic projects, i.e., those which were consistent with maximizing the joint gains to the two countries combined. On the other hand, the benefit division involved the division of the gross gain of the projects, evaluated in terms of their place in the sequence of project construction. Since the most economic storage projects were Canadian and thus qualified for first-added credit, the gross gain reflected in part the displacement values of the supramarginal United States projects subsequently added. Accordingly, for the protec-

Canada, subsequently, sought to obtain High Arrow–Duncan and Mica first-added, with Libby last-added on terms favorable to Canada. Ensuing discussion had provided for several contingencies which now were relevant for Canadian consideration.

First, Canada now concentrated its attention on a quantum of storage rather than on specific projects, diverting the discussion of storage from projects totaling 15.5 million acre-feet to a quantity of storage of 15.5 million acre-feet, and thus leaving to Canada the latitude to make up such storage with whatever projects it sought, regardless of the projects hitherto discussed. This focus, coupled with a reluctance to build the Mica project for storage without machining it to meet British Columbia loads, suggested the possibility of building a smaller Mica reservoir which might be used initially to regulate only flows for U.S. requirements. This in part would postpone Canadian expenditures; subsequently, construction of storage facilities at Surprise Rapids or Kinbasket, upstream, could be undertaken to meet Canadian stream regulation commitments to the United States. Mica could thus be machined and operated to fit the British Columbia loads as they developed. Some financial relief would be obtained since the capital outlays could be staged to be more consistent with domestic power requirements.

Second, a prospect for delaying Mica construction until it could be scheduled conveniently for British Columbia domestic requirements appeared to be provided. [12]

---

tion of the United States, a provision was made to the effect that the arrangements would have to result in a net advantage to each country.

The concept of "maximum economic advantage to each country" is a logical impossibility. It could not be invoked for each project in the arrangement without bringing about inconsistent consequences. For example, Libby might represent a net advantage to British Columbia over its domestic alternatives, whereas the Dorr–Bull River alternative would represent a net advantage to the United States over its domestic alternative (Libby). This results from the failure to make the IJC principles explicit with respect to separation of the efficiency aspects (criteria governing the most economic set of projects) from the equity aspects—i.e. (a) division of the gains initially to ensure to each country a position about which it would be indifferent as between the co-operative and the domestic alternatives, and (b) a further division of the residual or net gains from co-operation in such ways as to advance each country to a position superior to that which it would have achieved by independent action relying exclusively upon its domestic resources.

[12] The United States at this juncture was interpreted as being willing to permit scheduling of Canadian projects to mutual advantage, but actually such a proffer was implicitly contingent upon a credit for Libby storage as added second in the sequence in lieu of Mica.

Third, Canada could consider either proceeding immediately with the installation of turbines and generators at Mica, substituting this source of power for smaller and more conveniently scheduled increments, or plan to build only the storage facilities and delay machining the project until its generation was required in the British Columbia load.

The financial implications of each of the possible options were analyzed. First, six sequences were studied to evaluate the major issues. A condensed summary of the studies is shown in Table 19. [13]

The first four sequences all involve High Arrow–Duncan and High Mica, [14] which jointly provide 15 million acre-feet of storage in next-added sequence, with Libby last-added. They differ only in that facilities for at-site power production at Mica are installed

TABLE 19

Comparative Surplus or Deficits of Six Alternative Sequences of
Upper Columbia–Kootenay Storage Development

(million dollars)

| | | | | | Net Surplus (+) or Deficit (−) | |
| | Cumulative investment by completion (1980) | Annual cost on completion (1980) | Annual revenue on completion (1980) | Refinanc-ing costs by completion (1980) | Equal annual increments commencing (1981) | Cumulative to year after completion (1981) |
Sequence						
1) MA-5	1,234.0	93.2	113.3	40.9	+17.9	−19.4
2) MC-5	1,234.0	93.2	113.3	38.4	+17.6	−25.3
3) MB-5	1,234.0	93.2	113.3	48.0	+16.1	−52.2
4) DC-5	1,234.0	93.2	113.3	2.0	+22.3	+59.6
5) VB-5	1,284.0	96.9	119.1	17.4	+22.4	+25.3
6) MC-6	1,207.8	92.9	113.9	21.4	+20.6	+14.2

Source: Financial and Economic Aspects of the Present Position in the International Negotiations, B.C. Water Rights Branch, Victoria, August 1960.

[13] The assumptions underlying the analyses are as follows: All power generated at Canadian plants to be sold at 4 mills/kwh in British Columbia. Interest rates for projects and refinancing taken at 5.5 per cent, amortization over fifty years. Flood control benefits assumed to be transferred from Duncan Lake project to Libby account, others to be capitalized at 5 per cent. Flowage costs of Libby initially assumed to be borne by Canada, and transmission cost of repatriating Canada's share of benefits to the boundary by the United States, with Canada bearing cost of east-west transmission standby from the Columbia Basin in British Columbia to the lower mainland. Some of the foregoing assumptions were later modified in side calculations and will be noted in the text below.

[14] High Mica, with about 11.7 million acre-feet of storage capacity, would be operated with only 7.1 million acre-feet for seasonal storage purposes only in response to power objectives on the United States reaches of the system.

with different time lags. The sequence designated as MA-5 has Mica machined at the time of completion of the Mica storage facility in 1970; MC-5 delays the installation until 1972; and MB-5 calls for generators in Mica not before 1976. In all cases but one construction on the Mica storage facilities is begun early, with only the machining lagged in successive sequences. In the sequence designated as DC-5 the entire Mica project is delayed for four years (completion in 1974) contingent upon the United States accommodating this schedule without adverse consequences for Mica's credit position. In the sequence designated as VB-5, on the other hand, it is assumed that the U.S. negotiators would not be prepared to reserve Mica's credit position if the project were not built promptly; it therefore entails building a medium-sized Mica project, with sufficient storage to provide 7 million acre-feet when not used for power production, and, later, a supplementary project upstream to meet Canada's storage commitment when Mica would be converted from a storage to a power-producing function.

It can be clearly seen that Sequence DC-5 would have been most advantageous to British Columbia. But because the United States was not willing to schedule for mutual advantage in this case,[15] alternatives calling for construction of storage at the Mica site immediately, with various time lags for generator installation (MA-5, MC-5, and MB-5), were considered. The studies showed that the longer the lapse of time between Mica reservoir completion and generator installation, the larger would be the accumulated deficits in the early period of operation. This eliminated the possibility of delaying Mica generation to schedule more conveniently scaled plants on the lower Kootenay and Pend d'Oreille. As a consequence, the two-stage (VB-5) alternative was recommended for serious consideration, although attention was drawn to the sacrifice it would entail of the potentials for cyclical storage otherwise available in Mica.

Finally, a sequence designated MC-6 was analyzed. This was comparable in all respects to MC-5 except that it added a half-million acre-feet of storage credit at Mica (15.5 million acre-feet in total) consistent with the final Treaty provisions, and called for an annual standby transmission service charge in lieu of Canadian construction of standby facilities from the Columbia Basin to the lower British Columbia mainland. The study showed that the reduction in transmission costs in Canada more than offset the U.S.

[15] See footnote 12.

service charges, with the result that the cumulative deficit of $25 million in Sequence MC-5 would be converted to a surplus of $14 million in Sequence MC-6. Approximately the same ($39 million gain) would attend this substitution in all of the sequences previously discussed.[16]

If Canada decided in favor of MC-6, it could consider two supplementary options dealing with the means by which credit would be transferred to Libby. One proposal involved the assumption of Libby flowage costs by the United States. In return, the Duncan flood control benefits would be assigned to Libby, but the United States seemed to be prepared to increase Canada's share of High Arrow's flood control benefits from 50 to 65 per cent. Alternatively, Canada could assume cost of flowage for Libby and retain Duncan flood control benefits. The B.C. staff analysis is shown below:[17]

(a) Canada pays for Libby flowage in Canada and retains Duncan flood control benefits:

Annual cost to Canada of flowage................	$700,000
Annual value of Duncan flood control to Canada...	490,000
Annual net loss to Canada....................	$210,000

(b) United States pays for Libby flowage in Canada and Duncan flood control benefits are allocated to Libby; as an additional offset, the United States would pay Canada 65% rather than 50% of the flood damage prevented by High Arrow:

Annual value to Canada of 15% [sic] increase in High Arrow flood control.........................	$690,000
Annual value lost to Canada by allocation of Duncan flood control to Libby.......................	490,000
Annual net gain to Canada....................	$200,000

Net annual advantage of option (b) over (a)..........	$410,000

With this option a possibility, the report noted the merit of considering omitting Duncan entirely and allocating Duncan storage credit for power to storage-head possibilities such as Trout Lake, Kootenay Lake and/or Mica. The report continues:

From a rough analysis of the sequences included in this report wherein Duncan storage credit for downstream power benefits is allocated to

[16] *Financial and Economic Aspects of the Present Position in the International Negotiations* (Victoria: British Columbia Water Rights Branch, August 1960), p. 5.
[17] *Ibid.*, p. 4.

the Mica project, it is found that in each case, the deficit or surplus position of the sequence in 1981 was improved by about $13 million.[18]

In subsequent negotiations, the option given Canada was clarified and modified somewhat. It appears that no additional credit was to be allotted High Arrow storage for flood protection, and the offer to assume flowage costs was limited to about two-thirds of the total. On the other hand, flood control credit for Duncan was re-established, but on the basis of a quarter, rather than a half. The comparative economics from Canada's point of view would then appear as follows:

(a) Canada retains half share Duncan flood control credit, but assumes Libby flowage cost in Canada:
Flowage cost in Canada annually................ $700,000
Annual value of 50% Duncan benefits........... 490,000
Net annual cost to Canada of option (a)......... $210,000

(b) Canada retains quarter share of Duncan flood control credit and assumes one-third of Libby flowage costs:
Flowage costs in Canada annually............... $233,000
Annual value of 25% Duncan benefits........... 245,000
Net annual gain to Canada of option (b)......... $ 12,000

Net annual advantage of option (b) over (a)........... $222,000

Although the attractiveness of option (b) was reduced by almost one-half, it did represent a gain over option (a) which, capitalized at 5.5 per cent for the period of the Treaty, would amount to approximately $3.75 million. In addition, transfer of power storage credit to Mica and elimination of the cost of Duncan would have improved the Canadian position for all of the sequences studied.

Ultimately, British Columbia elected to decline the option. One proviso of the option as modified was to extend the grace period for the United States decision on Libby from five to ten years, and this was not favored by Canada. A second objection held that the assumption of costs by the United States for Libby flowage in Canada would have violated one of the major IJC principles calling for costs in each country to be borne by the country in question. At this stage in the negotiations, however, enough violence had been done to the IJC principles that it is unlikely this consideration could have influenced the outcome. Doubtless carrying more weight was the possible requirement by the United States to audit costs incurred for Libby flowage in Canada.

[18] *Loc. cit.*

CRITICAL APPRAISAL OF BRITISH COLUMBIA'S COSTS AND GAINS

From a review of British Columbia's staff studies, it appears that at each juncture where it was afforded an option, the province elected a course of action based on technical analysis and a careful weighing of the costs and gains, sociopolitical as well as economic. An overwhelming economic advantage would have been required to override the strong objection to flooding inhabited British Columbia territory. The potential difficulties of financing large-scale projects, given the magnitude of the power increments in relation to the size of the British Columbia market, and given the existence of an export ban on power, further created obstacles to a selection based on mutual economic advantage. In this instance, however, an inconsistency appears, connected with the option of avoiding the investment in Duncan ($25 million) and the flowage cost of Libby in Canada ($12 million) [19] in exchange for sacrificing only the flood control storage benefits of Duncan ($11 million). It is evident that in the staff study the computation indicating the loss to Canada under option (b) took explicit account of only the benefit reduction, overlooking the cost reduction associated with eliminating the Duncan project. From this one might infer a certain amount of slippage in the bargaining process which, in addition to policy considerations, may have helped to account for ultimate inclusion of the Duncan project in the Treaty system. In short, given the storage on the upper Kootenay sanctioned by the Treaty, there is scant justification for including Duncan in the system. And given the option afforded British Columbia, the project seems no more justified from the province's point of view.

While each decision grew out of an analysis of the implications of each alternative, this process itself had to be based on imponderables. For example, British Columbia's early decision to opt for Libby in Montana rather than provide storage within its own borders on Dorr–Bull River sites was based on the assumption that Libby could be made available "on conditions favorable to Canada." On the other hand, when it became evident to the United

---

[19] The $12 million flowage cost of Libby in Canada is roughly equivalent also to the modified proposal, namely, assumption by the United States of up to $8 million flowage cost of Libby in Canada, but with flood control storage benefits of only one quarter ($5.5 million) credited to Duncan in lieu of one half ($11 million) of the total estimated damage prevention. In this respect, we can consider the two proposals as equivalent.

States that British Columbia would not provide storage in the East Kootenay valley, the U.S. negotiators demanded substantial concessions in favor of Libby before presenting the Treaty to Congress. It may not be possible to identify precisely the monetary difference between the original expectations of returns based on building Libby "on conditions favorable to Canada," and those applying under the conditions in which Libby finally came into the Treaty system. Some indication can be obtained, however, from a comparison of the sequences which included Libby both before and after the British Columbia decision to withhold commitment of East Kootenay storage.

Sequence L-1 vs. Sequence MC-6. For this purpose, the Sequence L-1 of the May 1960 studies, which laid the foundation for the British Columbia position on the East Kootenay storage problem, can be compared with Sequence MC-6 of the August studies, which represents the projects, credit position, and scheduling associated with the actual Treaty terms. Both sets of studies are comparable in their assumptions governing the rate of interest and the rate at which the power would be marketed in British Columbia. But in other aspects several adjustments must be made. First, a close inspection of the work sheets suggests that in the early study a miscalculation occurred concerning the amount of flood control credit due to the Canadian storages; hence, an overestimate with a present value of between $47 million and $49 million must be deducted from the present value of the net income stream of L-1 before the results of the two studies are directly comparable. Second, refinancing costs were excluded from the May studies but included in the August studies, requiring an appropriate adjustment to obtain comparability. Finally, the May studies do not reflect the gain to Canada from the substitution of standby transmission charges in lieu of domestic construction of parallel facilities. With all the adjustments reflected, the results are presented in Table 20.

From this table it can be seen that a Libby compromise under conditions favorable to Canada (Sequence L-1) would have been more favorable for British Columbia than Sequence MC-6 which reflected the final Treaty terms, whether the standpoint is one of short-run financial considerations or one of long-run economic values.

Sequence MC-6 vs. Sequence N-2. It is instructive, also, to compare the actual results (MC-6) with a sequence that does not involve the

TABLE 20

Comparison of Anticipated with Realized Results of British Columbia's East Kootenay Storage Decision

(million dollars)

Year	(L-1) Revenue minus costs[1]	(L-1) Interest on cumulative difference at 5.5%	(L-1) Net surplus (+) or deficit (−)	(L-1) Cumulative surplus (+) or deficit (−)	(MC-6) Revenue minus costs	(MC-6) Interest on cumulative difference at 5.5%	(MC-6) Net surplus (+) or deficit (−)	(MC-6) Cumulative surplus (+) or deficit (−)
1965	+0.8	—	+0.8	+0.8	−6.2	—	−6.2	−6.2
1966	−5.0	−0.0	−5.0	−4.2	−5.8	−0.4	−6.2	−12.4
1967	−2.1	−0.2	−2.3	−6.5	−2.0	−0.7	−2.7	−15.1
1968	+0.7	−0.4	+0.3	−6.2	+0.6	−0.9	−0.3	−15.4
1969	+3.9	−0.4	+3.6	−2.6	+5.9	−0.9	+5.0	−10.4
1970	+2.8	−0.1	+2.7	+0.1	−9.3	−0.6	−9.9	−20.3
1971	+6.2	0.0	+6.2	+6.3	−4.4	−1.2	−5.6	−25.9
1972	−2.7	+0.3	−2.4	+3.9	+3.3	−1.5	+1.8	−24.1
1973	+0.3	+0.2	+0.5	+4.4	−3.0	−1.4	−4.4	−28.5
1974	−1.1	+0.2	−0.9	+3.5	−2.8	−1.7	−4.5	−33.0
1975	+3.7	+0.2	+3.9	+7.4	−4.8	−1.9	−6.7	−39.7
1976	+11.8	+0.4	+12.2	+19.6	+0.8	−2.3	−1.5	−41.2
1977	+10.0	+1.1	+11.1	+30.7	+8.7	−2.4	+6.3	−39.4
1978	+10.1	+1.7	+11.8	+42.5	+9.0	−2.1	+6.9	−34.9
1979	+17.6	+2.3	+19.3	+61.8	+7.8	−1.8	+6.0	−28.0
1980	+18.5	+3.4	+21.9	+83.7	+16.8	−1.3	+15.5	−6.4
1981	+18.5	+4.6	+23.1	+106.8	+21.0	−0.4	+20.6	+14.2
1982	+18.5	+5.8	+24.3	+131.1	+21.0	+0.8	+21.8	+36.0

Present value of 50-year stream of
net surplus or deficit.............$346.0
Less overestimate of flood control benefits......−49
Net difference in present worth of L-1 over MC-6.$ 28.9

Present value of 50-year stream of
net surplus or deficit.............$268.1

[1] L-1 sequence annual costs were systematically reduced by an amount equivalent to the difference between annual cost of MC-5 and MC-6, reflecting the savings from substitution of annual service charge in lieu of Canadian construction of east-west standby transmission facilities.

Libby compromise. This is shown in Table 21. Here, it is evident that a storage complex involving Dorr–Bull River is considerably more favorable to British Columbia in terms of both short-run financial and long-run economic considerations.

Sequence L-1 vs. Sequence N-2. Comparing the results of the studies available at the time of the decision to withhold upper Kootenay storage, there seems to be little to choose between the L-1 and N-2 sequences from a short-term financial standpoint, although the latter did and the former did not inundate a substantial portion of the East Kootenay valley. And from the longer-run standpoint, the N-2 sequence showed to an advantage of only $23 million based on the present worth of the fifty-year income stream. It is clear that British Columbia did not consider the difference sufficiently attractive to warrant flooding the East Kootenay valley.

TABLE 21

Comparison of Realizable Results of British Columbia's East Kootenay Storage Option

(million dollars)

	(N-2)				(MC-6)
Year	Revenue minus costs[1]	Interest on cumulative difference at 5.5%	Net surplus (+) or deficit (−)	Cumulative surplus (+) or deficit (−)	Cumulative surplus (+) or deficit (−)
1965	−5.5	—	−5.5	−5.5	−6.2
1966	−10.0	−0.3	−10.3	−15.8	−12.2
1967	−1.7	−0.9	−2.0	−17.8	−15.1
1968	+2.0	−1.0	+1.0	−16.8	−15.4
1969	+7.7	−0.9	+6.8	−10.0	−10.4
1970	+5.1	−0.6	+4.5	−5.5	−20.3
1971	+7.1	−0.3	+6.8	+1.3	−25.9
1972	+11.7	+0.1	+11.8	+12.1	−24.1
1973	−1.4	+0.7	−0.7	+11.4	−28.5
1974	−1.2	+0.6	−0.6	+10.8	−33.0
1975	+2.3	+0.6	+2.9	+13.7	−39.7
1976	+6.7	+0.8	+7.5	+21.2	−41.2
1977	+10.3	+1.2	+11.5	+32.7	−39.4
1978	+9.6	+1.8	+11.4	+44.1	−34.9
1979	+15.6	+2.4	+18.0	+62.1	−28.0
1980	+20.2	+3.4	+23.6	+85.7	−6.4
1981	+20.2	+4.7	+24.9	+110.6	+14.2
1982	+20.2	+6.1	+26.3	+136.9	+36.0

Present value of 50-year stream of net surplus or deficit......................$369.4 $268.1

Less overestimate of flood control benefits ..−49

Net advantage of N-2 over MC-6..............$ 52.3

[1] N-2 sequence annual costs were systematically reduced by an amount equivalent to the difference between annual costs of MC-5 and MC-6, reflecting the savings from substitution of annual service charges for standby in lieu of Canadian construction of the east-west standby transmission facilities.

Sequence MC-6 vs. Sequence N-2. On the other hand, the decision to withhold sanction for the Dorr–Bull River storages was to have consequences that could not have been fully anticipated. When the results of the actual terms on which Libby came to be included (MC-6) are evaluated on a comparable basis with the Dorr–Bull River alternative (N-2) the latter is favored by an appreciable margin so far as the financial position of British Columbia is concerned, and in terms of long-run economic values it would represent for British Columbia a gain in present values some $52 million greater than that obtained from inclusion of Libby in the international system.

To what extent these consequences had been anticipated during negotiations is not clear. The record gives no indication of the threshold values British Columbia may have reserved as sufficient to override its objections to flooding the East Kootenay valley. Thus, one can only speculate that the outcome might have been different if British Columbia could have made its decision with the benefit of hindsight.

Chapter 7

Problems in the Equitable Division of Co-operatively Achieved Gains

~~~~~~~~~~~~~~~~~~~~~~~~~~~~~~~~

The IJC General Principles reflect two elements critical in determining the benefits and defining the equitable division of gains in the international development of a river basin system. The first, embodied in General Principle No. 1, concerns the economic or efficiency aspect of a river basin design and/or development in which both parties have an interest provided that the resulting division of the gains is to be equitable. In this regard, the International Joint Commission recognized that the value of co-operative gains is dependent on (a) restricting mutually exclusive elements in the system to those that are most economical, and (b) constructing these in a sequence that permits the more economical projects to be built before the less economic (but still economically feasible) projects are added. Need for exclusion of uneconomic projects is self-evident. Attention to the order of construction is also a readily perceived requirement, since if the increased cost of the less economic projects can be delayed, the present worth of the total contribution will be larger than if the order were reversed.

The second element of the IJC General Principles relates to the matter of assurance that neither party to the co-operative venture will be penalized by pursuing a course of action that maximizes the net gain of the parties combined. In this respect General Principle No. 2 made provision for each party to retire from the venture with assurance that a net benefit accrued to him, as measured by the savings in cost compared with the cost of providing equivalent services by the most economical domestic means. It was not explicit, however, concerning the way in which the net gain should be shared. Rather, it sought to obtain a division of the gross benefits

119

so as to provide equal amounts of power and flood control benefits, subject only to the restriction that there would be a net advantage to each of the participants. In short, implicit in the benefit-division rule is the possibility that one party may be permitted to appropriate the preponderance of the *net* gain, provided only that there is some residual advantage accruing to the second party.

What do the Treaty terms provide for in this regard?

TREATY PROVISIONS FOR SHARING BENEFITS

The Treaty provisions are directed toward an equal division of the *gross* benefit, but on closer inspection it may be seen that they permit considerable latitude. In the case of flood damage reduction benefits, the Treaty provides that these will be divided equally, but since Canada cannot share physically in the benefit from flood management operations in the lower Columbia, the value of the mathematical expectation of flood damage prevention is to be shared. The procedure in computing this share is itself interesting, since in large part it abstracts from the sequence of project addition, which is the basis for division of the power gains. This is an outcome of the method used by the Corps of Engineers in calculating the benefit for flood protection works on the Columbia. Given the existence of a levee system capable of containing flows up to 800,000 cfs, the Corps of Engineers selected as a primary flood control objective storage in the system sufficient to reduce the peak discharge of the flood of record (1,240,000 cfs) to 800,000 cfs at The Dalles, the focal point for flood management operations. This objective requires a total of about 17 million acre-feet of effective flood control storage. In evaluating the benefits of any flood control storage up to 17 million acre-feet, the Corps attributes a constant value per acre-foot (i.e. $1.34) irrespective of the sequence in which it is built. Storage in excess of the primary objective requirements is credited with a constant value of $0.11 per acre-foot, reflecting the grossly diminished return to flood control storage between the two blocks.

It will be recalled from the discussion in Chapter 3 that the storage-benefit relation is actually a continuous function of storage such that incremental additions of storage in a sequence are attended by diminished incremental flood damage reduction. (See Figures 8–11.) Accordingly, the block of Canadian storage coming at the tail-end of the primary flood control objective requirements would have an average incremental benefit per acre-foot of only approximately half the benefit that was computed for purposes of benefit division. The Treaty terms in this connection permit the Canadian storage, last-added, to be computed proportionately with the existing United States flood control storage which preceded it, and require payment to Canada totaling $64.4 million ($U.S.) upon commencement of operations of the storage projects. This sum represents one-half the value of the ostensible average annual flood damage reduction, discounted at 3.87 per cent. [1]

Provisions with respect to power are different on several counts. Canadian national policy at the time prohibited the export of power; this was construed as requiring transmission back to Canada of the share of the incremental gain in U.S. power production resulting from Canadian storage operations. Under terms of the Treaty, Canada was obliged to pay a service charge of $1.50 per kilowatt annually for standby transmission capacity maintained by the United States.

To measure the increased power resulting from Canadian storage is complex and requires some explanation. The amount to be considered as resulting from Canadian storage releases is the difference between the power output from the U.S. plants then existing or under construction in the so-called U.S. base system, [2] and the output from that system when 15.5 million acre-feet of Canadian storage is evaluated as next-added to it. [3] Each country was to share equally in the increment in dependable capacity and average annual energy. "Dependable capacity," for this purpose, was defined as the difference in the amount of continuous energy available from the system with and without Canadian storage added to the base system, divided by the average critical-period load factor. [4] Now, the critical-period releases from storage, when supplementing interruptible energy available from the U.S. base system, in any event (except during the critical period) will produce a greater

---

[1] *Treaty Between Canada and the United States of America Relating to Cooperative Development of the Water Resources of the Columbia River Basin*, signed at Washington, D.C., January 17, 1961, Article VI. (Hereafter cited as *Treaty*.) And *Columbia River Treaty*, Hearings before the Committee on Foreign Relations, United States Senate, 87th Cong., 1st Sess., March 8, 1961, p. 43. The discount rate was based, not entirely logically, on the average *coupon* rate of long-term U.S. government bonds as of December 1961.

[2] *Treaty, op. cit.*, Annex B.

[3] *Treaty, op. cit.*, Article VII.

[4] Average critical-period load factor is defined as the average of the monthly load factors during the critical streamflow period. *Treaty, op. cit.*, Article I.

prime power gain than would the equivalent amount of energy released from Canadian storage at a uniform rate. (See Figure 13.) The increment of prime power is in part a blend of (a) otherwise salable secondary energy produced by the U.S. base system plants without additional storage, and (b) the releases from Canadian storage on a schedule calculated to firm up the U.S. secondary energy. Consequently, Canada is credited only with the amount of increased usable energy that it provides from storage, rather than with a share also of the pre-existing high-grade secondary energy from the U.S. base system plants with which it is blended. Nevertheless, the total gain in prime power attributed to the Canadian storage is used as the basis for determining Canada's dependable capacity benefits. As a result, while the dependable capacity based on prime power gain to the system is divided equally (1,331 mw under initial conditions), the prime power is shared approximately 1,142 mw for the United States and 763 mw for Canada. The Canadian prime power gain from the Treaty, however, is increased to 973 mw, the difference being provided through stream regulation over run-of-the-river plants on the lower Kootenay in British Columbia, resulting from Libby storage operations. The actual gain in energy, on the other hand, is shared equally.

The overriding question, then, is whether or not the division of the benefits in the above fashion is consistent with General Principle No. 2—that is, whether it represents a division by which both parties to the venture will advance to a position superior to that which each could have achieved through an independent course of action.

To answer this question, each country's independent alternatives to the Treaty system must be evaluated and compared. Here, as in Chapter 5, the analysis will be restricted to the alternatives over which the responsible parties had jurisdiction and on which they had information in 1960. This rules out for consideration, at this point in the study, alternatives such as the Peace River possibility, the Hat Creek thermal operation, and the Pacific Northwest and California and Southwest intertie, all of which emerged as relevant alternatives in succeeding years prior to ratification of the Treaty in 1964. These will be dealt with in Chapters 8 and 9. To a very large extent, therefore, the alternatives to a co-operative venture of the Columbia in 1960 were restricted to independent development of the Columbia by the United States and, similarly, independent development of the Columbia, in association with complementary developments on the Fraser, by British Columbia.

CANADIAN ALTERNATIVES TO THE COLUMBIA
TREATY SYSTEM PROJECTS

In order to establish a reserve position in negotiations concerned with the benefit division issue, both the Province of British Columbia and the federal Department of Northern Affairs and National Resources undertook analyses of Columbia River development in Canada, approached as an independent Canadian undertaking. The Province of British Columbia retained Crippen Wright Engineering Ltd. to undertake engineering investigations; Northern Affairs was assisted by the Montreal Engineering Company, Ltd., in developing a federal perspective on the questions at issue. Let us briefly examine the resulting reports.

Ideally, in order to determine the most economical independent alternative to the Columbia Treaty system for British Columbia, one would wish first to make as accurate a long-range forecast of provincial power needs as practicable, and then attempt to fit the energy resources to the projected load in a way calculated to result in the lowest long-run cost. However, while forecasts were made of the provincial load development, [5] these appear to have served more as general background data than as the means for making systematic load-resource studies that would compare independent and co-operative schemes of development. [6] The Crippen Wright study was comprehensive in terms of investigating alternative sites, scales of development at each site, combination of alternative sites and scales, and different permutations of development in order to identify an optimal staging strategy; nevertheless it was rather "broad brush" in approach. Consequently, it is not possible to use the Crippen Wright study data in combination with other sources of technical information to carry out a systematic load-resource study. With regard to the relevant data provided by the federal Department of Northern Affairs and National Resources,

[5] In connection with the *Documentary Submission* to the Royal Commission on Canada's Economic Prospects by the Government of the Province of British Columbia, August 1956; Crippen Wright Engineering Ltd., *Report on Electric Power Requirements in the Province of British Columbia*, April 1958; and Chantrill and Stevens, *Power Capabilities and Operating Aspects of a British Columbia Power Pool*, May 1961.

[6] The Chantrill-Stevens reports, done on behalf of the Peace River Development Company, Ltd., and the British Columbia Water Rights Branch and federal Water Resources Branch studies, in connection with analysis of negotiation issues, did develop load-resource studies. However, they were not addressed to the evaluation of British Columbia's independent alternatives to co-operative development of the Columbia.

they reflect the practice established in the ICREB report[7] and the studies of the U.S. Army Corps of Engineers, of selecting the year 1985 as "representative" of conditions spanning the time period over which benefits and costs are to be compared.[8]

Given the data available as of 1960, therefore, it is beyond the capability of this study to determine year by year the differences in costs associated with an independent as compared with a co-operative undertaking. The most that can be done is to compare the data on the alternatives presented by each source independently. Because the magnitude of the difference, or savings in cost of the Treaty system over the available alternatives on the Columbia, will not be the same using the two sources, one can establish only a range within which the net gains to Canada are likely to fall.

CRIPPEN WRIGHT ENGINEERING STUDIES

The investigations done on behalf of British Columbia, having in mind provincial power projects scaled appropriately to the size of the system and load requirements, contemplated bringing in comparatively small additions to capacity until, with the lapse of time and growth in load, larger blocks of capacity could be more conveniently accommodated. In this respect the Crippen Wright studies were unique at that time among engineering studies on the Columbia, being sensitive to the problem of scale, sequence, and timing of individual components of the development.

In order to scale the initial development efficiently in relation to the size of the projected load, the studies pointed toward the Clearwater tributary of the Fraser along with the Duncan Lake project (see Figure 22). A first stage would involve the construction of the Hobson and Azure projects on the Clearwater to meet load requirements in the Kamloops and possibly the Okanagan valley in the interior; and the Duncan project, along with additions of a unit each in the lower Bonnington and Brilliant plants on the lower Kootenay, to assist meeting the expanding demand in the Trail area serviced by the West Kootenay Power and Light Com-

[7] International Columbia River Engineering Board, *Water Resources of the Columbia River Basin*, report to the International Joint Commission, 1959.

[8] See the discussion of this procedure, p. 75, fn. 8. There is evidence of substantial study involving projected yearly loads and hydro resource scheduling to meet such loads in connection with the co-operative system, but I have been unable to find such an analysis of an independent system other than the Crippen Wright studies referred to above.

pany. This would be followed by construction of the Hemp Creek project on the Clearwater, with substantial capacity available to meet growing loads on the lower mainland. Next would be built a low dam at the Mica Creek site, followed by another structure (project X) on the Clearwater, and the development of the Seven Mile site on the Pend d'Oreille. When these developments had been completed and indicated load growth warranted, construction would begin on the diversion works on the Kootenay in the vicinity

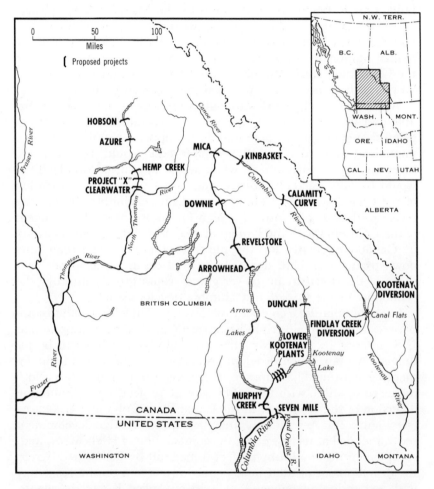

Figure 22. Plan introduced by Crippen Wright Engineering Ltd. for Canada's independent development of the Columbia River. (Source: Crippen Wright Engineering Ltd., *Upper Columbia Hydro-Electric Developments, Interim Report No. 5,* October 1958, Chapter IV.)

of Canal Flats. Findlay Creek would be diverted by tunnel directly into Columbia Lake, while the remainder of the Kootenay would be diverted by simple diversion works into the upper Columbia. This development would be complemented by a high dam at Calamity Curve to provide storage for regulation downstream on the Columbia, followed by construction of the Downie and Revelstoke Canyon head plants. Later, a dam and power plant at the Kinbasket site, between Calamity Curve and Mica Creek, would be built. Last to be constructed would be the Murphy Creek project between Castlegar and Trail, just above the international boundary, and the Arrowhead project at the upper Arrow Lakes. In order to realize significant integration benefits, operation of the plants on the Clearwater and Columbia would be co-ordinated throughout all phases in which power plants would exist on both streams.

While such a scheme was thought to represent the lowest realizable cost from Canada's independent development, it was recognized that considerable potential on the upper Columbia would go unrealized and that relatively high cost would be incurred, especially in the early phases when necessary transmission facilities would be only partially utilized and opportunities for integration of the Clearwater and Columbia would be negligible. It was also recognized that, in contrast, a plan for co-operative development of the Columbia with the United States, providing storage capacity in Canada explicitly for the purpose of regulating streamflows downstream over U.S. head plants, and assuming a 50 per cent share of the downstream power gains, would greatly improve the economics of the Canadian Columbia development.

In contemplating a co-operative development with which to compare results, Crippen Wright Engineering made the assumption that U.S. interest in the construction of Libby would have to be indulged. A plan which developed storage with the view of supplementing existing U.S. storage, therefore, would require developments compatible with the Libby storage project, thus eliminating diversion of the Kootenay in the Canal Flats–Columbia Lake area (see Figure 23). Accordingly, the plan of co-operative development recommended as its first phase the construction of High Arrow and, complementing the Libby project to be built by the United States, the development of the Canal plant downstream on the Kootenay with expansion of capacity at existing lower Kootenay plants. Development of the Seven Mile site on the Pend d'Oreille would follow. Additional storage would then be brought in on the upper Columbia in the Kinbasket reservoir, initially without power installations, for use in regulating streamflows to correspond with United States system requirements. With this degree of regulation on the upper Columbia, the Murphy Creek site was designated for next addition to provide at-site power to meet Canadian loads, followed by Duncan Lake and the installation of generators at the Kinbasket site. Then in sequence would come the low Mica, Downie Creek, and Revelstoke Canyon projects for generation to

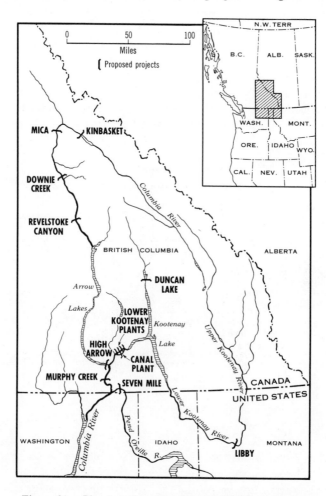

Figure 23. Plan introduced by Crippen Wright Engineering Ltd. for co-operative development of the Columbia River by Canada and the United States. (Source: Crippen Wright Engineering Ltd., *Upper Columbia Hydro-Electric Developments, Interim Report No. 7,* November 1958, p. IV-10.)

128   THE COLUMBIA RIVER TREATY

meet the growth in British Columbia loads. A summary comparison of the two schemes is given in Table 22.

While the Crippen Wright report did not visualize exactly the plan of development proposed in the Treaty, it does at least give some idea of the size of the benefit the Province of British Columbia anticipated from co-operative development. When the two plans are compared in Table 22, we see an increase of 1.9 billion kilowatt-hours per annum from the co-operative plan with downstream benefits credited to Canada, for a savings in outlay of $56 million. Assuming the value of this power at 4.5 mills per kilowatt-hour at the load center, and assuming a 5.5 per cent and 4.0 per cent discount rate, the present worth of this annual stream would capitalize at $144 million and $184 million. Adding to the co-operative plan the $56 million savings in outlay and the flood damage reduction benefits, the advantage would total upwards of $250 million as a crude estimate.

TABLE 22

Comparative Output and Cost of Independent Canadian Development and
Co-operative Plans, Crippen Wright Studies

Item	Independent development Clearwater–Calamity Curve scheme	Co-operative development High Arrow, Kinbasket, and Libby storage scheme
Estimated total generation and transmission costs:		
Investment ($ million)	1,628.5	1,572.5
Annual costs ($ million)	92.7	89.2
Estimated increased annual firm power at B.C. load centers (billion kwh)	29.3	31.2

Source: Upper Columbia Hydro-Electric Developments, ''Comparison of Alternative Schemes,'' Interim Report No. 7, Crippen Wright Engineering Ltd., November 1958, Chapter IV, p. IV-10.

NORTHERN AFFAIRS AND NATIONAL RESOURCES
DEPARTMENTAL STUDIES

As has been indicated, the federal government's studies of the costs of Canada's independent development of the Columbia are limited for our purpose by the fact that their evaluative results are based on conditions assumed to prevail for only the year 1985. Nevertheless, they provide useful supplementary information because they cover, more nearly than do the province's Crippen Wright studies, projects which were involved in the negotiation process and which dominated the results of the Treaty. Assuming a completely independent development of the upper Columbia and Kootenay, with no provision for storage to regulate flows of U.S. head plants downstream, the studies made by the Water Resources Branch of the Department of Northern Affairs and National Resources suggest that the most economic development would involve the so-called Canal Flats diversion. Incremental costs of added power from the Copper Creek and Dorr–Bull River diversions were judged to be, respectively, 4.06 mills and 4.10 mills per kilowatt-hour at the site of Canadian generation. When transmission costs are added, the total cost of these increments would be above the costs of thermal power at load centers.[9] The data provided on the Canal Flats alternative, then, appear to be the most favorable to use in a comparison of independent and co-operative development. As far as the latter is concerned the power output data associated with the non-diversion alternative analyzed in the Water Resource Branch studies[10] can be utilized.

Table 23 gives output data on these two schemes of development with appropriate adjustments to make the alternatives directly comparable. Table 24 converts these results to monetary equivalents.

The data employed by technical personnel of the federal Department of Northern Affairs and National Resources suggest that co-operative development (with Treaty terms for the division of the jointly produced gains) would mean a savings in cost of something on the order of a third of a billion dollars, compared with the cost of the most favorable alternative available to Canada.

The fact that estimates for only one year of the useful life-span of the facilities governed the calculations does, however, limit the precision of the method used and the accuracy of the results.[11]

[9] *Columbia River Treaty and Protocol, Minutes of Proceedings and Evidence*, No. 3, Standing Committee on External Affairs, House of Commons, Twenty-sixth Parliament, Second Session, April 9, 1964, pp. 192–93.

[10] The non-diversion even here, however, involves a relatively small partial diversion (1.5 million acre-feet) in the Canal Flats area after twenty years, rather than the full Dorr–Bull River–Luxor diversion scheme.

[11] See the discussion concerning the accuracy of data, particularly of output data, developed in Chapter 5, pp. 74–75, 97. In the matter of making a selection between mutually exclusive alternatives, the limitation on accuracy is perhaps of negligible significance in determining the *relative* merit of two alternatives. When evaluating a project as to its relative worth vis-à-vis alternative expenditures in competing sectors of the economy (i.e., the economic justification studies), the problem of accuracy becomes more acute, for it is the absolute magnitude of the incremental costs and gains that is determinative. In the present instance, while it is not particularly difficult to evaluate the *relative* merits of the co-operative and independent development plans, the *absolute* size of the advantage is not readily measured with accuracy.

TABLE 23

Comparative Output Data on Independent Canal Flats Diversion and Co-operative Non-diversion Alternatives for Columbia River Development in Canada (1985 Conditions)

Projects	Average critical period output (prime power mw)	Firm hydro energy at site (kwh x 10⁶)	Firm hydro energy at load (kwh x 10⁶)	Firm thermal energy at load (kwh x 10⁶)
CO-OPERATIVE COLUMBIA DEVELOPMENT				
Mica	703.2			
Downie	445.0			
Revelstoke	313.8			
Duncan Storage	0			
W. Kootenay additions	85.3			
Waneta–Seven Mile	540.1			
Murphy Creek	243.1			
Total Non-diversion System¹	2,330.5			
Plus				
Downstream Benefit Share¹				
High Arrow	570.0			
Mica	297.8			
Canal Plant	210.0			
Co-operative System Total	3,408.3	29,856.7	28,065.3	—
INDEPENDENT CANADIAN PLAN²				
Canal Flats diversion	—			
Calamity Curve	44.1			
Mica	768.4			
Downie	477.7			
Revelstoke	334.7			
Duncan Storage	0			
West Kootenay additions	45.8			
Waneta–Seven Mile	540.1			
Murphy Creek	240.7			
Hydro System Total	2,451.5	21,475.1	20,169.6	
Independent System Deficiency			7,895.8	
Required make-up thermal at load				7,895.8

¹ Summary of Water Resources Branch Power Output Studies of the Columbia River, Department of Northern Affairs and National Resources, Water Resources Branch, Study No. 24/1, Tables IV-8 and IV-11, divided by 2 and multiplied by 73.2% load factor for 1985 system conditions output estimates.
² Ibid., Study No. 43/2.

Perhaps all one can say, therefore, is that the estimated savings in cost are likely to be within the margin of error of plus or minus 33 per cent. In that event, the savings in cost for Canada resulting from the Treaty projects and terms regarding benefit division would, according to the federal government's data, be in the magnitude of a quarter- to a half-billion dollars.

TABLE 24

Savings in Cost of Co-operative Columbia River Development over Independent
Canadian Development

(thousand dollars)

	Annual costs of systems' output assuming 5.5% interest			
Plans of development	Annual at-site costs	Trans- mission costs	Thermal make-up costs	Total annual cost of power at load
Non-diversion System	57,094	28,779	—	85,873
Co-operative Plan[1]				
High Arrow	4,350	6,241[2]	—	10,591
Mica (d.s. benefits)	—	3,263	—	3,263
Canal plant and Libby flowage	3,864	2,759[3]	—	6,623
U.S. standby transmission charges	—	1,779[4]	—	1,779
Total annual cost of co-operative system................................				108,129
Independent Canadian System				
(Canal Flats diversion)	57,444[5]	29,581[5]		87,025
Cost of make-up thermal			39,380	39,380
Total annual cost of independent system...............................				• 126,405
SAVINGS IN COST OF CO-OPERATIVE SYSTEM ANNUALLY................				18,276
Present value of annual savings (5.5%)............................			309,491[6]	
Add flood damage reduction benefits (64.4).......................			373,891	

[1] *Columbia River Treaty and Protocol, Minutes of Proceedings and Evidence,* No. 3, Standing Committee on External Affairs, House of Commons, Twenty-sixth Parliament, Second Session, April 9, 1964, Appendix C, Table 3, p. 192 (based on Water Resources Branch Output Study 24/1).
[2] Based on 1.25 mills/kwh. *Ibid.,* fn. 3, Table 3, p. 192.
[3] *Loc. cit.*
[4] Computed on capacity charge of 1.50/kw/yr. *Treaty,* Article X-2.
[5] *Minutes of Proceedings and Evidence, op. cit.,* Appendix C, Table 3, p. 192.
[6] This computation understates the gain by about 4% for by 1985 the partial diversion permitted by the Treaty would be in effect.

From Canada's point of view, given the information available and the policies bounding the feasible range of alternatives in 1960, the Canadian negotiating team could rest satisfied that the advantages of co-operative development in terms of savings in cost over the relevant alternatives available to them were amply demonstrated.

UNITED STATES ALTERNATIVES TO THE COLUMBIA TREATY SYSTEM PROJECTS

On the United States side of the border, the test of the Treaty system projects and Treaty terms with respect to the division of gains evolved through a series of studies conducted in the course of

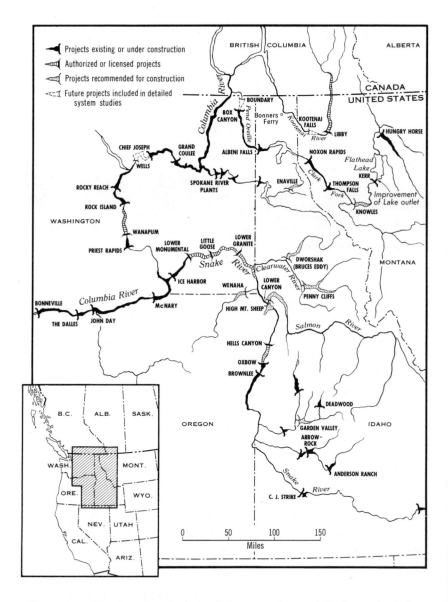

Figure 24.   Plan introduced by the U.S. Army Corps of Engineers for inde-
pendent development of the Columbia River by the United States. (Source:
Columbia River and Tributaries, Vol. I, H.D. No. 403, 87th Cong., 2nd Sess., 1963,
Plate 1.)

the U.S.–Canadian negotiations. In 1958, the U.S. Army Corps of Engineers had developed an independent U.S. Columbia Basin plan designated as "The Major Water Plan"[12] concurrently with the International Columbia River Engineering Board's survey of both countries' reaches of the Columbia. Elements of this plan are shown in Figure 24. The engineering investigations provided the U.S. technical staff with pertinent background for evaluating the comparative advantage of a co-operative scheme of development, involving various combinations of international projects at different stages, with an entirely U.S. system.

First, a domestic system made up of elements of the Major Water Plan was compared with an international system which included High Arrow, Dorr–Bull River, and Mica[13]—the projects initially advanced by Canada. The projects and their scheduling are shown in Table 25.

It can be seen from the table that the international system employs all of the major U.S. projects in the domestic U.S. system, excluding only the relatively small and high-cost Enaville, Ninemile Prairie, Quartz Creek, and Flathead Lake outlet improvement projects. Neither system, however, includes the Lower Canyon project of the Major Water Plan—a project that would seem to warrant consideration in a domestic system lacking the benefit of Canadian storage.

Since this study was preliminary in nature and represents an early stage in the evolution of the projects to be included in the ultimate Treaty system and also of the form that the division of benefits would take, the details of the load-resource study will not be dealt with. It is sufficient to say that based on the following assumptions:

1) storage projects would be added in the order of their economics irrespective of country of origin,[14] namely, Canadian storage projects would be added first;

2) benefits would be computed on the basis of the storage con-

---

[12] *Water Resources Development of the Columbia River Basin* (Review of House Doc. No. 531, 81st Cong., 2nd Sess.), a report by the Division Engineer, U.S. Army Engineer Division, North Pacific, to the Chief of Engineers, U.S. Army, June 1958 (republished with post-Canadian Treaty supplement, and related official reviews, in House Doc. No. 403, 87th Cong., 2nd Sess., 1963).

[13] *International Columbia River Studies, Costs of Analysis [sic] of a Canadian-U.S. System vs. an Alternative U.S. System*, U. S. Army Engineer Division, North Pacific, April 25, 1960.

[14] Subject only to the condition that a project's construction lead time was compatible with introduction in a sequence consistent with its relative economics.

TABLE 25

Schedule of Completion of Hydro Projects in the Columbia River Basin for the
Co-operative and Independent Systems of Development

Project dates	1970	1975	1980	1985	1990
Co-operative System					
High Arrow	x				
Dorr–Bull River	x				
Hells Canyon	x				
Lower Monumental	x				
Mica		x			
High Mt. Sheep		x			
Bruces Eddy		x			
Long Meadows		x			
Wells		x			
China Gardens		x			
Lower Granite		x			
Little Goose		x			
Knowles			x		
Garden Valley			x		
Boundary			x		
Asotin			x		
Penny Cliffs					x
Independent U.S. System					
High Mt. Sheep	x				
Long Meadows	x				
Flathead Lake outlet	x				
Lower Monumental	x				
Hells Canyon	x				
Bruces Eddy		x			
Knowles		x			
Ninemile Prairie		x			
Enaville		x			
Wells		x			
China Gardens		x			
Lower Granite		x			
Little Goose		x			
Garden Valley			x		
Quartz Creek			x		
Boundary			x		
Asotin			x		
Penny Cliffs				x	

Source: *International Columbia River Studies, Costs of Analysis* [sic] *of a Canadian-U.S.
System vs. an Alternative U.S. System*, U.S. Army Engineer Div., North Pacific, April 25, 1960.

tribution to the system in the sequence in which the projects
were added;

3) power benefits would be divided equally;
the resulting comparative evaluation shows the added cost to the
United States, under the above principles of benefit measurement
and division, to be greater by $290 million (1970 worth) with co-
operative development than it would be with an independent system which relied entirely on U.S. resources.[15]

[15] *International Columbia River Studies, Costs of Analysis* [sic] *of a Canadian-U.S.
System vs. an Alternative U.S. System, op. cit.*, p. 6. This estimate applies a 2.5 per cent
discount consistent with the rate used for estimates of annual costs.

This result could have been anticipated in view of the diminishing marginal yield from storage that occurs as increasingly large amounts of storage capacity are added to a hydro system. Since approximately 24 million acre-feet of Canadian storage was scheduled into the system (with existing 13 million acre-feet) before any credit for storage was attributed to U.S. projects, the 50 per cent split of incremental prime power incident on this 24 million acre-feet, coupled with storage values credited to U.S. projects on a fourth-added basis, totaled less than the storage value of U.S. projects alone first-added without benefit of sharing in Canadian storage regulation.

This is illustrated diagramatically in Figure 25. In the absence of Canadian storage, the Corps proposed to provide about 14 million acre-feet of storage from exclusively domestic sites. This volume of storage, if added next to the existing system, would

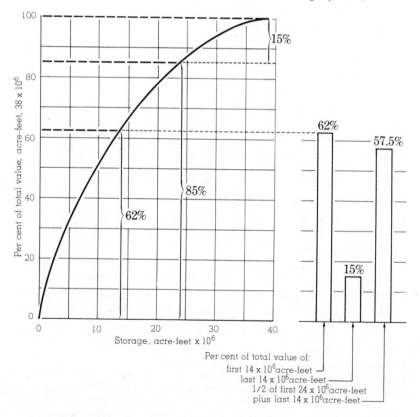

Figure 25. Percentage of total power value from storage under 1970 load and resource conditions, and alternative U.S. options.

provide about 62 per cent of the combined value of 24 million acre-feet of Canadian and 14 million acre-feet of U.S. storage. If the latter is credited following 24 million acre-feet of Canadian storage, however, its contribution has a value of only about 15 per cent of the total. Accordingly, if the benefits of 24 million acre-feet of Canadian storage (85 per cent of the total) are to be divided equally, the sum of the U.S. share (42.5 per cent) and its own storage evaluated as added following Canadian storage would provide only 57.5 per cent of the total value of the 38 million acre-feet addition, compared with 62 per cent were the United States to act independently pursuing alternatives available within its borders.

Something similar, but to an even more exaggerated extent, attends the computation of flood damage reduction benefits, a matter discussed earlier in this chapter.

Viewed another way, one can say that the amount of storage which has value to system operations is ultimately limited or approaches zero in the limit. However, the proposed storage in the United States would be provided by dams which also have appreciable head, and which it may be economic to build merely to install generator capacity. As the value of storage in system operations declines with the emergence of a predominantly thermal system, the plants could be operated alternatively as high head plants for peaking the base load operations. Accordingly, the Canadian storage is not likely to result in a substitution of Canadian construction expenditures for U.S. construction outlays.[16] It tends only to pre-empt the most valuable portion of the firming spectrum on the hydro system during the hydro phase of system operations, thus displacing the supramarginality of U.S. projects in the computation of benefit shares.

A situation in which all of the most economic storage is located in the upstream country (thus first-added, with prime power gain evaluated on that basis) and which requires that the power be divided equally, will create an impasse, making agreement infeasible.[17] In the case of the Columbia, the results of such a mode

[16] *U.S. Columbia River Power System, 1963; Advance Program, 1973*, U.S. Department of the Interior, Bonneville Power Administration, February 1963. See also *Pacific Northwest Electric Energy Costs with and without Canadian Treaty Projects*, Bulletin No. 8, H. Zinder and Associates for Division of Power Resources, Department of Conservation, State of Washington, February 1964, Chart 3 following p. 30.

[17] This, of course, would not be true if there were no storage sites available in the downstream country, as might be the case were the upstream country to occupy the highlands and the downstream country an alluvial delta.

of operation would adversely affect the United States and there would be no basis for a co-operative venture. If, however, it is considered desirable to preserve the appearance of an equal division while departing from its reality, several adjustments to the rule of equal division of power are possible. The Treaty negotiators considered several such changes. One of the reasons why the costs to the United States increased by $290 million when co-operative rather than domestic development was contemplated is rooted in the fact that Canadian storage regulation would have firmed up a substantial block of high-grade U.S. interruptible power for which there was a market—power that was available from 80 to 87 per cent of the time. Thus, despite only a 13 to 20 per cent supplement of energy from Canadian storage, the rule to share prime power equally would have given Canada 50 per cent of the combined energy. It was mutually agreed, therefore, that the United States should be permitted to deduct from the downstream storage benefits the amount of secondary energy which was estimated to be salable in any event, [18] subject to the restriction that no more than 40 per cent of the secondary energy not used for thermal energy displacement in the Pacific Northwest should be considered salable. [19]

It was also agreed to consider a reduction in the amount of storage to be provided by Canada. Prior to a decision on this point the U.S. technical staff analyzed four alternative possibilities, ranging in amount from 8.5 million acre-feet (High Arrow–Duncan) to 16.7 million acre-feet (Mica and Dorr–Bull River), to test the effect of both a reduction in the amount of storage and an adjustment to compensate for loss of U.S. salable secondary energy.

Each of the Canadian alternative storage complements in the "international system" was compared in turn with the U.S. domestic system discussed above. The results of this study [20] show that by eliminating the U.S. secondary energy from Canadian entitlement and varying amounts of reduced Canadian storage, the United

[18] This is in accordance with the IJC Power Principle No. 6. See *The Columbia Treaty, Protocol and Related Documents* (Ottawa: Departments of External Affairs, and Northern Affairs and National Resources, February 1964), p. 39 ff.

[19] *Treaty, op. cit.,* Annex B, para. 3c. This was to protect Canada from a drastic reduction in benefits were an electrical interconnection between the Pacific Northwest and Pacific Southwest to be built.

[20] *Alternative System Studies, U.S.-Canadian Development of the Columbia River,* U.S. Department of the Interior, Bonneville Power Administration; and U.S. Army Engineer Division, North Pacific, July 8, 1960.

States deficit from the co-operative undertaking would decrease from $290 million to a range between $72.5 million and $147.1 million, depending on the storage complement assumed to be provided by the Canadian resources. [21]

It was clear, therefore, that even with the adjustment of Canadian entitlement to reflect the loss of U.S. salable secondary energy, an equal division of the remaining downstream power would produce no advantage to the United States if that advantage is measured in terms of savings in the cost of supplying power requirements. [22]

A further change in the Canadian storage complement for the co-operative system was made, as noted in Chapter 6, reducing Mica Creek storage for U.S. system regulation from 11.7 million to 7.5 million acre-feet, substituting the Libby project at U.S. cost for the Dorr–Bull River storage in Canada, and providing the High Arrow–Duncan complex—for a total of 15.5 million acre-feet of Canadian storage. No systematic load resource study of the type referred to earlier in this chapter appears to have been undertaken by the United States to test out whether this configuration of projects and terms with respect to the division of benefits could be demonstrated to represent an advantage to the United States.

There is one bit of related evidence provided officially, however, which might be of some help in judging how the co-operative, as compared with the independent, system affected the position of the United States. Following the Treaty of 1961, the Corps of Engineers submitted a supplement to the Columbia River 308 Review Report, re-evaluating the benefits and costs of its projects in the Major Water Plan which would be affected by the Canadian storage being credited as first-added. The relevant portion of the exhibit is given in Table 26.

In this instance, returning to its more usual mode of analysis, the Corps provided data relevant to conditions assumed to prevail in one year, 1985. Observe that the value of the Major Water Plan projects is reduced by an estimated $23.6 million as an average annual sum if they are added after Canadian projects. When this sum is discounted at 4 per cent and 5.5 per cent, the reduction in terms of present values becomes $507.8 million and $467.1 million,

---

[21] When annual costs are discounted at 2.5 per cent, consistent with rate employed in the study.

[22] Appropriate adjustment in the estimated cost of supplying power was made to reflect the influence of the equal division of downstream flood damage reduction benefits, i.e., resulting in a different cost allocation to power facilities on multiple-purpose storage projects.

TABLE 26

Summary of Corps of Engineers' Economic Comparisons

(thousand dollars)

Project	Flood Control Benefits		Thermal Power Savings		Other benefits	Total Accomplishments	
	Without Canadian storage	With Canadian storage	Without Canadian storage	With Canadian storage		Without Canadian storage	With Canadian storage
Flathead Lake Outlet Impr.	656[1]	147[2]	—	114[3]	—	656	261
Knowles	2,999[1]	447[2]	19,866	11,292	58	22,915	11,797
Garden Valley	534[1]	143[2]	9,406[4]	9,236[4]	−34	9,906	9,345
High Mountain Sheep	1,819[1]	239[2]	25,733	23,312	16	27,568	23,567
Lower Canyon	285[2]	285[2]	19,768	17,858	75	20,128	18,218
Penny Cliffs	911[2]	911[2]	11,409	9,483	282	12,602	10,676
Bruces Eddy	2,277[1]	552[2]	8,043	6,801	553	10,873	7,906
Kootenai Falls	—	—	5,646	5,000	—	5,646	5,000
Asotin (W.O. Lock)	—	—	9,095	9,033	32	9,127	9,065
China Gardens (910)	—	—	5,440	5,423	13	5,453	5,436
China Gardens (895)	—	—	4,341	4,308	13	4,354	4,321
Totals	9,473	2,724	118,740	101,860		129,228	105,592
	Δ6,749		Δ16,887			Δ23,636	

[1] Based on project operating in basic flood control plan for control to 800,000 cfs at The Dalles.
[2] Based on project being placed in operation subsequent to attainment of basic flood control objective.
[3] Power benefit recognized but not evaluated in basic report.
[4] Power benefits.

Source: Columbia River and Tributaries, House Document No. 403, 87th Cong., 2nd Sess., Supplement to Report on Water Resources Development, Columbia River Basin, U.S. Army Engineer Division, North Pacific, February 24, 1961, Table 10, p. 41.

respectively.[23] It must be emphasized that these magnitudes do not represent the monetary equivalent of the *net loss* of the Columbia Treaty to the United States, but rather a gross relative reduction in the value of the U.S. complement of facilities (the displacement effect) which is partially compensated for by the net value of the Canadian storage services provided.

If we restrict ourselves to analyses made before 1961, we do not have sufficient information to demonstrate whether the arrangement involving the storage secured by the Columbia Treaty results in any net advantage to the United States, although the evidence suggests it to be questionable. To arrive at any sound judgment on this matter, it is necessary to utilize data from the 1963 analyses referred to above. These, in effect, simulate the development of the regional power system in the United States' portions of the Columbia system,[24] on the assumption that Treaty storage would be added as scheduled in the Treaty. They also provide a basis for estimating the cost of meeting power and flood control objectives in the Pacific Northwest with hydro resources available in the Treaty system, and with the Canadian downstream benefits returned to British Columbia. For comparative purposes, Resources for the Future in 1965 undertook a parallel set of studies simulating a domestic system from which costs could be estimated for meeting similar power and flood control objectives.[25] Because both sets of studies are based on 1963 concepts with regard to generator unit sizes, etc., and these concepts had undergone some change since 1960, cost data for 1960 cannot be used in comparing the costs of the Treaty and independent domestic systems. Instead, *cost estimates as of 1963*[26] are applied to the terms of the Treaty of 1961. Table 27 gives the results of this comparison.

The table shows that, under the conditions indicated above, the cost to the United States of meeting identical power objectives and

[23] Actually, since the annual costs were based on the use of a 2.5 per cent rate of interest, the average annual sum might have been discounted at 2.5 per cent, increasing the discounted value of the annual amount to $670 million. The substitution of different rates of interest for different components and/or purposes of analysis, however, leads easily to inadvertent miscalculations. In the analysis made by Resources for the Future (see Table 27 and text below) all data for purposes of evaluation are treated consistently employing a 4 per cent interest and/or discount rate.

[24] *Columbia River Development: Determination of Canadian Downstream Power Entitlement*, Technical Report, Work Group No. 1, November 1963.

[25] See Technical Note to this chapter for a description of the two systems and method of estimating costs for each.

[26] Supplied by U.S. Army Engineer Division, North Pacific, and U.S. Bureau of Reclamation for Grand Coulee's third powerhouse.

Item	1968–1969				
	Treaty System[1]		Domestic U.S. System[2]		Trea
	January peaking capacity	Critical period generation	January peaking capacity	Critical period generation	January peaking capacity
	(megawatts)				
1. Main hydro system...................................	14,771	8,535	14,781	8,248	15,756
2. Independent resources.............................	3,669	1,762	3,669	1,762	3,669
3. Total hydro..	18,440	10,297	18,450	10,010	19,425
4. Less Canadian entitlement[3]	−191	−105	—	—	−956
5. TOTAL HYDRO FOR N.W. LOAD......................	18,249	10,192	18,450	10,010	18,469
6. Thermal...	1,255	1,062[4]	1,255	1,062[4]	1,255
7. Less reserves required[5].............................	−1,344	−53	−1,344	−53	−1,493
8. TOTAL RESOURCES FOR N.W. LOAD..................	18,160	11,201	18,361	11,019	18,231
9. Estimated firm load...............................	16,614	11,109	16,614	11,109	17,694
10. Surplus or deficiency	+1,546	+92	+1,747	−90	+537
11. Thermal adjustments					
Energy...	—	—	—	94.5	—
Capacity.......................................	—	—	105	—	—
12. Hydro system annual cost difference ($000)............	—	—	—	—	—
13. Annual cost of differences in system components.......					
Capacity ($000)...................................	—		1,085.7		
Energy (net of displacement) ($000)................	1,211.3		1,800.6		1.
14. TOTAL ANNUAL COSTS OF SYSTEM DIFFERENCES					
($000).....................................	1,211.3		2,886.3		1.
15. Differences in system annual cost					
($000)...	—		1,675		
16. Present value of excess cost of Treaty system ($000)..............................	241,862				
17. Flood control adjustments					
Excess present cost of Treaty flood control measures ($000)......................	+62,184				
Excess present value of Treaty flood control benefits ($000)......................	−50,725				
18. Total excess cost of Treaty system ($000)......................................	253,321				

[1] *Columbia River Development: Determination of Canadian Downstream Power Entitlement*, Technical I
[2] Resources for the Future, Inc.
[3] *The Columbia River Treaty and Protocol* (Ottawa: Departments of External Affairs and Northern A
Table 9, p. 99.
[4] Hanford New Production Reactor and Existing Conventional Thermal Stations.
[5] Computed at 8% of firm load and 5% of thermal plant energy capability.
* Estimated.

TABLE 27

Comparative Cost of Treaty vs. United States Domestic Power Systems as of 1960

	1969–1970			1976–1977				1983–1984		
	Treaty System¹	Domestic U.S. System²		Treaty System¹		Domestic U.S. System²		Treaty System¹		Domesti(c)
	Critical period generation	January peaking capacity	Critical period generation	January peaking capacity	Critical period generation	January peaking capacity	Critical period generation	January peaking capacity	Critical period generation	January peaking capacity
	(megawatts)			(megawatts)				(megawatts)		
	9,485	15,552	8,278	21,426	12,550	21,042	11,089	23,866	12,420	22,511
	1,695	3,669	1,762	4,504	2,127	4,504	2,193	4,728	2,258	4,728
	11,180	19,222	10,040	25,930	14,677	25,546	13,282	28,594	14,678	27,239
	−540	—	—	−1,322	−700	—	—	1,235	507	—
	10,640	19,221	10,040	24,608	13,977	25,546	13,282	27,359	14,171	27,239
	1,062⁴	1,255	1,062⁴	1,600	1,440	1,600	1,440	6,745	6,070	6,745
	−53	−1,416	−53	−2,040	−69	−1,933	−69	−2,517	−289	−2,517
	11,649	19,060	11,049	24,168	15,348	25,213	14,653	31,587	19,952	31,467
	11,516	17,694	11,516	24,168	15,272	24,168	15,272	31,467	20,160	31,467
	+133	+1,366	−467	—	+76	+1,045	−619	+120	−208	—
	—	—	490	—	—	721	649	—	218	—
	—	544	—	—	—	—	—	242	—	—
	—	—	—	22,904		—	—	7,753		—
		5,624.9		—		7,455.1		2,502		
3.1		3,522.1		5,682.9		9,250.1		67,310		59
3.1		9,147.0		28,533.9		16,705.2		77,565		5(
		8,063.9		11,828.7		—		17,762		

eport, Work Group No. 1, November 1963.

airs and National Resources, April 1964),

similar flood control objectives would be greater by about a quarter of a billion dollars by means of the Columbia Treaty system than the cost of pursuing an independent domestic alternative.[27] It appears that the concessions won by the U.S. negotiators—deduction of the pre-existing salable secondary energy from Canadian entitlement, reservation of 4.5 million acre-feet of storage,[28] and other negotiating points calculated to make the Treaty potentially feasible—were in turn dissipated by the U.S. option to develop the Libby project.

[27] See Technical Note at end of chapter for details on the simulation and evaluation of the two systems. Incidentally, sensitivity tests were made with respect to rate of load growth, etc. At the high-load growth rate, the cost difference would be increased by approximately $10 million; similarly if a 5.5 per cent interest rate were assumed and the higher costs for thermal capacity and energy were employed. The $253 million deficit occasioned by the Treaty represents results from the most favorable constellation of assumptions with respect to conditions for use of Canadian storage.

In commenting on the above analysis, Brigadier General P. C. Hyzer, Division Engineer, and the staff of the U.S. Army Engineer Division, North Pacific, suggest that the two systems being compared are not strictly comparable. That is to say, the domestic system contains two storage projects which do not appear in the Treaty system, and one of these (the Lower Canyon project) in their judgment would remain economic to some degree despite the displacement effects of Canadian storage and Libby first-added, namely, 20.5 million acre-feet in excess of the domestic system's storage. Inclusion of the Lower Canyon project, along with correction of some incomparabilities arising out of a change in design of unit sizes at the Dworshak project between the time the Treaty system was evaluated and the RFF domestic system studies were undertaken, would result, in their opinion, in a reduction of the excess cost of the Treaty system during the periods 1983–84 and 1988–89 by as much as one-half, and for the last period (2010–11) by even more than one-half. There is no way of testing these judgments short of simulating the Treaty system during these later periods with Lower Canyon included and checking results thus obtained with those provided by the International Work Group studies. This, of course, is quite beyond the resources available to this study, albeit it represents studies which should have been undertaken preparatory to the negotiation of the Treaty terms. One point, however, bears noting: Even if the informed judgment of the technical personnel of the Corps of Engineers is accepted, the change would affect only the magnitude of the difference in costs between the Treaty and domestic systems (roughly to about $150 million, i.e., a reduction of about $100 million) but not the conclusions with respect to lack of net advantage to the United States by reason of the 1961 Treaty terms.

[28] Canadian storage exceeding 20 million acre-feet is available in the High Arrow–Duncan and Mica reservoirs; thus, by crediting only 15.5 million acre-feet, 4.5 million acre-feet represents a reservation of storage for the U.S. projects. It should be noted that this 4.5 million acre-feet is largely only cyclical storage which provides capacity benefits but little energy benefits, and hence is not directly comparable with the first 15.5 million acre-feet.

CONCLUDING OBSERVATIONS ON THE FIRST PHASE OF NEGOTIATIONS

The Columbia Treaty and the associated supplementary agreements concluded after the Treaty was signed in 1961 represent the entire set of arrangements that can be characterized as the international agreement for co-operative development of the Columbia River Basin. While analysis of data pertinent to the 1961 Treaty cannot be expected to cover all the relevant considerations, it may be useful to review the results at each stage in order to understand what was accomplished, or perhaps what was thought to be accomplished.

Several conclusions emerge from the analyses in Chapter 5 and the present chapter:

1. It is clear, in evaluating the results of the Treaty terms of 1961, that projects not qualifying under a strict interpretation of the IJC principles were included in the Treaty package.

2. In reviewing the studies made to test the application of General Principle No. 2, it is clear that inclusion of the most economic projects in the order economic criteria would indicate, *coupled with the rule that the attributed power gain be shared equally,* did not in the Columbia case represent a viable basis for successful negotiation of a treaty through which both parties could advance to economic positions superior to those they could have achieved independently.

3. It seems clear that while application of economic criteria will maximize the jointly produced gain for mutual sharing, if all the most economic storage sites are located in the upstream country the share of the power gains must reflect the displacement of supramarginal opportunities downstream in the country with the developed head.

4. It seems clear, also, that while deduction of a part of the secondary energy in computing the power gain to the United States did improve the U.S. share, this benefit was obtained partly in response to a decision which permitted much of the improvement to be dissipated—the decision to substitute the Libby project for more economic alternatives.

As a result, there is a demonstrable gain to Canada from the Columbia River Treaty, but there is no similar net gain to the United States. It should be borne in mind, however, that economic considerations alone did not dominate the principals to the negotiations on the United States side, and that the IJC principles themselves offered a degree of flexibility in interpretation. Among the objectives voiced by members of the United States negotiating delegation during the hearings on Treaty ratification was one of no small significance for the results:

> Thirdly, we were anxious that this agreement operate to progressively reduce power costs in British Columbia; firstly and obviously because if there was going to be an agreement it had to operate in that direction for the Canadians; secondly we regard Canada as a partner in the free world, and its growth, its economic growth, as being important to the United States.[29]

There can be little question that the course of action taken by the United States contributed to the realization of this objective.

Another consideration motivating the U.S. negotiators was the interest in obtaining a large block of power on a basis that would permit maintenance of the rate structure on the federal system, i.e., the Bonneville Power Administration's $17.50-per-kilowatt prime power rate.[30] I believe it must be concluded that in this they were unsuccessful.[31] Moreover, it is anything but clear that their behavior was consistent with seeking such an arrangement.[32]

A final consideration, and one which apparently loomed large in the minds of participants, was the question of dealing with the flood hazard in the lower Kootenai in the vicinity of Bonners Ferry, Idaho. There can be little question that the Treaty of 1961 makes very substantial provisions for flood control storage to meet flood management objectives in the United States and especially in the Bonners Ferry area. It is equally true, however, that it relies on a more expensive complex of projects than would have emerged from the IJC economizing principle. When it was clear that British Columbia was irrevocably opposed to flooding the East Kootenay valley to provide upper Kootenay storage, a more economical alternative would have been to protect the Bonners Ferry area by means of the comparatively inexpensive and high-returns local flood protection measures investigated by the Corps

---

[29] *Columbia River Treaty,* Hearings before the Committee on Foreign Relations, United States Senate, 87th Cong., 1st Sess., March 8, 1964, Statement by Ivan B. White, Deputy Assistant Secretary of State, pp. 33, 44.

[30] *Columbia River Treaty, op. cit.,* p. 33.

[31] See *Pacific Northwest Electric Energy Costs with and without Canadian Treaty Projects, op. cit.,* pp. 33–34. Consistent with this, Bonneville found it necessary to request a rate increase of the Federal Power Commission. See Federal Power Commission, Release No. 14150, Washington, December 14, 1965.

[32] Persistence in urging the adoption of Libby was simply not consistent with the apparent objective of obtaining low-cost power for the Northwest.

of Engineers.[33] There is no evidence in the record that the local flood management possibility was considered. This suggests that there may have been a breakdown in the information flow from the Corps of Engineers to other parties concerned with negotiating the Treaty.

TECHNICAL NOTE ON THE EVALUATION OF THE COST DIFFERENCES BETWEEN THE COLUMBIA RIVER TREATY SYSTEM AND THE UNITED STATES DOMESTIC SYSTEM, 1961

POWER ASPECTS

In evaluating the comparative cost of meeting Pacific Northwest power loads in the United States with and, alternatively, without the Canadian–United States Columbia River Treaty, six specific system conditions over time were selected. These specific points in time were identified by the International Work Group in the preparation of a technical report entitled *Columbia River Development, Determination of Canadian Downstream Power Entitlement*, November, 1963. They include for two rates of load growth the various years when the components of Canadian storage become usable, the time at which additional thermal is first required to meet the firm energy load, and the time at which the ultimate hydro system becomes fully developed. System data on these specific points in time are available in exhibits C-2 through C-14 of the International Work Group report. Parallel data for an exclusively domestic resource system were obtained through comparable simulation studies undertaken by H. Zinder and Associates with the co-operation of the Bonneville Power Administration on behalf of Resources for the Future, Inc.

For the year 1968–69, the first year in which a portion of the Canadian storage would become operable, the total hydro resources consist of the principal Columbia system plus "independent

---

[33] *Report on Survey for Flood Control of Kootenai River in Kootenai Flats Area, Idaho*, U.S. Army Engineer Division, North Pacific, Seattle District, December 1, 1958. Although this report shows a 1.65:1 benefit to cost ratio, the Corps *recommended against the project* as being uneconomic for the reason that it was assumed Libby would be built in any event, rendering the local flood protection works superfluous. In reality, with the advent of the large amount of Canadian storage in the upper Columbia, this storage along with the local flood protection alternative for Bonners Ferry rendered Libby superfluous.

resources," the latter composed of projects which are either dis-associated hydraulically from the Columbia River system or whose operations do not materially affect the streamflows available to the Treaty base system or other projects included with the main Columbia power system. For the Treaty system, the Canadian entitlement [34] has been deducted to obtain the hydroelectric power available for meeting power loads of the Pacific Northwest. In addition to the hydro, 1,255 mw of thermal capacity have been included in the system studies, consisting of the Hanford New Production Reactor (786 mw of peaking capability and 669 mw of energy) and existing fossil fuel steam electric plants of 469 mw of peaking capability and 393 mw of energy. Reserve requirements of hydro are taken at 8 per cent of peak loads, and of energy at 5 per cent of thermal plant energy capability.

If a system including the above resources is shown to be deficient in energy, as is the case with the domestic U.S. system, the indicated energy deficiency is adjusted to include the necessary reserve energy (5 per cent) and this total is associated with thermal capacity (assumed operated at 90 per cent plant factor), as such capacity is required to meet the thermal deficiency despite the fact that excess peaking capability may exist on the hydro system.

The cost of the annual fuel bill associated with the fossil fuel plants is computed at $19.71 per kilowatt, corresponding to fuel costs at 25 cents per million Btu. The amount of fuel actually consumed, however, is computed net of fuel displacement by available secondary energy. For example, of the 1,062 mw of thermal shown, 669 mw are deducted as the nuclear reactor will not be subject to displacement by secondary hydro and the remainder 393 less 92 mw (for the Treaty system), or 301 mw, will have a fuel consumption equivalent to only 61.5 average mw net of energy displacement from secondary hydro. Surplus secondary energy was obtained from thirty-year regulations undertaken by the Bonneville Power Administration in its study designated as 69-1. In the case of the domestic U.S. system, the net fuel requirements for the nominal 487 mw of fossil fuel requirement is 91.3 average mw net of fuel displacement obtained in turn from secondary energy data of the H. Zinder simulation designated as RFF-1. (See Table 28.)

Since the hydro system for 1968–69 is the same in terms of U.S. costs for both systems (only the Duncan Lake project provided at

[34] Obtained from *The Columbia River Treaty and Protocol, op. cit.*, Table 9, p. 99, for both the low-load and the high-load forecast conditions.

Canadian expense distinguishes between the two systems) the total difference consists of the difference in amount of thermal capacity and energy used by the two systems.

The evaluation of cost differences for the two systems for 1969–70 is similar in all respects to that for the previous year. Only the Arrow Lakes storage is added, again with no expense to the United States, and to balance the increased capability of the Treaty system an additional 439 mw of thermal capacity are required to support 385 mw of required additional thermal energy. Net fossil fuel requirements for this year are 55 average mw and 179 average mw respectively for the Treaty and the domestic U.S. system. Available secondary energy data were taken from BPA study 70-1 for the Treaty system and RFF-2 for the domestic system. Incremental capacity costs for thermal plant is computed at $10.34 per kilowatt.

For the year 1974–75 (high load forecasts) or 1976–77 (low load forecasts) a difference in hydro system costs occurs with the addition of the Libby and Kootenai Falls projects in the Treaty system, in addition to the expansion common to both systems. The annual costs (computed with interest at 4 per cent and amortization over fifty years) to the United States in connection with the Treaty system thus is $22.9 million greater than for the domestic system. The added thermal costs for the domestic U.S. system required to make up energy deficiency is computed as in the previous cases. In this connection the fossil fuel costs associated with meeting energy requirements are for 295 average mw and 469 average mw respectively for the Treaty and the domestic systems, with secondary energy data obtained respectively from BPA study 75-1 and RFF-3. In this case, the full capability of 717 mw of energy is attributed to the Hanford New Production Reactor.

By the year 1983–84 (low load forecasts; 1978–79, high load) several differences occur in the hydro components of the two systems; these are shown below:

Treaty System			Domestic System		
Projects	Units	Annual costs ($000)	Projects	Units	Annual costs ($000)
Grand Coulee	4	6,126	China Gardens	1	457
John Day	4	2,288	Penny Cliffs	4	11,298
Libby	4	18,094	Lower Canyon	4	11,828
Kootenai Falls	3	4,828			
Total		31,336	Total		23,583

Net difference in hydro component ($000)....7,753

U.S. System²	1988–1989				2010–2011			
	Treaty System¹		Domestic U.S. System²		Treaty System¹		Domestic U.S. System²	
Critical period generation	January peaking capacity	Critical period generation	January peaking capacity	Critical period generation	January peaking capacity	22 Months continuous power	January peaking capacity	Critical period generation
		(megawatts)				(megawatts)		
12,122	25,111	12,411	25,165	12,132	33,725	12,646	34,541	12,549
2,298	4,728	2,240	4,728	2,298	4,717	2,222	4,717	2,222
14,420	29,839	14,651	29,893	14,430	38,442	14,868	39,258	14,771
—	1,140	374	—	—	—	134*	—	—
14,420	28,699	14,277	27,893	14,430	38,022	14,738	39,258	14,771
6,070	10,514	9,463	10,514	9,463	45,581	41,024	45,581	41,024
−289	−2,938	−450	−2,938	−450	−6,285	−1,954	−6,285	−1,954
20,201	36,275	23,290	37,469	23,443	77,318	53,808	78,554	—
20,160	36,730	23,443	36,730	23,443	78,562	53,841	78,562	53,841
+41	−455	−150	+739	—	−824	−37	—	—
—	—	158	—	—	—	39	—	—
—	630	—	—	—	868	—	—	—
—	—	—	2,009		159		—	—
—	6,514	—		—	8,975		—	
03.3	123,424		114,456		741,766		731,109	
03.3	129,938		116,465		750,900		—	
—	13,473		—		19,791		—	

In addition, the Treaty system is deficient by 218 mw of energy and 242 mw of thermal capacity as compared with the thermal installation of the domestic system. To determine the amount of energy required net of secondary hydro, in this case, reliance had to be placed on the secondary energy data available from the 1974–75 system regulation, as neither twenty- nor thirty-year regulations were performed for the Treaty system. The average energy and surplus secondary available from the Bonneville Power Administration study 75-1 was used for this purpose and is believed to provide a good index of the amount of secondary available for fuel displacement as all of the storage in the system is assumed to have been developed and in operation in the BPA 75-1 system study. Average energy and surplus secondary from twenty- and thirty-year regulations were available on the domestic system (RFF-4) as the total system storage is not assumed to be in operation before the 1983–84 period. With the secondary energy data drawn from the above studies, the fossil fuel requirements net of fuel displacement energy for the Treaty and domestic systems respectively are 3,415 and 3,034 average mw.

The hydro configuration for the year 1988–89 (low load forecast; 1981–82 high load) shows the following differences:

Treaty System			Domestic System		
Projects	Units	Annual costs ($000)	Projects	Units	Annual costs ($000)
Libby	4	18,094	The Dalles	2	961
Kootenai Falls	3	4,828	John Day	2	1,144
Kerr	1	100*	Penny Cliffs	4	11,298
Hells Canyon	1	200*	Lower Canyon	4	11,828
Total		23,222	Total		25,231

Net difference in hydro component ($000) 2,009
*Nominal values as direct estimates were not available.

Attention should be drawn to the fact that the International Work Group study for 1988–89 shows only three units at Knowles, whereas in the above comparison it was assumed the Treaty system would have the same number of units installed at Knowles as did the domestic (four each), especially since the Treaty system for the previous period indicated four units installed at Knowles. Accordingly, the capacity adjustment appropriate to the inclusion of one unit above that shown in the International Work Group study has been made in the system comparisons for 1988–89 in this study.

Neither twenty- nor thirty-year regulations were available for the total system, whether Treaty or domestic, for the 1988–89 system configuration. Again, to estimate the net fossil fuel requirement, the secondary energy given in the BPA study 75-1 was used for the Treaty system, and the corresponding data for the domestic system were taken from the RFF-4 twenty- and thirty-year regulations. In both cases the average energy may have been understated slightly as the increased units in the 1988–89 system configurations would on the average tend to reduce some spilling. In any event, as an estimate of the fuel displacement, the data used will reduce fossil fuel requirements for both systems approximately in the right proportions. Thus, fuel requirements for the Treaty and domestic systems are, respectively, 6,262 average mw and 5,807 average mw.

The cost differences in the hydro system configurations for the year 2010–11 are given below:

Treaty System			Domestic System		
Projects	Units	Annual costs ($000)	Projects	Units	Annual costs ($000)
Libby	4	20,934	Penny Cliffs	4	11,298
Kootenai Falls	5	5,545	Lower Canyon	8	14,998
Total		26,388	Total		26,229

Net difference in hydro component ($000)....159

In the case of the year 2010–11 system, some ambiguity may arise in the comparison of the Treaty and domestic alternatives. When the domestic system was regulated for maximum energy it was shown to be capacity deficient. Similarly, when regulated without regard to maximum critical period energy the system appeared energy deficient. As a result, the reservoirs were drafted in the simulated regulations in such a manner as to balance the capacity and energy. For the Treaty system, again there was no true critical period. To obtain the energy component of the system, the Corps of Engineers study C-37 was used to obtain the twenty-two-month continuous power generation, using the capacity data as given in exhibits C-12 and C-14 in the International Work Group's technical report. I am not clear whether this comparison results in as "lean" a thermal requirement for the Treaty system as might be possible with some modification of the reservoir operations. It has been used above, however, in the absence of a system simulation that achieves greater comparability with the RFF-5A simulation. With this qualification, the fossil fuel requirement, net of secondary hydro replacement, is 37,634 average mw and 37,093 average mw, respectively, for the Treaty and domestic systems.

FLOOD CONTROL ASPECTS

To evaluate the difference in performance of the two systems with respect to flood damage reduction provided by each, the differences in the amount of flood control storage and its timing were taken into account. Damage estimates were not available for each of the possible storage quantities; where unavailable, therefore, they were estimated by interpolation between the controlled discharge levels for which damage estimates had been prepared. [35] These involved estimates of damages for the 1894 flood flows controlled alternatively to 1,030,000 cfs (present flood control facilities), 920,000 cfs (with and without levee improvements), 800,000 cfs, 700,000 cfs and 600,000 cfs.

It was assumed that Duncan Lake would be first operable for one year before other elements of the flood damage reduction facilities could be added. This Canadian project would provide 1,270,000 acre-feet of usable storage [36] and would provide an estimated average annual equivalent of $1,220,000 in flood damage reduction (based on conditions appropriate to year 1985). During the next four years, Arrow Lakes storage with 3,135,000 additional acre-feet of usable flood control storage [37] would be operating along with Duncan Lake, to provide about 4.4 million acre-feet in total, controlling the discharge at The Dalles to about 900,000 cfs, and for a total damage reduction from present protection facilities of about $3,700,000 as an average annual equivalent. By the year 1973–74, it was assumed that all three Canadian storages along with Libby, Knowles, Dworshak, and High Mountain Sheep, would be in operation in the Treaty system, controlling discharges to about

[35] Determination of Average Annual Damages (work sheets), NPP Form 285, U.S. Army Engineer Division, North Pacific, Portland District.

[36] *Columbia River Negotiations, Views of the United States Negotiation Team, Flood Control*, May 15, 1960.

[37] *Ibid.*

600,000 cfs at The Dalles. The domestic system was assumed to have Knowles, Dworshak, and High Mountain Sheep, in total controlling discharges equivalent to the flood of 1894, to 860,000 cfs at The Dalles. The difference in flood damage reduction of $2,500,000 as an average annual equivalent favored the Treaty system, and was assumed to remain for a period of seven years. By the year 1980–81, it was assumed that Penny Cliffs and Lower Canyon would be added to the domestic system, capable of controlling flood discharges to about 750,000 cfs at The Dalles. This would reduce the difference in the damage prevention between the two systems to about $1,090,000, as an annual average equivalent for the remainder of the fifty-year period of evaluation. These average annual equivalent sums discounted at ˙4 per cent gave a present value of approximately $41,225,000, or the increased value of flood protection provided by the Treaty system as compared with the domestic system.

In addition, the Treaty system would make unnecessary local flood protection works on the Kootenai in the vicinity of Bonners Ferry, representing an additional saving of about $9.5 million,[38] for a total of approximately $50,725,000 as a present value.

[38] *Report of Survey for Flood Control of Kootenai River in Kootenai Flats Area, Idaho,* U.S. Army Engineer Division, North Pacific, Seattle District, December 1, 1958.

PART III

The Columbia River Treaty, 1961-64

Chapter 8

Second Phase of Negotiations

Although possibilities for international development of the Columbia had been explored since 1944, it was not until 1960 that negotiations on the Treaty itself began. This being the final year of the Eisenhower Administration, it was natural that both the United States and Canada should want to finalize the Treaty before a change in administration took place. If for no other reason, the agreement was put together with a shared sense of urgency, and as a result some matters essential to implementing the Treaty were reserved for later attention.

In Canada, one of the significant matters left unsettled involved arrangements for financing the Canadian-based Treaty projects and definition of the respective roles and responsibilities of the provincial and federal governments. Even when the Treaty was signed, an early resolution of the issues was not very promising and, in point of fact, the complex issues were not ultimately resolved before July of 1963, more than two years after the Treaty had been signed by the two countries and ratified by the United States.

Part of the difficulty revolved around the degree of control which the federal government in Ottawa was to exercise over the Columbia River power policy and associated matters. And part of the difficulty may have resulted from related developments in British Columbia which will be outlined here.

As far back as 1956, investigations of the potentials of the Peace River were taken over by the Wenner-Gren B.C. Development Company, Ltd., under arrangements with the government of British Columbia. In 1958, a series of investigations commissioned by the Wenner-Gren interests was undertaken, at which point the Peace River Power Development Company, Ltd. was formed to take over the commitments of the Wenner-Gren B.C. Development

153

Company. A report on the power development was completed in December of 1959, [1] and steps were taken toward securing a license for development.

To British Columbia, one of the attractive features of the Peace development was its location in the central interior of the province, much of which was undeveloped. (See Figure 26.) The government of British Columbia, therefore, regarded the potentialities of the Peace River project as an instrument for the economic development of the interior.

In the course of the protracted negotiations between the province and the federal government, the provincial authorities moved along with plans for the Peace River country. In fact, even shortly before the signing of the Treaty, the British Columbia Energy Board had been requested to study the comparative costs of power from the Peace and the Columbia, the relationship between the two, and the conditions under which they would be complementary developments. [2]

The report of the British Columbia Energy Board, based on the investigation of a consortium of consulting engineers, [3] was made during mid-1961. [4] Among its significant findings was one to the effect that if the Peace were developed as a public undertaking of the kind called for in the plans for the prospective Columbia development, and if the returns from the proposed flood control benefits of the Columbia were excluded, the cost of power from the two sources would be approximately equal. A choice between the two developments, if one was to be made, would have to be based on considerations other than comparative power costs. The report went on to say that some advantages would be realized from simultaneous development of both power sources, but in this event the market in British Columbia would not be sufficient to absorb the power from both. Considering the necessity for exporting power surplus to British Columbia's needs, the report identified the Pacific Northwest in the United States as the most promising potential market. [5] The advantages which the Columbia would enjoy

[1] *Peace River Hydro-Electric Project*, Peace River Power Development Company, Ltd., December, 1959.

[2] Minute No. 2905 of the Lieutenant-Governor in Council, December 27, 1960.

[3] Sir Alexander Gibb and Partners and Merz and McLellan, *Columbia and Peace Power Projects: Report on Power Costs*, report to the British Columbia Engineering Board, July 1961.

[4] *Report on the Columbia and Peace Projects* (Victoria, B.C.: British Columbia Energy Board, July 31, 1961).

[5] *Ibid.*, pp. 28–29.

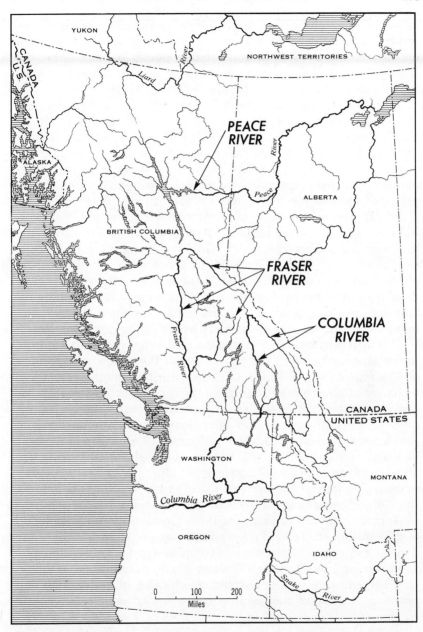

Figure 26. Location of the Peace, Fraser, and Columbia rivers in British Columbia. (Source: R.L. Chantrill and Jack D. Stevens, *Power Capabilities and Operating Aspects of the Peace River Project and a Pacific International Power Pool*, Peace River Power Development Co., Ltd., Vancouver, May 1960.)

as a source of the export power were emphasized, since a substantial part of the power gain from Canadian storage development on the Columbia would be generated at plants downstream in the United States in any event, thus requiring no transmission facilities to be built in Canada for this purpose.

Following this report by the B.C. Energy Board, the government of British Columbia took over ownership of the Peace River Power Development Company, B.C. Engineering Company, and the B.C. Electric Company—a stockholder in the first and parent company of the second.[6] The conversion of these private companies to Crown corporation status had two significant effects: It prepared the way for development of the Peace project with financial arrangements somewhat more favorable than would have been the case under private auspices. And it gained control over the major power market in British Columbia (the former B.C. Electric Company's service area) which, in the absence of sanction to export power, was essential to the viability of any large-scale power development in British Columbia. The province coincidentally reaffirmed its determination to pursue its "two-river policy" and announced that an immediate start would be made on the Peace.

This turn of events complicated the problem of reaching a mutual understanding between the province and the federal government of Canada. Two years were to elapse, during which Canada saw a change of government in Ottawa, before an accord between the province and the federal government could be reached.[7] Among other matters covered by the agreement was the intent to sell in the United States Canada's entitlement of downstream power benefits, and to use the proceeds of such sale for financing the Treaty storage projects. The agreement also provided for Canada's undertaking formal negotiations with the United States to achieve these objectives along with certain modifications and/or clarification of the terms of the Treaty of 1961. Upon successful completion of this mission the federal government was prepared to submit the Treaty and related agreements to Parliament for ratification.

The negotiations to which Canada was now committed, it should be observed, were for the purpose of achieving objectives that had been ruled outside the feasible range under policies governing

[6] Power Development Act, 1961 (Second Session, Ch. 4), assented to August 3, 1961.

[7] Canada–British Columbia Agreement, July 8, 1963, reprinted in *The Columbia River Treaty, Protocol and Related Documents* (Ottawa: Departments of External Affairs, and Northern Affairs and National Resources, February 1964).

during the original negotiations leading to the Treaty of 1961. When at that time Canada rejected the invitation to make power available to the United States from Canadian development and declined the proffer of financial assistance in constructing the Treaty projects, some of the alternatives relevant to the Columbia River in Canada were precluded from serious consideration. It will be recalled from Chapter 6 that accelerated development appropriate to U.S. power requirements with consequent excess capacity in relation to B.C. power loads had been dominant considerations in early negotiations when British Columbia advanced its proposals for the Kootenays. Now, however, technical information previously held by the B.C. Engineering Company was publicly available, and the launching of the Peace development in British Columbia further enlarged the range of information on technical alternatives within which consideration of the Columbia development could take place. In short, during the two and one-half years between the signing of the Treaty and the Canada–British Columbia agreement of July 1963, the course of events had produced some fundamental changes in circumstances which differed markedly from the assumptions underlying the negotiation of the Treaty of 1961.

In the United States, similarly, the circumstances that dominated the Treaty negotiations had changed considerably. The projected growth in load in the Pacific Northwest failed to materialize quite as had been anticipated, thus eliminating the need for an early block of low-cost energy previously thought to be required by 1965. Moreover, a change in administration in Washington had produced a more sympathetic attitude toward federal development of domestic resources in the Pacific Northwest. The Dworshak project was authorized and its construction begun, providing some of the required storage for power and flood control in the Columbia Basin. Aggressive executive branch support for the Knowles project on the Pend Oreille in the upper Columbia system improved the prospects for its authorization and construction, in the absence of Treaty storage. Downstream on the Pend Oreille the Boundary project was getting under way, and the Federal Power Commission had licensed the High Mountain Sheep project for private development. Arrangements for construction of the Hanford New Production Reactor were completed, adding a substantial source of new power to the regional power supply in the Pacific Northwest. And, partly as a result of the stimulus provided by the Federal Power Commission's National Power Survey and advances in extra-high voltage transmission technology, interest in electrical interconnection among regional power systems was heightened. Hence the prospect for interconnecting the Pacific Northwest with the systems in California and the Southwest was improved. An intertie of this sort promised to substitute in part for storage in the Columbia Basin by making use of the large amounts of otherwise unsalable secondary energy as well as improving prospects for a market for the excess peaking capability in the Columbia hydro system.

The significance of these shifts in parameters had implications of two sorts for the negotiations which began in August of 1963. First, the question could be raised whether the change in circumstances permitted a more efficient design for the Treaty system than had been available under the original policy, technical, and informational constraints. Second, since the reopening of negotiations now looked toward the disposition of Canada's share of downstream power in the United States rather than its repatriation to British Columbia, how would the results of the negotiated terms of sale conform to the IJC principles: that is, would both countries, as a result of the co-operative undertaking, advance to a position superior to one that could have been achieved if each, acting independently, had relied on its domestic resources alone?

BASIC ISSUES

Given the circumstances outlined above, two alternative courses of action could be taken. First, in the light of the broader range of information and possibilities now available, the entire question of system design and benefit sharing could be opened anew with a view to revising the original agreement prior to ratification by the Canadian government. This, however, would entail resubmission of the Treaty in its revised form to the United States Senate. Second, since opening the Treaty for major revision would require extensive new negotiations with unpredictable outcome, the provisions of the Treaty of 1961 might be left unaltered except for arrangements for the disposition of the Canadian downstream power entitlement and financing the Treaty projects in Canada. If the latter course were chosen there would be no necessity to resubmit the Treaty for U.S. ratification.

The first course of action would subject to investigation once again the whole matter of determining the potential sites to be developed. For example, in 1963, with prospects for an advance of capital for the construction of projects of mutual interest in Canada, and the option to sell large blocks of energy in the United States, the problem of surplus capacity and financial stress that had been significant in influencing the selection of the Treaty projects in 1960 would no longer appear so oppressive to British Columbia. The difference of up to 1½ per cent in rate of interest on Canadian Treaty project costs as compared with domestic sources of financing, which figured in the original studies affecting the decision, would represent a present worth on the order of a hundred million dollars, or a reduction of that amount in Canadian Treaty project costs and financing.

A consideration of this sort also had economic implications for a choice between the Peace and the Columbia developments. If both were financed by domestic public capital, comparative costs of power for the two were approximately equal under certain conditions; but an advance of funds from the United States in exchange for Canada's downstream entitlement would reduce Canadian outlays for the Columbia to approximately the same level as for the Peace project, with close to 400 mw of additional power available from at-site generation at Mica and complementary power production from run-of-the-river plants on the Columbia River in Canada.

However, should the Peace, for policy reasons in British Columbia, be considered as independent of any decision with respect to the Columbia, its independent existence with enormous storage capacity would raise questions about the design capacity on the Columbia. Interconnection of the Peace and Columbia hydro systems through transmission facilities to load centers on the lower mainland would permit the sale of otherwise unusable secondary energy from the Columbia whenever good water years made it available, while storing energy in the Peace reservoir for release to firm the Columbia secondary energy during years of low flow. [8]

In addition, Pacific Northwest loads were increasing at a slower rate than had been expected. Moreover, alternative arrangements for power supply were scheduled for the mid-1960's (which High

[8] With only the Mica project and Downie Creek and Revelstoke Canyon run-of-the-river projects considered as added to the existing facilities on the Columbia, the load-carrying capability of the Peace and Columbia systems, if interconnected as above, would be increased by a million kilowatts of firm power. See R. L. Chantrill and Jack D. Stevens, *Power Capabilities and Operating Aspects of the Peace River Project and a Pacific International Power Pool* (Vancouver, B.C.: Peace River Power Development Co., Ltd., May 1960).

Arrow had been initially calculated to meet). These factors affected
the justification of the Arrow project as an integral part of an efficient power system. The value of Arrow Lakes storage, considered
incremental to Kootenay storage and Mica, was not very large
either with respect to power production or flood damage reduction.
The function of the Arrow Lakes and Duncan storages, in fact,
could be discharged by Mica and East Kootenay storage if the
Peace and Columbia hydro systems were integrated. [9]

With these changed conditions in Canada, plus the new markets
for secondary energy in California and the Southwest opened up
by the Northwest-Southwest intertie, it is clear that the justifiable
volume of storage on the Columbia surplus to the need for flood
control (6.5 million acre-feet) required re-evaluation.

It has been mentioned that when the government of British
Columbia took over the B.C. Engineering Company, Ltd. and
related facilities, it obtained access to hitherto privately owned
technical information. A part of this information dealt with thermal
alternatives based on coal deposits in the Hat Creek area which had
been investigated by B.C. Engineering on behalf of its parent company, B.C. Electric Company. [10]

Sufficient low-cost, albeit low-grade, coal was available in the
vicinity of Hat Creek to provide for up to 2 million kilowatts of
power over the service life of steam electric stations at costs comparable to any known source of supply in British Columbia. [11] In
some respects, in the absence of arrangements to export power from
large-scale hydro development, these thermal facilities afforded a
flexible means by which to bring inexpensive power to load centers
in increments scaled appropriately to the size of the British
Columbia market; whereas the Columbia developed under co-
operative conditions could involve so sizable an increment of
capacity that some part would remain unutilized for varying peri-

[9] Cf. testimony of Richard Deane, in *Columbia River Treaty and Protocol, Minutes
of Proceedings and Evidence*, No. 21, Standing Committee on External Affairs,
House of Commons, Twenty-Sixth Parliament, Second Session, May 7, 1964,
pp. 1042, 1049, and 1053-54. It has been suggested to me that this is true only
if the Canadian and United States portions of the Columbia were fully integrated.
Negotiations between the two countries would be required to achieve this, and
absence of storage below Mica Creek (namely, Arrow), it is maintained, would
deprive the Canadians of a viable negotiating position.

[10] *Hat Creek Power Project*, British Columbia Engineering Company, Ltd., 1961.

[11] John C. Davis, "Power Benefits and Costs in British Columbia," paper presented before the Benefits and Costs Workshop, Resources for Tomorrow Con-
ference, Montreal, October 1, 1961.

ods, depending on the development of electrical loads. Hence, the Hat Creek thermal operation enjoyed some advantages over both the Peace and Columbia developments, and could have been regarded as a logical step in building up the system to the point at which the British Columbia market for power could accommodate efficiently additional capacity of the scale represented by the larger lower-cost hydro developments.

On the other hand, while the thermal development could be postponed without critically affecting its ultimate economy for British Columbia, the Peace could not be delayed without ill effects upon the developmental thrust its construction and operation was expected to impart to the central British Columbia economy; neither could the Columbia Treaty projects be deferred indefinitely without adverse implications for the value of the downstream benefits originally secured through skillful and arduous negotiation. These being highly specific to conditions in 1960, any postponement of the Treaty projects beyond the point the United States would indulge would erode if not eliminate the benefit Canada could hope to realize from any future co-operative effort on the Columbia.[12] Canada also recognized that in the absence of substantial gains from a co-operative undertaking, development of the Columbia River by Canada would be a marginal undertaking. Thus, it was conceded that deferring the Treaty projects in favor of some alternative source of power would not in the long run be wise if Canada should ever have to rely on the Columbia for power.

While the Columbia as a source of energy for British Columbia seemed likely to provide power more economically than the Peace,[13] government policy in British Columbia tended to regard the two hydro developments not as alternative sources of near-term supply, but as separate instruments for achieving different goals. In the autumn following the B.C.-Canada accord of July 1963, the government of British Columbia went to the people, in effect submitting the power policy of the government to a referendum at the polls. While additional issues crept into the campaign locally, if the central issue remained the "Two-River Policy" of the

[12] John V. Krutilla, *The Columbia River Treaty, an International Evaluation* (Washington, D.C.: Resources for the Future, Inc., 1963), pp. 15 ff.

[13] This assumes reduction in the cost of the full development of the Columbia by an amount equal to the receipt of funds for sale of downstream power entitlement, and relying upon the at-site generation from Mica and the complementary run-of-the-river plants on the Columbia River in Canada. See Sir Alexander Gibb and Partners and Merz and McLellan, *op. cit.*

government it was supported by the electorate. The question of choice between the Columbia and the Peace, therefore, no longer remained at issue. The Peace would become an instrument for economic development of the interior of the province. The Columbia, with prospective advances of investment funds from the United States in return for downstream storage benefits, could provide one of the lowest-cost reservations of energy on the North American continent when it became expedient to employ the Columbia's potential to meet British Columbia's requirements.

With such prospects in mind, and with the knowledge that conditions in the United States had become less favorable for winning concessions of the sort obtained by the Treaty of 1961, Canada was unwilling to risk reopening old issues in pursuit of a more efficient total program.[14] Thus, Canada adopted a course of action which looked toward protecting all provisions of the Treaty of 1961, with the exception of repatriation of downstream power entitlement and capital advances to finance the Treaty projects.

TECHNICAL ISSUES

With Canada now looking toward the sale of its power entitlement and, as it developed, having as an objective a prior lump-sum settlement which would provide funds for the construction of Treaty projects, the negotiators were confronted with the problem of making an advance determination of the amount of power that would represent Canada's power entitlement.[15] It became clear that many assumptions would need to be made[16] with respect both to the conditions in the future and to the resolution of questions on which the Treaty had not been explicit. Over a dozen assumptions were identified that had implications for the quantum of power to which Canada would be entitled. Of these, about two-thirds were regarded to be either of minor significance or, if potentially so, of

[14] Notwithstanding this fact, the pressures of domestic Canadian politics appear to have made both Canadian governments, albeit for different reasons, highly motivated to harden the bargain in the limited negotiations that did take place.

[15] Since the assumptions underlying the original Treaty arrangements did not contemplate the sale of Canadian entitlement, provision was made only for periodic evaluation of its size under actual operating conditions, which would become known at some future time when the repatriation deliveries were to be made.

[16] *Columbia River Development: Determination of Canadian Downstream Power Entitlement*, Technical Report, Work Group No. 1, November 1963.

an indeterminate character. Several, however, were quite significant and attention was given them in negotiating the final agreement.

The matter of estimating future loads in the United States was carefully considered. A rapid rate of load development implied an accelerated installation of thermal plants in the Pacific Northwest, with the attendant possibility of using river flows more nearly as they occurred to displace fuel requirements, and thus limiting reliance on storage. The Canadian entitlement could be affected by up to 18 per cent, it was estimated, depending on whether a high or low load forecast was assumed to be appropriate.[17] Another matter of perhaps equal significance was the difference in Canadian entitlement depending upon whether the streamflows of twenty years, as indicated in the Treaty, were to be used, or the longer thirty-year period of record. Canadian entitlement would be about 14 per cent greater if the thirty-year flows were to be adopted.[18]

A point of disagreement revolved about the Grand Coulee irrigation pumping load. In the United States the Bureau of Reclamation had reserved a quantity of power to pump irrigation water supplies from the reservoir into a retention basin before the remainder was permitted to enter the Bonneville Power Administration marketing system. For this purpose, the pumping requirements at Grand Coulee were considered "negative generation" and deducted from area loads in conventional BPA calculations. In the absence of large blocks of storage such as were envisaged in the Treaty, Bureau of Reclamation pumping requirements utilized dump power because the pumping occurred during the season of high flow when large amounts of surplus non-salable secondary energy were available. With the addition of Treaty storage, however, the critical period would be extended from the current seven months to an over-the-year twenty-month period during which there would be generation for pumping purposes. The Canadian capacity entitlement had been defined in the Treaty as the difference between the average rates of generation during the critical streamflow periods with and without such storage operating in the system.

[17] While this was felt to be the order of magnitude of the difference depending on what assumption was made regarding the rate of growth of load, my own sensitivity analyses do not support so large a difference on this account.

[18] In my analysis of the value of Canadian storage to the United States, in Chapter 9, the low load forecast is used as well as a thirty-year period of record, so as to provide the most favorable conditions for evaluation of Canadian storage.

This would make a difference in the Canadian entitlement of up to 70–80 mw of capacity compared with the conventional way in which the Grand Coulee pumping loads were treated for BPA purposes, and would be reflected in a 4 to 5 per cent difference in the present worth of the Canadian entitlement.

A further difficulty of critical dimensions developed when the Canadian and U.S. technical personnel differed over an interpretation of the term "base system"—central to the determination of Canadian capacity entitlement. In the pre-Treaty work by joint technical teams, the base system used to illustrate the application of procedures for measuring Canadian entitlement had included existing thermal capacity, and the results obtained had reflected a pattern of capacity benefit decline over time which was accepted by all parties, both in joint endeavors[19] and in independent evaluations.[20] In drafting Annex B of the Treaty of 1961, however, a reference to existing thermal resources had been inadvertently omitted from Paragraph 2—a key paragraph specifying the limitation on Canadian capacity credit—although it had been included in Paragraph 7, which deals with the procedure for determining Canadian benefits. Canada, for negotiation purposes, chose to rely on a literal interpretation of Paragraph 2 which did not acknowledge existing thermal capacity in the base system. The capacity creditable to Canada under this interpretation would be limited only by its ability to peak the hydro energy of the Columbia.

The consequences of such an interpretation could be drastic. For example: At a time when capacity benefits would be reduced to zero under established practice, under the Canadian interpretation the United States would be liable for installing over a million kilowatts of thermal capacity to meet Canada's capacity entitlement. Nevertheless, the wording of the paragraph in question appears to support the Canadian position, and it thus provided the basis for further negotiation whereby the United States ultimately was prepared to concede on technical issues, such as the thirty-year record and Grand Coulee pumping, in order to have the interpretation set aside.

[19] E.g., *Columbia River Negotiations, Summary Report No. 1*, International Work Group, May 10, 1960.

[20] E.g., *Report on the Columbia and Peace Power Projects, op. cit.*, and staff studies by the Water Rights Branch of the provincial government and Water Resources Branch of the federal government.

FINAL ARRANGEMENTS

By the time the terms of sale of Canadian downstream entitlement entered the decisive phase of negotiation, it had been established that the Bonneville Power Administration, under its enabling legislation, was not permitted to purchase power for resale except for firming energy. It could, however, in the interest of facilitating an acceptable arrangement, serve as a broker between the British Columbia Hydro and Power Authority and third parties in the United States which would be interested in purchasing Canadian entitlement. Toward this end, a consortium of utilities in the Pacific Northwest undertook to form a corporate entity to become known as the Columbia Storage Power Exchange, which would be the initial recipient of Canadian Treaty entitlement. Accordingly, representatives of this group, along with the Bonneville Power Administration, the U.S. Army Corps of Engineers, and the U.S. Department of State, participated in the negotiation of the final terms of sale.

In brief, a figure equivalent to approximately $305 million (payable in eight annual installments), plus the flood control advances totaling $64 million (payable in three parts on the initiation of flood control operations at each of the three Canadian storage projects) were the terms of ultimate settlement.

In addressing the question concerning the precise time at which the funds for construction would be required if Duncan storage was to be in operation during 1968, High Arrow during 1969, and Mica by 1973, and the time required by the United States interests to complete arrangements with respect to organizing the Columbia Storage Power Exchange, it was decided that October 1, 1964 be designated as the target date for exchange of ratification and transfer of funds, and that all capital sums would be computed on the basis of worth as of that date. It was mutually agreed, therefore, that $254 million (U.S.) would constitute the advance payment for the Canadian power entitlement, and $54 million the flood control equivalent as of October 1964. An interest rate of 4.5 per cent was designated as the rate by which these sums would be adjusted if the actual exchanges departed in any direction from the target date.

The agreement was formally executed January 22, 1964,[21]

[21] Annex to Exchange of Notes Dated January 22, 1964 between the Governments of Canada and the United States regarding the Columbia Treaty, Washington, D.C., January 22, 1964.

whereupon the Canadian government prepared to submit the Treaty and related agreements to Parliament for ratification and the United States set into motion the organization of the independent consortium of Pacific Northwest utilities which was to serve as the entity for purchasing the Canadian entitlement. The Treaty was ratified by Parliament in May of 1964; the consortium was established and a bond issue of $314 million was successfully floated at an effective interest rate of 3.875 per cent. The formal exchanges of ratification took place on September 16, 1964, bringing to a conclusion twenty years of international co-operative effort in search of agreement.

During the second phase of negotiations culminating in the exchange of ratification, British Columbia had successfully accomplished its major objectives. It was to receive a capital sum equivalent to the cost of constructing all the Treaty projects in Canada, with a residual equivalent to almost half the cost of installing generators at the Mica project.[22] By obtaining a lump-sum advance settlement in exchange for the downstream benefits occurring in the United States reaches of the Columbia, it secured beneficial stream regulation for itself from the Mica reservoir which increases the amount of firm power to be ultimately produced at the Downie Creek and Revelstoke Canyon run-of-the-river plants by about 700 mw as well as additional firm power at the Murphy Creek project on the mainstem in British Columbia. In addition, regulation provided by the Kootenay storages affords both flood protection in the Creston Flats area and increased firm power on the lower Kootenay. At the Mica site alone, the savings in cost of producing power resulting from the international arrangements have been estimated to approximate $16 million annually,[23] with additional savings realized at the run-of-the-river plants on the Columbia and lower Kootenay. The precise sum as a present worth, however, cannot be readily computed; this will depend on the timing of the generation at Mica and construction of complementary facilities in Canada. It is clear that while the benefits in total will be very large,[24] the present value will be somewhat diminished by

[22] *The Columbia River Treaty and Protocol: A Presentation* (Ottawa: Departments of External Affairs and Northern Affairs and National Resources, April 1964), p. 96.

[23] H. L. Keenleyside, "The Columbia River Agreement," an address to the Vancouver Board of Trade, February 10, 1964.

[24] As an example, the present value of $16 million/year over a fifty-year term at 4 and 5.5 per cent comes to $343 million and $271 million, respectively.

the deferment of the Columbia as a source of power to meet British Columbia requirements. The difference in present worth of the savings in Mica generation, for example, will be approximately $46 million, depending on whether it is machined for operation in 1973, upon completion of the storage, or in 1980 to pick up the Canadian load which by then will exceed the capability of the Peace project. Thus, while British Columbia's objective to provide for a large block of low-cost power potential in the Columbia for future use was successfully accomplished, the present worth of this reservation is somewhat smaller the longer development of the Columbia for British Columbia loads is deferred.

In view of the imponderables governing even the above calculations, one can do no more than speculate whether or not the potential benefits to British Columbia would have been greater had the second phase of negotiations opened the original Treaty to renegotiation. Doubtless, several opportunities to effect economies might have been realized, given the accumulation of new information, enlarged technical opportunities, and changes in policy parameters. But if, as is more than likely, substantially different projects, sequences, and technical combinations had emerged, it is not at all clear that the resulting benefit division would have better served British Columbia objectives. The only gains in economy resulting from the second phase of negotiations were achieved through the use of superior financial resources. In this respect, the effective rate for British Columbia's project financing was reduced from 5.5 per cent to 4.5 per cent. It may be noted also that since the effective rate for the Columbia Storage Power Exchange bond issue was ultimately 3.875 per cent, the United States entity, in effect, shared to an extent in the gain in economy resulting from the use of superior financial resources.

The Protocol and Sales Agreement results have implications for the United States somewhat more complex than for Canada. The consequences of the second phase of negotiations for the United States merit considerable attention and will be dealt with in Chapter 9.

Chapter 9

Comparative Cost of Columbia Treaty System and United States Domestic System

In Chapter 7 an effort was made to evaluate the cost behavior of the Columbia Treaty system as compared with alternative domestic means of achieving equivalent results in the circumstances existing in 1961. This was done in order to determine whether or not the benefit division met the test of IJC General Principle No. 2. As closely as could be determined, the provisions of the Treaty of 1961 were quite favorable to Canada, resulting in a savings in cost of approximately one-quarter to one-half billion dollars. A substantial share of these savings to Canada did not result from increased economy due to co-operation, but from the heavy costs to the United States of its portion of the Columbia system, given the division of the downstream benefits. Excess costs of the Treaty system for the United States were found to approximate a quarter of a billion dollars. One important reason for this was that the amount of power obtainable from the Columbia as a result of the Treaty storage and benefit division averaged less for the United States than that available from the Columbia under independent development (see Table 26). But perhaps equally important was inclusion of the very high-cost Kootenai developments which were a related product of the Treaty.

To the extent that the cost of the United States portion of the Columbia system is increased by inclusion of the Libby and Kootenai Falls projects, nothing in the Protocol Note and Sales Agreement resulting from the second phase of negotiations would alter this particular cost factor. On the other hand, since the terms of the Treaty of 1961 were altered to require the United States to

169

buy the Canadian share of the nominal downstream benefits, more power would be available from the hydro system under the Treaty than under a completely domestic alternative. The comparative cost of the alternatives could be expected to be largely a function of the price which the United States was required to pay for retaining the Canadian entitlement; i.e., if the price of the net gain in power output resulting from Canadian storage operations were less than the cost of alternative sources of supply for the United States, the previously demonstrated disadvantage of the Treaty system could be narrowed or eliminated. If the price were greater than the cost of alternative sources of power, however, the excess cost of the Treaty system would be increased.

The problem of evaluating the alternative, however, is additionally complicated. Aside from the change in requirements to repatriate the Canadian power entitlement, a new element had been introduced by the time the exchange of ratification took place, in 1964. The efforts to negotiate an understanding among United States domestic interests looking toward the construction of the Pacific Northwest–California and Southwest intertie culminated in success coincident with completion of all arrangements preliminary to implementation of the Treaty.

While the intertie was required partly to aid in the disposal of Canadian entitlement which the United States was obligated to take, its construction greatly reduces the value of the storage for power purposes. Instead of a gradual reduction in the value of storage as the Northwest power system evolves into a predominantly thermal system, the interconnection of the Northwest system with the thermal systems of California and the Southwest immediately provides conditions comparable to those expected in the Northwest after fifteen or twenty years of Treaty storage. More of the unregulated streamflows could be used as they occur, since a market for secondary energy as fuel replacement in the Southwest becomes available immediately. Moreover, the Northwest's importation of economy energy during periods of adverse streamflows is an alternative way of firming up a substantial portion of the Columbia system secondary energy. This latter aspect of the intertie has significant implications for the value of storage in the hydro system, because important displacement effects characterize the relation between storage and intertie operations.[1] Accordingly, before the cost behavior of the Treaty system, as reflected in the 1964 terms

---

[1] See Chapter 3, pp. 46 ff.

of the international agreement, can be compared with that of an alternative domestic system, we need to address the economics of the intertie operation.

We shall consider below the amount and disposition of secondary energy associated with the hydro system operated to maximize its firm load-carrying capability. In this respect, the intertie is treated as "second-added" to the storage in place at any point of time.[2] On the other hand, because in the domestic system the intertie is combined with a much lower volume of storage at any point in time than is the Treaty system, we can observe the extent to which the intertie may substitute for Treaty storage. Details of the cost performance of the two alternatives are given in the last section of this chapter. From them we can infer the shortfall, from the United States power supply standpoint, of the 1964 Treaty terms and provisions for sharing the nominal benefits.

ECONOMIC EFFECTS OF THE INTERTIE

The extra-high-voltage transmission interconnection of the Northwest and Southwest will have numerous economizing features. Among the more significant are: (1) the reduction in required reserves in the two power regions by virtue of the reduced probability of simultaneous forced outages; (2) a possible reduction in the amount of thermal capacity required in both regions (in future) by reason of potential seasonal load diversity; (3) probable increased firm power without associated capacity installation by virtue of the potential hydrologic diversity between the Columbia and the Colorado River in the Southwest; (4) the increase in firm power in the Northwest by use of diurnal off-peak economy energy from the Southwest; and (5) increased use of secondary energy through sales of surplus secondary in California and Southwest markets via the intertie.

If one were asking whether or not the intertie is an economic undertaking, all of the economizing aspects of the intertie would need to be evaluated to determine if their estimated present value

[2] This procedure has the effect of considering the intertie second-added after storage provided subsequent to the intertie, but was required to simplify the computer simulation of the hydro systems. However, since we have the analyses conducted for two levels of storage, i.e., Treaty system and the lesser domestic system storage, the performance of the systems can be compared to infer the net gain of the Treaty system due to Treaty storage.

for each scale increment exceeds the incremental intertie cost, and if the total of such benefits exceeds the total costs. This question, however, is not relevant to the particular problem[3] of this study. Here, the intertie's existence is taken as given for both the Treaty and domestic system and what is evaluated is only the differential effects of the intertie with, or alternatively without, the Treaty storage in the hydro system.

It is unlikely that economizing features (1) and (2) would have any differential impact on the two alternatives; thus, we do not concern ourselves with them. Feature (3), the increase in firm power for the Northwest, due to hydrologic diversity between the Columbia and the Colorado, would probably have a differential effect favoring the domestic alternative, as this system will have less storage than the Treaty system. Neither existing analyses nor the scope of this study, however, permit our addressing this question, but it is unlikely that the differential effects due to this characteristic will be of the same order of significance as the differential impact of the intertie on the Treaty and domestic systems felt through characteristics (4) and (5) noted above. For this reason, analysis of the intertie will be confined to evaluating the increased firm load-carrying capability of the intertie for the Northwest, and the increased sales of surplus energy from the Northwest to markets in California and the Southwest.

How much firm power will it be economical to obtain in the Northwest by means of the intertie? This will depend on quite a number of factors: (1) amount of excess hydro capacity in the system; (2) amount of secondary energy; (3) the price of energy sold as secondary energy; (4) the price of energy sold as firm; (5) the amount and cost of economy imported energy; (6) the

---

[3] The economics of the intertie have been investigated by Joel Bergsman in *Economic Problems in Electric Power System Planning*, Publication EEP-6 (Stanford University, July 1963), and by Edouard André Sautter in *Studies in the Long-Range Planning of Interties between Electric Power Systems*, Report EEP-11 (Stanford University, Institute in Engineering-Economics Systems, July 1964). Bergsman evaluated the optimal capacity of the intertie in terms of energy flows from the Northwest to the Southwest. Sautter evaluated the optimal scale of the intertie in the light of seasonal load diversities between the systems. In both cases about an 1,800-mw capacity intertie was identified as optimal. The capacity of the intertie as finally authorized has been set at 4,400 mw, and I shall use this capacity, although the maximum capacity for firming the secondary energy in the Northwest is found to be equal to or less than 1,800 mw. The use of the intertie for this purpose, incidentally, is compatible with its use simultaneously as visualized by Bergsman, i.e., will serve both purposes.

efficiency with which imported economy energy can be used in response to anticipated adverse streamflow conditions; and (7) the comparative cost of firming secondary energy with local thermal operations.

We can put these factors into relation with the following model: Let

Z_{ijk} = Megawatts of secondary energy in year i and month j[4] of system condition k ($k = 1,$---$,6$),

T_k = Optimal megawatts of increased firm power from intertie ($0 \leqslant T \leqslant \beta_k$), ($k = 1,$---$,6$),

K_s = Value per megawatt month of energy sold as secondary,

K_c = Cost per megawatt month of imported economy energy,

K_p = Value per megawatt month of firm power,

$1/\alpha$ = Per cent efficiency with which imported energy is used,

B_k = Megawatts of excess hydro capacity during system condition k,

R_{ijk} = Net gain in dollars in year i and month j of firming secondary energy with intertie imports during system condition k,

$\overline{R}_k$ = Average annual net gain from firming secondary energy with intertie during system condition k;

then

$$\overline{R}_k = \sum_{i}^{30} \sum_{j}^{12} R_{ijk} \Big/ 30$$

where

$$R_{ijk} = \begin{cases} K_p T_k - K_s T_k & Z_{ijk} \geqslant T_k \\ K_p T_k - K_s Z_{ijk} - K_c \left[\alpha (T_k - Z_{ijk}) \right] \\ \qquad + (\alpha - 1)(T_k - Z_{ijk}) K_s & Z_{ijk} < T_k \end{cases}$$

---

[4] The values of the Z_{ijk} are obtained from the simulation of the Treaty and domestic systems (Chapter 7, including Technical Note) for each of the six periods defined by additions of storage, hydro capacity, or thermal capacity to the system (see Table 28). The above model then permits the selection of optimal T_k for each of these periods. It should be noted that while the model is a net revenue maximizing model, the simulation model of the hydrologic system is one in which loads are met by a feasible program without explicit assurance that elements of the program have been selected in such a way and introduced in that sequence which will maximize system net benefits.

What this model indicates, in effect, is what the net monetary gain will be from firming up secondary energy for any specified amount of increased firm power sought, subject to the capacity of the intertie and the excess hydro capacity (January peaking capability less peak load requirements) in the system. [5] Given a specified level of increased firm, for any month in which the secondary energy available is equal to or greater than the increment of firm power ($Z_{ijk} \geqslant T_k$), the net gain from firming the power will be the difference between the value of the energy as firm ($K_p T_k$) and its value if sold as secondary ($K_s T_k$). That is, power used as part of the firm power commitment represents an equivalent amount that can no longer be sold as secondary.

For any month in which the amount of secondary energy available is less than the specified increment in firm power ($Z_{ijk} < T_k$), the computation becomes a bit more complicated. Since the amount of required imported energy ($T_k - Z_{ijk}$) cannot be known with perfect foresight, some multiple of the amount actually required, as seen in retrospect, will doubtless be imported owing to errors of forecasting. Accordingly for months in which the incremental firm power exceeds the secondary energy, the net gain is computed as follows: Value of the prime power increment ($K_p T_k$) less the value of the secondary energy ($K_s Z_{ijk}$) less some factor (α) times the required imported energy ($T_k - Z_{ijk}$) multiplied by its cost (K_c). However, since in retrospect it will be obvious that more energy has been imported than required, the difference $[(\alpha - 1)(T_k - Z_{ijk})]$ can be resold as secondary and the proceeds added to the computation of the net gain.

Given the data corresponding to the model, the range of firm power increments from zero to the appropriate constraint level can be investigated. The optimal level of increased firm power from the intertie is given by the condition that the average annual net gain ($\overline{R}_k$) be a maximum.

What can be said about the data in the model? The monthly megawatts of secondary energy are given by the hydro system simulations at each level of development for system configurations

---

[5] In order to remove the restriction with respect to excess hydro capacity, a change in the price relationships is required which will reflect the cost of installing additional generating capacity in the system. The effect can be incorporated as a reduction in the value of the firm power equal to the cost per unit of generating capacity.

for which thirty-year regulations have been completed. [6] These system studies also provide information on the amount of excess hydro capacity, a datum that is employed as a constraint on the amount of firm power that can be obtained from the intertie, and that assists in estimating the significant price relationships. The prices used are given below:

K_c = 3.25 mills/kwh plus 10 per cent line loss or $2,609.75/mw-month,

K_s = $17.50/kw less 5 per cent line loss or $1,385.00/mw-month,

K_p = 3.75 mills/kwh at 65 per cent load factor or $2,737.50/mw-month.

The use of the particular price relatives can be rationalized as follows: In attempting to ascertain the amount and cost of economy energy off the diurnal peak in the California and Southwest power regions, all thermal stations with *average* fuel cost of 3.25 mills/kwh or less were noted, along with the plant factor at which they were operated. [7] The difference in production between the actual output of such operations and generation at an average annual 85 per cent plant factor was shown to be approximately 10 billion kwh during 1963. It can be assumed that this amount would increase greatly, perhaps even doubling, between 1963 and the decade of the seventies when the intertie will be in operation. Examination of the Federal Power Commission load duration curves for the areas (1960) and the projected 1970 and 1980 load duration curves reveals that the amount of energy available off of the diurnal peaks will exceed the 4,400-mw capacity of the intertie about 70 per cent of the time by 1970, and a substantially greater proportion of the time thereafter. [8] It can be assumed, therefore, that up to 3,100 mw of energy could be imported by the Northwest by means of an intertie of 4,400-mw capacity. But it is not necessarily true that as much as 3,100 mw could be obtained at 3.25 mills/kwh. As it turns

[6] Thirty-year regulations have been made for the majority of the system configurations and levels of development used in this study. These are available from the Bonneville Power Administration; the U.S. Army Engineer Division, North Pacific; and Resources for the Future, Inc.

[7] *Steam Electric Plant Construction Costs and Annual Production Expenses*, Sixteenth Annual Supplement, 1963 (Washington: Federal Power Commission, 1964).

[8] Unpublished tabulations prepared by the Federal Power Commission in connection with the National Power Survey, 1964.

out, however, the amount of energy it is economical to firm up is largely restricted to the amount of surplus hydro capacity, and as this is only a fraction of our 3,100-mw constraint we need not be concerned about the availability of enough economy energy at this price by the 1970's.[9] Accordingly, while the problem was investigated in earlier stages with the price of imported power varying between 3.25 and 4.0 mills/kwh, it does not appear that K_c in our model needs ultimately to be set above 3.25 mills/kwh.

The price of secondary energy is set by the Bonneville Power Administration's marketing policy, and it will be used here for our own analyses because it represents a rate which, adjusted for transmission losses en route, should remain attractive as fuel replacement energy throughout most of California and the Southwest. The value of firm power is set to reflect what is thought to represent the cost of its most economical alternative source.

One additional parameter requires specification, i.e., the efficiency of utilization of imported energy for firming power. In this study we assume that the imported energy will be used with only 67 per cent efficiency. That is, 50 per cent more energy typically will be imported than will be seen in retrospect to have been required owing to normal errors of forecasting runoff. We assume, however, that all such imported energy found to be in excess of requirements can be resold subsequently at the general secondary energy rate. Accordingly, the effective cost of imported energy is taken to be first the nominal 3.25 mills/kwh plus 10 per cent for line losses or 3.57 mills/kwh at the northern terminals. This must in turn be adjusted for the net efficiency losses, i.e., 1.5 (3.57) − 0.5 (1.90), giving 4.4 mills/kwh as the effective costs of imported energy.

The question arises: Does such energy represent a more economical source than energy from local thermal operations in the Northwest? To answer this question, we shall need to estimate the plant factor at which the local thermal plant would operate. We do this initially by setting the incremental firm power obtained from the intertie at its constrained maximum, i.e., 3,100 mw/month, and compute for each system the proportion (P) of the incremental firm power representing the required imported energy, namely:

$$P_k = \sum_{i}^{30} \sum_{j}^{12} (T_k - Z_{ijk})/360\,T, \text{ except}$$

$$T_k - Z_{ijk} = 0 \text{ when } Z_{ijk} \geqslant T_k$$

[9] The amount of 3.25 mills/kwh power available in 1963 would have been almost enough to meet the highest level of firm power increments identified in the analyses.

which is simultaneously equivalent also to the plant factor at which a Northwest thermal plant would need to operate in order to firm the given increment of power. These results are shown in Table 29.

TABLE 29

Proportion of Imported Energy to Provide 3,100 mw Firm Power from Intertie

Study input identification	k	Year (system development)	Firm power increment T_k	Proportion of increment that is imported P_k (per cent)
BPA 69-1 (Treaty)	1	1968–69	3,100	40
RFF-1 (Domestic)		1968–69	3,100	35
BPA 70-1 (Treaty)	2	1969–70	3,100	56
RFF-2 (Domestic)		1969–70	3,100	35
BPA 75-1 (Treaty)	3	1976–77	3,100	53
RFF-3 (Domestic)		1976–77	3,100	42
BPA 75-1 (Treaty)	4	1983–84	3,100	53
RFF-4 (Domestic)		1983–84	3,100	49

Table 29 reveals that firm power increments up to the line capacity can be obtained with the imported energy representing around 50–55 per cent of the total for the Treaty system and 35–50 per cent of the total for the domestic system. This can be compared with thermal costs for various plant factors, as shown in Table 30.

TABLE 30

Cost of Firming Secondary Energy With Northwest Thermal Plant at Fuel Costs of 25 cents/million Btu and Various Plant Factors

Capacity cost	Plant factor in per cent									
	35	40	45	50	55	60	65	70	75	80
	Mills per kilowatt-hour									
$10.34/kw	5.6	5.2	5.0	4.6	4.4	4.2	4.0	3.9	3.8	3.6
13.80/kw	6.8	6.2	5.6	5.4	5.1	4.9	4.7	4.4	4.2	4.1

The table suggests that imported energy up to 55 per cent of the amount firmed could be accommodated at a nominal rate of 3.25 mills/kwh before a thermal plant with costs at $10.34 per kilowatt could provide competitive firming energy locally.[10] For assumed capacity costs of $13.80 per kilowatt, imported energy equivalent

[10] It has been brought to my attention that some amount of fuel in the Pacific Northwest might be available at between 17 and 18 cents per million Btu. In that event, the percentage of the imported component of the firmed energy for thermal plants of $10.34 and $13.80 per kilowatt would fall to 40 and 55 respectively.

to 70 per cent of the increase in firm power would still be competitive with local thermal energy used for the purpose.

In computations with the prices given and the secondary energy corresponding to each one of the systems and levels of development, the net gain $(\overline{R}_k)$ continues to increase up to the capacity of the intertie. The price relatives will hold, however, only to the extent there is surplus hydro capacity in the system to service the firm energy. Since we have assumed a 65 per cent system load factor, in no case does the excess capacity permit the firm power available from the intertie to exceed 1,300 mw. When the price relatives are modified to take into account the additional cost of installing capacity to service the firm power in excess of available hydro capacity, in no case does the amount of firm which it appears economical to obtain in this manner exceed 1,500 mw. [11]

Given the actual amounts of increased firm power with which we work, therefore, the proportion of the firmed energy for which imports account falls well below the critical levels at which local thermal could be used to firm secondary energy competitively.

Table 31 shows the optimal amounts of firm power, with the associated net gain from conversion of secondary to firm through intertie imports of economy energy.

Since there is substantially more storage in the Treaty system than in the domestic system at any comparable point in time, there will be less secondary energy to combine with imported energy. Accordingly, the cost of equivalent blocks of intertie firm power would be greater for the Treaty system, as a larger proportion of the block would have to be imported than in the domestic system. For this reason, subject only to there being adequate hydro capacity in the system, the domestic system typically will be able to firm up a greater amount of secondary energy than the Treaty system, and at a substantially larger average net gain.

Aside from the use of the intertie to convert secondary into firm power, the intertie will be used also for transmitting surplus secondary energy to California and the Southwest. In the legislation setting up the intertie, preference was accorded the Northwest for use of power generated in the Columbia, permitting the export of

---

[11] The procedure used to obtain the additional firm justified by installing additional hydro capacity was as follows: The original model and price relatives were used to obtain the gains from the intertie firm up to the level of existing excess hydro capacity. Then a side calculation was performed substituting for K_p a price ($1,978.00/mw-month) representing the installation costs of capacity ($5.05/kw as a weighted average) deducted from the prime power value for firm power at 65 per cent load factor.

TABLE 31

Intertie Firm Power and Corresponding Net Gains from Intertie Operations

Level of development and system identification	k	T_k Intertie firm power (mw)	$\bar{R}_k$ Average annual gain from intertie operations ($000)
1968–69			
Treaty system	1	900	10,000
Domestic system		1,200	13,491
1969–70			
Treaty system	2	300	3,528
Domestic system		1,300	14,725
1976–77			
Treaty system	3	200	1,358
Domestic system		1,300	11,389
1983–84			
Treaty system	4	800	5,066
Domestic system		0	0
1988–89			
Treaty system		400	2,620
Domestic system		634	6,026
2010–11	6	—	—

only the surplus. Use of secondary energy in the Northwest will consist of sales of high-grade interruptible (about 552 mw to electro process industries in the early years) and fuel displacement for the initially small amount of thermal in the Northwest. To estimate the average annual surplus secondary (S_k) net of Northwest requirements we have:

$$S_k = \sum_i^{30} \sum_j^{12} [Z_{ijk} - (T_k + I_{ijk} + D_k)]/360$$

except

$$Z_{ijk} - (T_k + I_{ijk} + D_k)$$

$$\begin{cases} = 0 \text{ when } Z_{ijk} < (T_k + I_{ijk} + D_k) \\ = 4{,}400 \text{ when } Z_{ijk} - (T_k + I_{ijk} + D_k) > 4{,}400 \end{cases}$$

where

Z_{ijk} = megawatts of secondary in year i and month j of system condition k,

T_k = megawatts of firm power from intertie operations during system condition k,

I_{ijk} = megawatts of high-grade interruptible power in year i and month j of condition k,

D_k = megawatts of secondary energy required for fuel displacement under condition k.

The data employed and computed results are given in Table 32.

TABLE 32

Estimates of Surplus Secondary Energy Available for Sale to Southwest

(megawatts)

Level of development and system identification	k	Value of T_k	Value of D_k	Value of I_k	Available average annual surplus secondary S_k
1968–69					
Treaty system	1	900	393	552	1,181
Domestic system		1,200	393	552	1,375
1969–70					
Treaty system	2	300	397	552	1,168
Domestic system		1,300	397	552	1,592
1976–77					
Treaty system	3	200	345	0	2,404
Domestic system		1,300	345	0	2,369
1983–84					
Treaty system	4	800	4,199	0	686
Domestic system		0	5,310	0	938
1988–89					
Treaty system	5	400	8,118	0	94
Domestic system		634	8,081	0	279
2010–11	6	All secondary energy can be used for fuel displacement in Northwest.			

Table 32 gives comparative results for the two systems not dissimilar from those shown in Table 31. In Table 32 we see a substantially larger amount of secondary energy available for sale to California and the Southwest in the domestic system in spite of a substantially larger amount of secondary conversion to firm via the intertie. This is particularly noticeable in the 1969–70 level of development, in which the Treaty system has 8.5 million acre-feet of storage in excess of the domestic system by virtue of the combined storages of Duncan Lake and High Arrow. This difference in the volume of storage between the two systems has the effect that the intertie functions more productively in the domestic system since it can, to an extent, substitute for Treaty storage in power operations, and its supramarginality in this sense is partially displaced by such storage in the Treaty system.

COMPARATIVE COSTS OF TREATY AND DOMESTIC SYSTEMS, TAKING ACCOUNT OF SALES AGREEMENT TERMS AND NORTHWEST–SOUTHWEST INTERTIE OPERATIONS

Using the estimates of additional firm power which the intertie operation can provide economically for each system, we can make a comparison of the cost performance of the Treaty and the domestic systems as it appeared in 1964, as was done in Chapter 7 for the conditions prevailing in 1961. First, however, it may be useful to present the formal model for the estimation of fossil fuel requirements and cost for the two systems, since this was not done explicitly in Chapter 7.

We wish to determine the difference in the fossil fuel displacement by secondary energy corresponding to each of the two systems at each level of development. Actually, what we wish to know for purposes of comparing the cost behavior of the two systems is the amount of fossil fuel required (C_k) net of displacement by secondary energy which is surplus to the needs of conversion to firm, and provision during the early years of some high-grade interruptible power. This is computed for each system for each level of development as follows:

$$C_k = \sum_i^{30} \sum_j^{12} (F_k - \Upsilon_{ijk})/360$$

$$\text{except } F_k - \Upsilon_{ijk} \begin{cases} = 0 \text{ when } \Upsilon_{ijk} > F \\ = F_k \text{ when } \Upsilon_{ijk} < 0 \end{cases}$$

where all terms are defined as previously and

$F_k = $ critical period average thermal generation
$\Upsilon_{ijk} = \mathcal{Z}_{ijk} - (T_k + I_{ijk})$.

The fossil fuel requirement computed in this way, it should be mentioned, assumes that secondary energy will not be used to displace nuclear reactors, as it is unlikely that such would be subject to fuel displacement, nor is there any plan to do so with the Hanford New Production Reactor.[12]

[12] For purposes of determining net fossil fuel thermal requirements, the New Production Reactor was credited with 786 mw capacity and 669 mw energy for 1968–69; 786 mw capacity and 665 mw energy for 1969–70; and 843 mw capacity and 717 mw energy in the period 1976–77 and beyond.

The results of these computations are given for reference in Table 33.

TABLE 33

Average Annual Megawatts of Fossil Fuel Requirements for Treaty and Alternative Domestic Systems, and the Several Levels of Development

(megawatts)

Level of development and system identification	k	Values of F_k	Values of Y_{ijk}		Average annual generation with fossil fuel, C_k
1968–69					
Treaty system	1	393	Z_{ij1}	$-1,452$	138.7
Domestic system		393	Z_{ij1}	$-1,752$	157.2
1969–70					
Treaty system	2	397	Z_{ij2}	-852	250.5
Domestic system		397	Z_{ij2}	$-1,852$	159.8
1976–77					
Treaty system	3	345	Z_{ij3}	-200	154.2
Domestic system		345	Z_{ij3}	$-1,300$	143.9
1983–84					
Treaty system	4	4,199	Z_{ij4}	-800	2,617.9
Domestic system		5,310	Z_{ij4}	0	3,034.1
1988–89					
Treaty system	5	8,118	Z_{ij5}	-400	5,727.8
Domestic system		8,081	Z_{ij5}	-634	5,531.7
2010–11					
Treaty system	6	40,210	Z_{ij6}	0	37,502.0
Domestic system		40,307	Z_{ij6}	0	37,092.8

Source: Bonneville Power Administration, Branch of Power Resources, December 1964.

Table 33 indicates that the comparative net fossil fuel requirements of the two systems vary among the levels of development. At the 1968–69 level, the difference in the amount of storage between the two systems is small, being accounted for only by Duncan Lake's 1.4 million acre-feet. This slightly larger amount of storage in the Treaty system does not have as much effect on availability of secondary energy for fuel displacement as does the greater amount of secondary conversion to firm power in the domestic system. Accordingly, the fossil fuel requirements of the domestic system are slightly larger than for the Treaty system. This relationship changes substantially with the addition of 7 million acre-feet of High Arrow storage. More fossil fuel is required for the Treaty system from 1969–70 onward, with the single exception of the 1983–84 system conditions.

Tables 31 through 33 provide data on the way the several components of costs and revenues of the two systems are affected by changing and differential amounts of storage in combination with the intertie operating in the system. A synoptic view of the entire system, functioning at each of the several levels of development in combination with the intertie, is given in Table 34.[13]

We might have been led to anticipate, given the substitution relation between the intertie and storage, that the excess costs of the Treaty system shown in Chapter 7 would be increased unless the price in the terms of sale of the Canadian entitlement were especially low. Perhaps this can be further clarified with an illustration. Consider the 1976–77 system conditions for the two systems. Item 7 of Table 34 gives the total power resources to meet load and export. The Treaty system has but 384 mw of capacity and 295 mw of firm energy greater than the domestic system.[14] The Treaty system contains, in addition to Canadian storage, the Libby storage project and the Kootenai Falls head plant. The *at-site generation of these two U.S. plants* will, by itself, account for the difference in system output. That is to say, the domestic system operating with the intertie would have an output equivalent to that of the Treaty system save for the output of the two U.S. plants included (excluded) in the Treaty (domestic) system, at a cost less than the cost of the Treaty system charged with the average annual equivalent of the United States prepayment for downstream power benefits.

Similarly—though the comparison is not quite so dramatic—in general the output of the domestic system plus the intertie firm always will nearly equal the output of the Treaty system, despite the substantially lesser amounts of storage in the domestic system. Consider the 1969–70 entry in which only the High Arrow–Duncan storage projects with 8.4 million acre-feet of additional storage are in the Treaty system. The firm power capability of the hydro system is 1,207 mw greater than the domestic system capability (entry 1, Table 34). With the optimal intertie firm power added to *both* systems, however, the capability of the Treaty system exceeds the domestic system's by only 140 mw. This is indicative of the extent to which the intertie may substitute for Treaty storage or,

[13] A detailed discussion of the source of data and computational procedure for each of the entries in Table 34 is given in the Technical Note to this chapter.

[14] The amount of pre-existing thermal is identical for both systems, hence the difference in system capability is given by the hydro installations and intertie.

conversely, indicative of the extent to which Treaty storage pre-empts the supramarginality of the firming function of the intertie. [15]

Apparently, therefore, as a result of the negotiated price for the nominal Canadian entitlement and the technical possibilities inherent in the intertie, the settlement of 1964 represents a position under General Principle No. 2 which deteriorated between 1961 and 1964 another hundred million dollars. [16] That is to say, the United States appears to have been able to achieve its power and flood control objectives through alternatives that would save approximately a third of a billion dollars as compared with its cooperative undertaking with Canada. This is due largely to the fact that the displacement of U.S. storage by Canadian storage, observed earlier, was augmented by displacement of the supramarginality of the U.S. Northwest-Southwest intertie. [17]

[15] It should be noted that this conclusion is consistent with the conclusions of the Department of the Interior Task Force Report, "Pacific Northwest, Pacific Southwest Extra-high Voltage Common Carrier Interconnection," December 15, 1961, namely: "Our conclusions are that the extra-high voltage common carrier interconnection facility would provide greater benefits should the Treaty between the United States and Canada not be ratified." (P. 44) And again, "The firming of secondary in the Pacific Northwest area by purchase of off-peak economy steam in California would also prove beneficial for a longer period of time and at much less cost." (P. 45)

[16] We should recall here the criticism of Brigadier General P. C. Hyzer and his staff (see Chapter 7, footnote 27). It is not clear to me, however, that the quantitative significance of the exclusion of the Lower Canyon project from the Treaty system would be as great for the situation in 1964, involving the intertie, as it would be under the conditions of 1961, analyzed in Chapter 7.

[17] It may be thought that the conclusions reached here, with respect to the economic disadvantages of the Columbia Treaty, apply only to the Northwest regional power system, and not necessarily to the whole of the United States when possible advantages of Canadian entitlement to the power systems of California and the Southwest are taken into account. On this point, it is significant that the Bonneville Power Administration was required to subsidize transmission of that portion of the Canadian entitlement power that was to be sold in California and the Southwest, because there was not sufficient incentive for the recipient utilities to purchase the power at the rate negotiated by the two countries. See "International Development of the Columbia River, Its Significance upon Western Power Developments," paper presented by Bernard Goldhammer, Assistant Administrator for Power Management, Bonneville Power Administration, at the Western Political Science Association meetings, Victoria, B.C., March 19, 1965, p. 4.

TECHNICAL NOTE ON THE EVALUATION OF THE COST
DIFFERENCES BETWEEN THE COLUMBIA RIVER TREATY SYSTEM
AND THE U. S. DOMESTIC SYSTEM, 1964

POWER ASPECTS

This note addresses in detail the data and method used in the preparation of Table 34.

Lines 1, 2, and 3 are taken directly from the power system studies which provided the data on hydro installations and output used in analysis of the two systems under terms of the 1961 understanding between Canada and the United States for each of six distinguishable periods. Line 4 gives the amount of firm power which is obtained from the intertie, constrained in amount to the extent of excess hydro capacity. Line 5 gives the thermal capacity and critical-period average generation as before, for the first three time periods in which thermal capacity is given by the presently existing capacity in the system. In later periods the thermal is somewhat reduced as compared with the earlier conditions, since the Canadian entitlement is retained in the United States; the increment of firm power via the intertie also is available. In this line (5) the thermal requirements are shown as identical for both systems and in amount sufficient to have only one system meet its critical-period energy requirements. The deficiency thus shown for the other system will give the differential amount of thermal capacity and fossil fuel requirements (net of displacement). For all time periods between 1968–69 and 1976–77 the surplus capacity and energy shown for both systems are assumed available for sale in California and the Southwest. Reserve requirements in Line 6 are computed as before, i.e., 8 per cent of peak load requirements and 5 per cent of thermal generating capability. Lines 7 and 8 are self-explanatory, and the difference between these gives the system surpluses or deficiences (Line 9).

Line 10, indicated as "Intertie Offset," represents a deduction of the amount of intertie firm and associated capacity from the actual surplus or deficit. The deduction is required because the intertie firm differs for the two systems, and, since the net gain of the firm has been separately computed as a side calculation, we want the differences between the two systems' surpluses and deficits net of the intertie firm power for purposes of comparability. This is shown as "Adjusted Surplus or Deficit" in Line 11.

The entry "Thermal Adjustment" (Line 12), first shown in the U.S. domestic system in 1983–84, is provided to take account of the reserve requirements associated with the indicated deficiencies. All of the above entries are indicated in physical terms, namely, megawatts.

Lines 13 through 22 have entries in value terms in order to evaluate the net difference in the cost behavior of the two systems. Line 13 gives only the fuel costs for the system configurations 1968–69 through 1976–77, as the systems, in fact, have identical thermal capacity which is given at the outset. For the period 1983–84, the difference in both thermal capacity and fossil fuel thermal energy is shown. Thermal capacity is taken as $10.34 per kilowatt-year and energy at $19.71 per kilowatt-year.

The entry "Annual Gain from Intertie Firm" (Line 14), was obtained from the model described in this chapter. It should be noted that $\bar{R}_k$ gives a net figure, i.e., has taken account of losses of potential secondary energy sales for fuel displacement, high-grade interruptible, or sales to California.

Line 15 is computed to provide the difference between the two systems with respect to their surplus or deficiency, adjusted for having computed the intertie firm power separately as the side calculation giving maximum $\bar{R}_k$ values. Since this model did not account for costs of using excess hydro capacity, the amount of hydro capacity required to service this intertie firm needs to be deducted also in order to make the indicated surpluses or deficits comparable as between the Treaty and domestic systems.

Line 16 is a straightforward application of the model previously described which provides the amount of secondary energy surplus to the needs for intertie firm, high-grade interruptible power (early years only), and use of secondary for fuel displacement. This is assumed to be sold at the indicated secondary rate of $17.50 per kilowatt less line loss to the California border.

The algebraic sum of the entries from Lines 13 through 16 is given as Line 17, and the net difference between the two systems as Line 18. Line 19 represents the annual average interest and amortization charges on $297 million as of 1968–69, computed at 4 per cent and thirty years appropriate to the Treaty system. It also includes the differences that exist between the two systems in average annual cost for hydro installations, and remains the same as observed in connection with the cost performance for the 1961 terms of agreement described in the Technical Note to Chapter 7.

The algebraic sum of the entries from Lines 18 and 19 gives the total difference in average annual costs of the two systems for each point in the time span reviewed.

Since we do not have system components for each year of the fifty-year period of analysis, the values given for the indicated periods were assumed to hold for some part of the interstitial period between dates actually employed. These were as given below:

> 1968–69 for one year, i.e. 1968–69
> 1969–70 from 1969–70 through 1972–73
> 1976–77 from 1973–74 through 1979–80
> 1983–84 from 1980–81 through 1985–86
> 1988–89 from 1986–87 through 1999–2000
> 2010–11 from 2000–01 through 2018–19

The average annual differences in costs were discounted to 1968–69 at 4 per cent, giving the present value of the excess cost of the Treaty system in Line 21.

FLOOD CONTROL ASPECTS

To evaluate the difference in performance of the two systems with respect to flood damage reduction provided by each, the analysis accompanying Chapter 7 had to be modified to account for the fact that the Dworshak project was undertaken during the interval between the ratification of the Treaty by the United States Senate in 1961, and the ratification of the Treaty and related supplementary documents by the Canadian Parliament in 1964. The Dworshak project, therefore, is considered as though it were part of the "base system" of projects existing or under construction and, as such, preceding the Treaty storage. With Dworshak in the system, the flood damage reduction provided by Duncan Lake, reducing peak discharge from about 980,000 cfs to 950,000 cfs at The Dalles, would provide for an average annual damage reduction of about $1 million greater than would be the case with the domestic system. This would prevail for a year until High Arrow's storage, reducing peak discharge from about 950,000 cfs to 880,000 cfs, would provide an additional $1.6 million, for a total of $2.6 million flood management benefits in excess of the domestic system. By the year 1973 it is assumed that Mica as well as the High Arrow–Duncan storage projects are in the system along with Libby, Knowles, and High Mountain Sheep in addition to Dworshak, thus controlling in total the peak discharge of flows equivalent to the 1894 flood of record below 600,000 cfs at The Dalles. The domestic system was assumed to have, in addition to Dworshak, the Knowles and High Mountain Sheep projects, in total controlling discharges equivalent to the flood of 1894 to 860,000 cfs at The Dalles. The difference in flood damage reduction of about $2.36 million as an average annual benefit favoring the Treaty system was assumed to remain for seven years. By 1980–81, it was assumed the Penny Cliffs and Lower Canyon projects would be operating in the domestic system, capable of reducing peak discharges to 750,000 cfs at The Dalles. This would narrow the difference in the damage prevention between the two systems to about $950,000 as an average annual equivalent for the remainder of the period of evaluation.

These sums, prevailing over different segments of the time span under consideration, were discounted at 4 per cent, which gave a present value of the estimated greater flood management benefits of the Treaty system of $31 million. As in the original case described in Chapter 7, the Treaty system would make unnecessary the construction of local flood protection works on the Kootenai in the vicinity of Bonners Ferry, giving a net gain from Treaty storage for flood damage reduction and related benefits of around $40.5 million.

SENSITIVITY ANALYSES

To test the sensitivity of our results to the particular assumptions employed in the analysis, several modifications were introduced one at a time, to determine whether or not significant differences would occur.

It has been noted previously that the present value of the Treaty storage is related to the rate of growth of power requirements and hence the thermal component in the system. The analyses in both cases (Chapter 7, 1961 terms and conditions as well as the present case) were carried out on the assumption that a low rate of growth prevailed, and thus favoring by this assumption the economics of the Treaty system. If a high rate of growth were substituted, however, only a modest (3.5–4.0 per cent) difference would result. The present excess cost of the Treaty system would be increased by only about $10 million.

If a higher capacity cost were assumed—i.e., substituting $13.80 for the $10.34 used in the analyses—the results would differ for the two sets of conditions. In the 1961 terms of the agreement, the United States was required to repatriate the Canadian entitlement, and in this connection was required to install thermal capacity to honor its dependable capacity commitment to Canada. Accordingly, an increase in the assumed cost of thermal capacity to $13.80 would be reflected in approximately a $7 million addition to excess cost of the Treaty system, computed as a present value. Under the terms and conditions prevailing in 1964, however, substituting a cost of $13.80 for thermal capacity results in a small reduction (1.25 per cent) in the excess cost of the Treaty system.

Results of the intertie analyses presented in the text of the present chapter were restricted to the case in which the intertie firm was constrained by the amount of existing excess hydro capacity. When this assumption was relaxed to permit addition of hydro capacity to service additional intertie firm power, the result favored the Treaty system by about 1 per cent. In no case was the amount of increased firm power very large, and the net return on such, given the need to absorb cost of capacity installation in the system, was quite modest. An illustration of the relationship is given in the tabulation below:

System	Development	Intertie firm as in text (T) (mw)	Increased intertie firm through added capacity (T') (mw)	Net gain of T (R) ($000)	Added net gain of T' (R') ($000)
Treasury........	1968–69	900	500	300,980	6,419
Domestic......	1968–69	1,200	200	404,718	1,977
Treaty........	1969–70	300	400	105,847	24,056
Domestic......	1969–70	1,300	200	441,763	2,449

After all the Treaty storage is in, beginning 1973–74 for the Treaty system, and a substantial portion of the domestic storage in the domestic system (1976–77 system conditions and beyond), the quality of the secondary remaining after conversion to firm up to the excess hydro capacity, is "too thin" to absorb any cost of capacity installation on its account. It is obvious, merely from inspection of the net gain associated with the increment in firm power, that firming secondary beyond the point at which excess hydro capacity is exhausted is attended by slim margins.

Given the variation in the results for which sensitivity analyses were conducted, the margin of error possibly due to the assumptions made in the study is shown to be very slight—well within ±5 per cent. However, there were other assumptions which were potentially significant, but which could not be checked either because they dealt with imponderables, or because they would have required considerably more computer time and research resources than were available for this study. A few examples will be mentioned.

The system configuration for the Treaty was given by the selection of projects in the International Work Group's study of the Canadian entitlement. It is doubtless true that of the remaining storage and head, the Libby and Kootenai Falls plants are not the most economic. On the other hand, the Treaty makes provision to accommodate Libby; in fact one of the major *de facto* objectives of the Treaty was to obtain Canadian clearance for its construction and thus Libby will be included whether or not it is economic. In this connection, a test might have been made to find out whether or not the Lower Canyon and Penny Cliffs projects included in the domestic system would also be economic in a Treaty system with 20 million additional acre-feet of storage, and what effect their inclusion in the Treaty system along with the Libby and Kootenai Falls projects would have on comparative system performance.[18]

Another assumption that could have been checked for sensitivity, had resources permitted, was one concerning the efficiency with which imported economy energy would be used for firming, and the extent to which the comparative performance of the two systems is dependent on this assumption.

With several such assumptions embedded in the analysis, it is clear that the over-all analysis cannot be considered within ±5 per cent accuracy. On the other hand, it should not be dismissed on this account as too crude. For all its shortcomings, the analysis is substantially more refined than any of those conducted by official parties to the Columbia agreement on which a resource allocation decision amounting to several billion dollars rested.

[18] Recall the observations of Brigadier General P. C. Hyzer and his staff, Chapter 7, footnote 27.

Chapter 10

The Columbia Treaty: Concluding Observations

~~~~~~~~~~~~~~~~~~~~~~~~~~~~~~~

This study has attempted to establish whether certain assumptions underlying a co-operative undertaking to develop an international river for mutual benefit of the participating countries are, in fact, borne out by the resulting terms of agreement.

International arrangements to permit the integration of diverse energy sources and markets appear to be justified when there are prospects for realizing significant benefits or for avoiding costs which would occur if development were to take place unilaterally. In the case studied, that of the Columbia River Treaty, one would expect the results to reflect more efficient exploitation of the water resources of the river and its tributaries. Certainly, the guidelines for negotiation laid down by the International Joint Commission support this view. Although they embody numerous qualifications which are subject to interpretation, in the main the IJC principles were directed toward realizing through co-operative development economies which would not be possible through independent action. Further, they provided means by which action undertaken for the benefit of system economy (i.e., for the two countries combined) should not result in adverse consequences for either one of the parties to the venture. In spite of these precautions the features of the Columbia development secured by the Treaty left such expectations unrealized.

SUMMARY OF THE TREATY'S ECONOMIC RESULTS

Under the conditions prevailing in 1960, storage appeared to be needed in considerable volume on the upper Columbia and Koote-

191

nay. This the Treaty provided by adding 20 million acre-feet of storage. However, our examination has shown that the storage in question was obtained by means that were not consistent with the fundamental objective of co-operative resource development—i.e., the achievement of shared economies. Of the mutually exclusive projects proposed—Dorr–Bull River and Libby—the former was the more economic yet the latter was selected. Granting for the moment that the Dorr–Bull River sites would not be developed for good and sufficient reasons internal to British Columbia, it does not necessarily follow that the Libby project was the only relevant alternative for accomplishing power and flood control objectives. The benefit from Libby, considered incrementally after the High Arrow, Duncan, and Mica storages, is scarcely equal to the cost. From a strictly national point of view, the benefits to the United States are substantially less than the costs. Since under the terms of the Treaty the project is optional rather than required, the desirability of its construction may still be questioned. If Libby were not built, regulation of the lower Kootenay would have to be performed by the Duncan storage, and flood damage reduction achieved by means of local flood protection measures in the Bonners Ferry area of the lower Kootenai in Idaho; this would be the economic way of meeting objectives whose value would warrant the cost. If, on the other hand, the Libby project represented a *sine qua non* of Treaty ratification by the United States Senate, a question arises as to the justification for expenditures on the Duncan storage project. With 5 million acre-feet of storage in prospect in the Libby storage reservoir on the Kootenai, and 14 million acre-feet on the upper Columbia in Canada, the incremental contribution of the Duncan project to the system can be regarded as negligible. Rationally, one might expect, therefore, that if the only objective were to realize economies, negotiations would have led either to the Dorr–Bull River storage project for regulation of flows on the Kootenay, or the Duncan project in conjunction with local flood protection measures in the area of recurrent Bonners Ferry flooding. Alternatively, if the Dorr–Bull River project had been unconditionally unavailable and the Libby project a *sine qua non* of the Treaty, one has reason to question the outlays for the Duncan storage project.

Finally, if we consider the choices that were available in the context of 1963 policies, the technical possibilities, and the increased amount of information regarding feasible alternatives, one might well question the role of the High Arrow storage. High Arrow is a pure storage project, not suited to conversion to hydro peaking as the demand for storage gradually declines. Its inclusion in the original Treaty in 1960 was at least partly justified by the short lead time required to bring it into the system and the expectation that load growth would leave a gap in power supply which High Arrow alone could fill in time. By 1963, when the second phase of negotiations was in progress, it was clear that High Arrow was not required to forestall an imminent power shortage. Co-ordinated operations of the Peace River storage and integrated Columbia hydro facilities by means of transmission facilities from both developments to the Vancouver, B.C. and/or similar Northwest power market areas would accomplish at little additional cost the purpose the Arrow Lakes storage was intended to serve in the regional power system. In fact, the increase in firm power load which such co-ordinated operations could accomplish would greatly exceed the incremental contribution of the Arrow Lakes storage, and at a savings in cost nearly equivalent to the outlays for High Arrow.

What then is the quantitative significance of these observations? If the Dorr–Bull River sites can be regarded as having been conditionally available for use in lieu of the Libby storage, and if the Arrow Lakes and Duncan projects are eliminated, an economy over the actual Treaty storage could have been realized in the neighborhood of $250 million to $300 million. On the other hand, if the Dorr–Bull River project is regarded as having been unconditionally unavailable and the Libby project to have been a *sine qua non* of the Columbia Treaty, Libby's operation coupled with the co-ordination of the Peace and Columbia systems operation would have substituted satisfactorily for the High Arrow–Duncan storage, and an efficiency gain (economy) of about $150 million could still have been realized. In short, in this international undertaking the opportunities for realizing significant economies through pooling technical possibilities were, on the whole, missed. It is not at all clear, in fact, that the returns to Canada and the United States combined are greater than they would have been if each country had proceeded independently. We can evaluate this point better after reviewing the Treaty consequences bearing on the division of the gains from Treaty storage operations.

It will be recalled that the International Joint Commission's principles for guidance regarding the measurement and division of these gains required, first, a selection of Treaty system components which would yield the maximum net gain to the *Columbia system*, i.e., to the two countries combined. This was to be achieved by introducing storage projects into the Columbia system in such a sequence that the most economic would be first-added, and no project would be included that would preclude a more economic means of achieving the same or greater benefits. The benefits were to be so divided that the increment in power from Treaty storage would be equal for the two countries and the flood control benefits would be shared by means of monetary compensation equal to one-half the estimated value of such flood damage reduction. While the provisions of the IJC principles appear to promise that each party to the co-operative venture will receive something that is somehow equal, the circumstances of the case in question permitted a division of the real gains predominantly to Canada. This is so because the most economic storage was available in Canada and, according to the IJC principles, would qualify for inclusion in the system first. The amount of storage offered by Canada ultimately was only so much as to provide largely the seasonal storage which, representing use over a short critical period, was attended by disproportionate gross returns. Because any additional storage would qualify only as cyclical storage, to be used over a much longer critical period and thus with greatly reduced yields, an equal share of the increment in power associated with the first block of storage added had the effect of pre-empting values which otherwise could be realized in any event by United States storage. Such measurement and division of the increment attributable to Canadian storage would, of course, remove incentive for United States participation. Accordingly, provision was made in the IJC principles to permit altering the division marginally so that some (nominal) advantage would accrue to each country while maintaining the basic terms of division. Thus, the preponderance of the net benefits would still accrue to Canada, but the United States would receive token gains. The extent of the latter was dependent upon an adequate assessment of the displacement effects of the Canadian storage for subsequently added U.S. storage projects.

What, then, is the result of the actual division of benefits? The answer, which can only be approximate, is arrived at by calculating how much each country was able to save as compared with independent alternatives available to each.

In the case of Canada, if the United States payments for the Canadian power entitlement and flood control benefits are deducted from the costs of developing the whole of the Columbia River in Canada, the remaining cost is approximately equal to the cost of the Peace development. The full development of the Columbia in

Canada, however, would provide about 400 mw of power more than the Peace development. The benefit of this in monetary terms —on the order of $225 million to $275 million—can be regarded as the benefit to Canada from the Columbia Treaty as measured by the savings in cost compared with alternatives available to Canada.

In the case of the United States, after considering the problem of meeting power supply and flood management objectives by such means as developing domestic storage and the Northwest-Southwest intertie, we find that the Treaty results in a relative loss to the United States of about $250 million to $375 million. [1] There is no evidence that a net economy has been achieved; on the contrary, there is reason to suspect some net loss.

SPECIAL CIRCUMSTANCES RESPONSIBLE FOR THE TREATY OUTCOME

When the Columbia River Treaty and its various economic consequences are viewed with the benefit of hindsight, there seems little to commend it in terms of realizing, through co-operation, economies unavailable to each riparian independently. British Columbia, as a quasi-autonomous entity, realized a substantial gain, but this did not result from exploiting economies arising from co-operation. Rather, the gain to British Columbia was offset by increased costs for the United States. In retrospect this is quite clear.

Several factors suggest reasons for such an outcome, and most of them are not economic. Perhaps most significant was the changing policy environment as negotiations progressed through three governments in Canada and three administrations in the United States.

In the beginning, when engineering investigations on the Columbia had progressed to a point at which negotiations could begin, the government in Canada was reluctant to enter into a co-operative undertaking which would involve an advance of capital from the United States and/or sales of electricity to the United States. The problem of developing the Columbia River, from the standpoint of the Province of British Columbia at least, was one of finding suitable financial means and a choice of projects which would represent

---

[1] The lower figure represents adjustments in an amount suggested by Brigadier General P. C. Hyzer and staff, U.S. Army Engineer Division, North Pacific. See Chapter 7, footnote 27.

initially the minimum capital commitment. These reasons, at least in part, prompted the British Columbia authorities to avoid commitment of the East Kootenay sites to development—i.e., to avoid making available on a schedule to accommodate U.S. power objectives all three groups of storage which qualified under IJC principles. Capital constraints, in the light of policy restrictions on sale of energy and/or receipt of funds from the United States, played some if not the dominant part in the ultimate decision regarding the choice of storage sites on the upper Kootenay. Whether the change in Canadian energy policy, had it preceded negotiation of the Treaty of 1961, would have led to a different choice of storage on the Kootenay, cannot be known, but certainly a large obstacle to providing Kootenay storage in Canada would have been removed with the removal of these policy constraints. [2]

Policy environment in the United States also bears on the acceptability of the original Treaty terms with respect to the division of benefits. As we have seen, during the period of negotiation of the Treaty of 1961 power policy in the United States sought to reduce the role and significance of the federal government in the provision of the nation's power. Toward this end a "Partnership Policy" had been developed which, in effect, discouraged the construction of hydro projects as federal undertakings so long as any non-federal alternative remained in prospect. In this way, a very substantial amount of the remaining head on the mainstem of the Columbia, along with head on the tributaries, was developed by non-federal entities. The matter of efficiency in the design and operation of the Columbia hydro system was sacrificed to the goal of reducing the influence of the federal hydro system in the power program of the Pacific Northwest.

While this policy of the administration during 1953–61 resulted in a stepped-up development of head plants on the Columbia, storage lagged severely. This was due partly to that provision of the Federal Power Act which requires non-federal developers of storage, as a condition of their FPC license, to provide regulation for federal head plants downstream without compensation. With so large a proportion of the existing head developed under federal auspices, much of the incentive for non-federal development of

----

[2] There is no doubt that reasons additional to financing governed the decision on East Kootenay storage. One factor, the recognition of the adverse effect on an unusually valuable wildlife resource with a wintering range in the Kootenay reaches which would be occupied by the Bull River–Dorr–Luxor complex, was coming into prominence by the time the 1963 negotiations began.

storage was eliminated. Accordingly, at the time of the negotiation of the Columbia Treaty storage in the system was grossly deficient; Canadian storage could be looked upon as meeting this deficiency without resort to federal construction of storage in the Pacific Northwest. That such an arrangement would have adverse implications for the economy of future power supplies in the Pacific Northwest was a matter of subsidiary concern and entirely consistent with the results obtained from application of the "Partnership Policy" in other instances from its inception. Canadian storage and the terms concerning division of benefits alike were consistent with, and advanced the objectives of, the "Partnership Policy" of the national administration.

With the change in administration immediately following the signing of the Treaty, the policy premises on which the Treaty was based no longer had relevance. A number of alternatives to Canadian storage, which had not been encouraged by the previous administration, now came under active consideration. Accordingly, the terms of the Treaty of 1961 began to assume an air of unreality.

While national power policies in both countries were subject to change after the signing of the Treaty, the evolution of power, economic development, and related resource development policies in the Province of British Columbia, which came to a head after the Treaty had been signed, had important implications also for the design and operation of the Columbia system. The economic development goals of British Columbia for its central-north interior relied on the Peace Power Project as a primary element. With the Peace development as a *given* in the power systems of the Pacific region, a reconsideration of the head-storage balance on the Columbia became a relevant technical matter. The enormous storage capacity of the Peace Power Project, in co-ordinated operations with the Columbia, would serve to make salable a very large additional amount of energy from the Columbia. In fact, as we have seen, it offered a technical opportunity to substitute Peace storage for High Arrow–Duncan, thus saving the expenditure on these Treaty storages without incurring significant costs in addition to those required in any event for the Peace project. The emergence of the Peace Power Project as an independent development after the Treaty of 1961 by itself provided the opportunity of obtaining a half of the total potential economy from an international agreement or, in effect, reducing the expenditures for Treaty storage on the Columbia.

A similar circumstance attended the change in Canadian policy which altered the Treaty terms regarding repatriation of Canadian power entitlement. After the Treaty was negotiated, and during the years its ratification was held in abeyance in Canada, power planning in the U.S. Pacific Northwest proceeded on the assumption that Canadian entitlement would be returned to Canada. Arrangement for supplies of power exclusive of Canadian entitlement proceeded so that an ample supply for the Pacific Northwest was in prospect prior to the final negotiations leading to the Protocol Note and Sales Agreement. In addition, the rate of growth in load in the Pacific Northwest diminished somewhat, making the load-resources relationship for the latter part of the 1960's comfortable if not overly abundant. The shift in Canadian position regarding the disposition of its downstream entitlement, therefore, required access to new markets in the United States in order to accommodate the British Columbia objectives. This was eventually accomplished through arrangements with California and other Southwest utilities made possible by a commitment to proceed immediately with the construction of extra-high-voltage transmission facilities connecting the Pacific Northwest with California and the Southwest power systems. An interconnection of this sort, however, along with the potential Peace-Columbia co-ordinated operations, largely eliminates the rationale for Columbia Treaty storage for power purposes. In fact, given the intertie and domestic storage possibilities (excluding co-ordination of Peace and Columbia operations), power objectives of the Pacific Northwest could be met with a saving of about $120 million (in addition to the $250 million given by the 1961 Treaty terms) as compared with a system on the Columbia involving Treaty storage and terms agreed upon for benefit division and sale of Canadian entitlement.

It should be observed that while each one of a number of technical possibilities would show large yields when evaluated in combination with the Columbia system, owing to the storage-head imbalance which was permitted to develop, it does not follow that all the possibilities—i.e., Peace storage and interconnection with the Columbia through the Vancouver market, Columbia Treaty storage, and Northwest-Southwest electrical interconnection— when taken in combination or simultaneously would produce a joint yield equal to the sum of the yields taken alternatively as next added. As illustrated in Chapter 3, there is a significant diminishing marginal productivity of storage for any given head development, and a substitution relation between storage in a hydro system and electrical interconnection with adjacent thermal systems. An opportunity was therefore available for eliminating excess facilities the function of which could be displaced by alternative means of accomplishing the same results while achieving additional objectives. In this respect, the failure to consider these possibilities sequentially or, if in combination, to consider the elimination of some single function facilities—e.g., pure storage projects—became a failure to perceive the potential economies which could reduce the cost of the co-operative venture, without corresponding reduction in over-all benefits.

The changes in the policy environment, which had the effect of broadening technical possibilities and financial bases, opened up these very significant possibilities for realizing economies which had not been available when the Treaty of 1961 was negotiated. However, because the original Treaty had been signed by both countries and ratified by the United States Senate, freedom of action was restricted. Whether or not, during the second phase of negotiations, the terms of the original agreement could have been opened up sufficiently to permit good prospects for a more economical arrangement, cannot be known. Apparently, in the judgment of those entrusted with the matter, the more conservative approach was preferred.

The restrictive policies governing negotiation of the original terms and the inflexibility of the Treaty document in the light of subsequent events are the two major factors accounting for the consequences of the international agreement. But there may have been contributing influences. The differing emphasis placed on the undertaking by the United States and Canada was reflected in the differing mechanisms each country used for making technical information available to the negotiators. There was, of course, far greater public interest in the Columbia development in Canada than in the United States, and this may have had a bearing on the efficiency with which Canadian policy and Canadian technical information were meshed. Canadian technicians left a voluminous record of careful and detailed analysis of the implications of alternative proposals, and Canadian negotiators generally had excellent information on the economic implications of proposals coming up for consideration; their skill in diverting the course of discussion to proposals, terms, and conditions which had the benefit of prior evaluation by Canadian technical staff stands out in the dialogue leading to the international agreement.

In the United States, the organization of the information generating, retrieving, and evaluating process was less systematic. No doubt, the Columbia Treaty was a matter of substantially less moment in the United States than in Canada; hence, the approach to negotiations was more relaxed. An advisory committee representing largely technical-level staff from several federal agencies had been appointed, but basically the research and analysis to support the negotiating team was handled by the staffs of the Bonneville Power Administration and the U.S. Army Engineer Division, North Pacific: both field staffs in the lower Columbia area. These were directed by Washington-based liaison personnel— high-level staff people whose long experience had developed special skill and competence in negotiating settlements in which resolution of conflict and achievement of consensus are primary objectives. Conditioned by this experience, they tended to approach problems requiring analysis as issues to be resolved rather than problems to be solved. As a consequence, to a large extent the technical personnel at the field level, many of whom possessed analytical competence of a very high order, were directed to search for compromises, formulas for resolving divergent viewpoints, etc., rather than to analyze technical problems or to evaluate the implications of alternative positions with respect to points at issue. Only two quite simplified studies, referred to in Chapter 7, were undertaken to evaluate two possibilities as to Treaty terms from the United States viewpoint.

A careful survey of the studies undertaken by technical personnel of the United States provides no evidence that the Treaty results were checked for consistency with the International Joint Commission's General Principle No. 2, to determine if there were benefits to the United States or savings in cost as compared with alternatives available to it. The U.S. negotiators were not unaware of the diminishing marginal productivity of storage, nor of the displacement effects among storages; these points found expression often in the dialogue leading to the final terms. Nevertheless, the quantitative significance of these relationships was not systematically evaluated. This leads one to speculate that at the highest levels in the United States there may have been greater interest in concluding an amicable settlement with Canada regarding future development of the Columbia—an objective with which few would quarrel—than in realizing positive economic advantage from the co-operative undertaking. Such an attitude would not foster the development of economic analyses which might prove to be of negative value in the trading of concessions or the insurance of ratification. One can only assume that creating an incentive for Canada to provide storage for the system in the United States may have been consistent with internal U.S. power policy as well as with the furtherance of good neighborly relations during the 1960 negotiations, and that after 1961 the latter objective alone provided reason for supporting the Treaty negotiated under the previous administration. If such were the motives at the highest levels, critical analyses of long-run costs of the Treaty to the United States doubtless were not encouraged.

THE SIGNIFICANCE OF THE COLUMBIA EXPERIENCE FOR ARRANGEMENTS ON OTHER INTERNATIONAL RIVER SYSTEMS

In reviewing the results of the international understanding for the development of the Columbia, we should be aware that a great disparity existed in the size, wealth, and economic resources of the two riparian countries. To the United States, the Columbia development in relation to total U.S. productive capacity, or even power-generating capacity, was comparatively small. Accordingly, a sizable misjudgment about the economics of the undertaking could be accommodated without serious consequences for the country's economy, credit status, or capability for undertaking effective public works activities in future. This may not have been the case with Canada, and most certainly was not so for British Columbia.

If we consider the problems faced in general by small political units, or by emerging, developing nations, the care exercised by British Columbia to function within its capital constraints and to secure a sufficient margin to cover any contingent miscalculation in return for committing its resources is an example that warrants emulation. There is no doubt that Canada, and British Columbia in particular, figured with a very sharp pencil. Analysis was used to illuminate policy choices and to evaluate the magnitudes in the trade-offs when economic and political, long-run and short-run, and similar conflicting objectives were being weighed in the balance.

The organization of the Canadian information generating-retrieving-evaluating process bears close study to determine whether it represents an inherently effective means of processing information and ensuring its distribution to all the principals, or whether the peculiarities of the case ensured that the relevant questions would be raised, researched, and accorded competent technical attention. For in this case there did exist a divergence of viewpoint between the provincial and federal authorities in a number of respects which doubtless helped to ensure the employment of relevant information no matter how unwelcome it may have been to one or other of the parties. Whatever its origin, maintenance of the distinction between technical analysis and policy choice was an outstanding Canadian accomplishment.

But the Columbia experience provides examples of things to be avoided as well as to be emulated. In this respect perhaps two matters warrant attention.

First, in the identification of sites for development and contingency plans as alternatives to co-operative undertakings, there is need to guard against psychological and/or political commitment. Development agencies, planning personnel, and project designers may all be somewhat susceptible to precommitment to a particular project, mode of procedure, or course of action before alternatives (representing the neighboring riparian's resources) have been sufficiently explored. Such commitments may become irreversible, restricting the flexibility with which the design of an efficient international water resource system should be approached, and having serious implications for the kind of bargains that are struck. A weakly rationalized commitment, for example, may exact a penalty, or "clearance ransom," reflected in the terms of agreement finally reached to accommodate an indefensible project. In the Columbia case, selection of the upper Kootenay storage is an example of the kind of thing likely to be encountered whenever the development of international streams is at issue. Here, the Libby storage site, viewed in the context of an exclusively domestic U.S. system, promised substantial benefits in excess of costs. However, the headwaters of the proposed project would extend across the international boundary and thus the site could not be developed by the United States without an international agreement. Moreover, prospects for a co-operative development of the upper Columbia were being investigated by the two countries. This would place Libby in competition with additional and mutually exclusive sites in British Columbia. Alternatives to Libby, we have seen, were economically superior from a system standpoint, but over the years enough domestic support had developed for the Libby project to make it, at least in the view of the congressional delegation from the Northwest, one important objective of the Treaty.

Despite its favorable characteristics within the context of a purely domestic undertaking, the Libby project was not ultimately an economic project in relation to alternatives when the Canadian reaches of the Columbia were pooled for the consideration of co-operative storage. Since, under the principles formulated by the International Joint Commission, Libby did not qualify, obtaining clearance from Canada for this project could be expected to come at a very high cost. The price for the project became so high, in fact, that the United States negotiators were ultimately released from an obligation to secure Libby. Nevertheless, in the final analysis, the price the United States was prepared to pay appeared more advantageous to Canada than a reduced share of the greater savings from a more economic system configuration.

Second, there is need to guard against building inflexibility into the Treaty document itself. Securing a treaty may not become as complex a process for all nations as it did for the riparian countries in the Columbia case. Nevertheless, such an instrument may have to run the gamut of polycentric decision mechanisms and, once negotiated and validated, it is exceedingly difficult to alter. It would seem that the hazards to which the Columbia Treaty would be exposed if opened for renegotiation in 1963, when formal negotiations were resumed, effectively discouraged consideration of the wider range of alternatives then available for achieving comparable end results with less cost. There is reason to think that if the negotiators had sought an agreement similar to a commercial contract in an environment akin to a utility industry bargaining situation, either the Libby or the Duncan Lake project would have been dropped. The High Arrow project would also have been eliminated, in view of the different situation introduced by the Peace Power Project and the Northwest-Southwest intertie. But the cumbersome nature of the decision apparatus deterred the principals from reopening the Treaty for review and revision lest the achievements already secured might be endangered.

Circumstances such as these lead one to the belief that an international agreement between riparians should not seek to address planning and operating details, these being matters that should remain subject to review and modification. Had the Columbia Treaty articulated objectives in the broadest terms, embodying general principles to guide the development of the Columbia, leaving the details to be worked out by a designated planning body, much greater flexibility would have attended the negotiations; once reached, the decisions could have been reviewed and modified as technical circumstances warranted. In short, a treaty would serve riparians well if it were confined to policy governing the planning and operation of co-operative undertakings. Planning and operating detail should be delegated to the operating agencies, but it might be wise to provide for review procedure in order to ensure that decisions were reached consistent with the general policy governing the co-operative venture.

Finally, let us review the requirements of an analytic approach to the identification of an efficient program of development and the sharing of co-operative gains. Here it seems desirable to retain the distinction between the co-operative and conflictive aspects of an international undertaking. In the first instance, all parties to an international undertaking should be able individually to identify the most economic means of achieving the objective for which a water resource development is undertaken. If, in order to maximize the joint gain for mutual sharing, system components are selected without regard to their location with respect to one or another of the countries involved, the possibility of an arrangement advantageous to all parties is maximized. With this accomplished, it is likely that a share of the joint gains will be found which will advance each participant to a position superior to that which each could have achieved independently. Where this is not the case, there is evidence that the undertaking is uneconomic in any event, whether undertaken individually or co-operatively, and it should be abandoned in favor of domestic alternatives.

The selection of efficient components of a large and complex system is not itself without difficulty. It is not sufficient to compare the original increment in system output with associated costs for two or more feasible components if their roles, and hence their values, are subject to change in the course of time. Where this is the case, it is necessary to simulate the system in operation over the entire planning horizon in order to compare the present value of the net benefits of a given system alternatively with each of mutually exclusive components in the system. This is particularly important when the cost of meeting objectives by means of a co-operative system is compared with the cost of achieving similar objectives domestically. Where storages are involved, this procedure appears to be efficient in evaluating the displacement effects among storage possibilities of co-operating riparians.

The alternative to such an analytic approach as is outlined above is to risk introducing excess costs into the co-operative system—a hazard that could defeat the basic purpose of the co-operative effort.

Index

205